DONIPHAN'S EXPEDITION

TEXAS A&M UNIVERSITY
MILITARY HISTORY SERIES

56

Doniphan's Expedition

BY
JOHN
TAYLOR
HUGHES

with an introduction by
Joseph G. Dawson III

Texas A&M University Press
College Station

First Texas A&M University Press edition, 1997
Manufactured in the United States of America
04 03 02 01 00 99 98 97   5 4 3 2 1

Originally published in 1847 by U. P. James, Cincinnati;
reformatted edition published in 1914 by the Government Printing Office, Washington, D. C.

The paper used in this book meets the minimum requirements
of the American National Standard for Permanence
of Paper for Printed Library Materials, Z39.48-1984.
Binding materials have been chosen for durability.

Library of Congress Cataloging-in-Publication Data

Hughes, John Taylor, 1817–1862.
    Doniphan's expedition / by John Taylor Hughes ; with an introduction by Joseph G. Dawson III. — 1st Texas A&M University Press ed.
        p.   cm. — (Texas A&M University military history series ; no. 56)
    "Reformatted edition published in 1914 by the Government Printing Office, Washington, D.C."—T.p. verso.
    Includes bibliographical references.
    ISBN 0-89096-795-4 (alk. paper)
    1. Doniphan's Expedition, 1846–1847—Personal narratives. 2. Mexican War, 1846–1848—Personal narratives. 3. Hughes, John Taylor, 1817–1862. 4. Soldiers—Missouri—Biography. I. Title. II. Series: Texas A&M University military history series ; 56.
    E405.2.H943   1997
    973.6'23—dc21   97-33376
                                                                                            CIP

INTRODUCTION

by Joseph G. Dawson III

During the 1840s, Alexander William Doniphan and John Taylor Hughes agreed with thousands of Americans who believed that the United States was destined to expand across the continent, between the Mississippi River and the Pacific Ocean, including large portions of Mexico. Writing in 1845, John O'Sullivan, a journalist who favored the Democratic party and contributed to the *Democratic Review,* gave the popular concept of expansion a meaningful sobriquet, "Manifest Destiny," stating that God ordained America's westward movement. Although thousands of Americans ardently favored Manifest Destiny, critics of territorial expansion branded such men as Doniphan and Hughes as "annexationists" and were worried that taking western lands would also expand the institution of slavery and lead to international wars, with either Great Britain or Mexico or both.[1]

Campaigning on an annexationist platform, James K. Polk, a Democrat from Tennessee, had been elected president in 1844 and inaugurated in March 1845. Polk's campaign promises called for annexing Oregon in the northwest, Texas in the southwest, and purchasing the Mexican states of New Mexico and California. Nationalistic Americans joyfully contemplated these acquisitions and delighted in the idea that these blocks of land would fill in the map of the United States, confirming its national reach across the continent. Doniphan and Hughes, though both had supported Senator Henry Clay, leader of the Whig party and Polk's rival for the presidency, endorsed their new president's call for obtaining these lands. Shortly before Polk had taken office, outgoing president John Tyler arranged for an unusual joint resolution of Congress to approve statehood for Texas, then in its tenth year as an independent republic. Early in Polk's term, American and British diplomats settled the Oregon question by dividing the region neatly along the forty-ninth parallel, leaving the remaining matters of New Mexico and California, what many Americans all too simply considered to be only a major real estate deal.[2]

More than twenty years of antagonism marked relations between Mexico and the United States. Disputes over boundaries and debts and participation by Americans in the Texas Revolution of 1835–36 were among the disagreements that divided the two countries. It appeared to Mexicans that the United States had helped Texas secede from the Republic of Mexico, and Mexicans demonstrated remarkable consensus that they must regain control of Texas, viewed as a wayward province that unfortunately had strayed from the fold.

After ten years of trying and several failed military expeditions, Mexico still had not regained Texas by 1846. Ill feelings reduced the likelihood that Mexican leaders would accept any offer of money for large portions of their national lands. Although estimates indicated that only one percent of Mexico's citizens resided in California and New Mexico, many Mexicans considered these northern provinces their "national patrimony"—the region for future national growth and development. Settlers expected to find deposits of gold and silver in both states, and each contained an important economic center of great potential. San Francisco, California, was the best natural harbor in North America and offered the prospect of a commercial gateway to Asia for the nation that developed it. Although modest if compared to Chicago, St. Louis, and New Orleans, Santa Fe, New Mexico, was the busiest trading center between the Mississippi River and the Pacific. None of the leaders of Mexico's political parties had any interest in selling California and New Mexico to the United States, and Polk's offer to buy them for only around thirty million dollars added insult to the injury of past disagreements.[3]

Disagreeing over the status of Texas brought on the war between Mexico and the United States. In 1846 Mexican national maps still showed Texas as a state in Mexico, despite the fact of its ten years as an independent republic. Therefore, when the United States annexed Texas, it had taken a step tantamount to an act of war, and Polk compounded that act by dispatching U.S. Army troops into Texas. Further complicating matters, the old boundary of Texas as a Mexican state was the Nueces River, which empties into the Gulf of Mexico at Corpus Christi. Winning their independence in 1836, Texans had made the brash claim that their new boundary would be the Rio Grande. Mexico never recognized either Texas independence or the Texans' claim of the Rio Grande boundary. But in 1846 the United States sent military patrols along that river; President Polk had accepted Texas' claim of the Rio Grande and insisted that it was the boundary between the United States and Mexico.

On April 25, 1846, Mexican troops encountered an American patrol on the northern side of the Rio Grande, winning a skirmish in which several U.S. soldiers were killed and wounded. Already preparing a call for war, President Polk learned of the skirmish and hastily made some additions to his message, including the stirring cry that "American blood had been shed on the American soil." Soon, both houses of the U.S. Congress approved a declaration of war against Mexico, and the president recognized that thousands of volunteer soldiers would be needed to supplement the small U.S. Regular Army, which had an enrollment only around eight thousand men.[4]

When Polk called for volunteers in the spring of 1846, Alexander Doniphan and John Taylor Hughes stepped forward to enlist, willing to prosecute a war to consolidate America's hold on the Rio Grande boundary, protect Texas, capture Santa Fe, and take California. They were among some three-thousand Missourians and seventy-three-thousand Americans who signed up and some fifty-two thousand who actually served for one year as volunteer soldiers during the war.

Although other soldiers were also recruited to serve in the U.S. Regular Army, the war could not have been carried out, and the United States could not have won it, without such citizen-soldiers as Doniphan, Hughes, and their fellow volunteers.[5]

Alexander Doniphan was born near Maysville, in Mason County, Kentucky, on July 9, 1808. His father, Joseph Doniphan, was a local man of mark, owning a substantial farm and eighteen slaves and holding the office of sheriff of Mason County. Joseph Doniphan died in 1813, leaving his wife, Ann, with a house full of children. The challenge of raising a family on her own proved to be too much for her, and she arranged to send Alexander to live with an older brother, George Doniphan, in Augusta, Kentucky, twenty miles away. In 1822 Doniphan matriculated at Augusta College, a Methodist Episcopal academy in town. He graduated four years later and aspired to become an attorney. He read law and passed the Kentucky bar examination in 1829.[6]

The next year Doniphan moved to Missouri and passed that state's bar examination. Too many young lawyers were already practicing in St. Louis so he headed west again, settling eventually in Liberty, a village of three hundred persons. In western Missouri, he made his reputation as an excellent public speaker and outstanding trial attorney, taking on a variety of cases, including ones defending members of the Church of Jesus Christ of Latter Day Saints—the Mormons, who at the time were under attack by other Christian denominations. Using his meritorious legal record and running as a Whig, Doniphan won a two-year term in the house of representatives in the Missouri General Assembly. He also gained an appointment as a brigadier general in the Missouri state militia, though that commission gave him little practical military experience.[7]

When Congress declared war against Mexico, Doniphan enlisted as a private for one year of service in a company from his home in Clay County. It marched to Fort Leavenworth, in modern-day Kansas, to rendezvous with other companies coming together to form the First Regiment of Missouri Mounted Volunteers. A few days after arriving at Fort Leavenworth, Doniphan capitalized on his popularity, winning election as colonel of the regiment, defeating John Price, a former volunteer officer from Missouri and veteran of the Second Seminole War in Florida.[8]

As colonel of the regiment, Doniphan was responsible for training and leading more than eight hundred volunteers. As for the training, the U.S. Regular Army played an important role, providing officers from the First Dragoons to teach the citizen-soldiers the basics of army tactical drill. Doniphan himself benefited from the advice and guidance of the dragoons' commander, Col. Stephen Watts Kearny, a consummate professional and one of the best regular officers in the army. Kearny profoundly influenced Doniphan in the weeks to come. Soon, President Polk, acting through Secretary of War William Marcy, directed Kearny to take command of the "Army of the West," with Doniphan as second ranking officer. Kearny's "Army" totaled sixteen hundred officers and men, including three hundred regular dragoons plus Doniphan's regiment along with five other attached volunteer companies. Their mission: capture Santa Fe, New Mexico. Confident of success, after taking Santa Fe Kearny and a detachment of regulars would go on to California while Doniphan would continue the invasion southward through New Mexico and into Chihuahua.

Starting from Fort Leavenworth in June 1846, Doniphan's regiment made contributions to the U.S. war effort, and its long march through enemy territory caught the imagination of the American public. Following the capture of Santa Fe, capital of New Mexico, in August 1846 and after occupying the city for several weeks, Doniphan and a committee of volunteers wrote a set of laws and a territorial constitution. Thus, Doniphan helped to secure New Mexico for the United States. Resuming his march deeper into Mexico in December 1846, Doniphan and his men fought a Mexican force outside of El Paso del Norte (modern Juárez, Mexico), occupied the town, and then maintained the offensive by aiming to take Chihuahua City in February 1847. A few miles north of Chihuahua City another Mexican army, waiting in field entrenchments, blocked the regiment's path. Doniphan directed a determined attack that dislodged the Mexican defenders, sending them streaming from the battlefield. Doniphan and his regiment then captured their second state capital.[9]

The Doniphan Expedition not only engaged Mexican forces and captured provincial capitals, it endured numerous tribulations and hazards along the way. Doniphan's March eventually totaled some 5,500 miles over land, through the Gulf of Mexico and up the Mississippi River. The regiment crossed some of the roughest country in North America. Supply wagons broke down, and animals went lame or sick and had to be abandoned. Constant shortages of supplies required that Doniphan's soldiers routinely subsist on "half rations," half of the normal allotment of food that the army usually issued to its soldiers. Traveling across dry stretches of the West and through the Chihuahuan desert also meant constant shortages of water for both men and animals. Always a precious commodity in the West, water became a delicacy while the regiment was on its march. The considerable distances of Doniphan's March, traversed in only one year, added to the making of an epic adventure and what some considered a test of American hardihood. The regiment returned to public acclaim in St. Louis in June 1847.[10]

Nationalistic American newspaper writers and politicians praised America's successful military officers during the Mexican War, and Doniphan won some of the highest accolades. In addition to winning a military victory in the war, Americans enjoyed making comparisons between the government of their nation and those of the republics of ancient Greece and Rome. Some of these comparisons were filled with hyperbole, but they also expressed much about the confidence and belligerence of the American nation. Several writers, most notably William Cullen Bryant, founder and editor of the New York *Evening Post,* compared Doniphan with the famous Greek commander Xenophon, who had led a group of Greek soldiers on a 3,500-

mile march across Persian territory around 400 B.C. Bryant suggested that Doniphan's March was even more remarkable than Xenophon's Anabasis and, like Xenophon, Doniphan should write an account of his march. The colonel probably decided not to write a memoir because of the publication of the book by Hughes, one of the soldiers from his regiment.[11]

Like Colonel Doniphan, John Taylor Hughes was a native of Kentucky. He was born on July 25, 1817, near Versailles and moved with his family to western Missouri in 1820. Hughes later graduated from a frontier academy, Bonne Femme College, outside of Columbia, Missouri. At the outbreak of the Mexican-American War, Hughes was teaching school in Liberty, Doniphan's hometown. Joining the First Regiment of Missouri Mounted Volunteers as a private, Hughes audaciously announced that he planned to write a history of the unit. As it turned out, several other soldiers also wrote personal accounts of Doniphan's March. Some of them were published in the nineteenth century and others many years later, but Hughes' was the most detailed.[12]

Like the other Missouri volunteers Hughes took great pride in his military service; but unlike most of them he took steps to cash in on the attention given to Doniphan's March. Turning his attention to his notes, personal journal, and letters to his hometown newspaper, the Liberty *Weekly Tribune,* Hughes worked diligently to produce a comprehensive account of his year-long experience as a soldier, highlighting the leadership and accomplishments of Alexander Doniphan in the process. *Doniphan's Expedition; Containing an Account of the Conquest of New Mexico* was published in 1847 by the U. P. James printing company of Cincinnati, Ohio. The author was pleased by the warm reception given his book, which went through several printings in the months after it was published. Numerous handsome woodcuts enhanced its appeal.

After the publication of his book, Hughes worked for the U.S. Government Land Office in Missouri and was elected as a Whig to the state legislature in 1854. Purchasing several slaves and a plantation north of Plattsburg, Missouri, raised his economic and social status. During the secession crisis of 1860–61 Hughes first stood for the Union, but his advocacy of states' rights and slavery prompted him to support the Confederacy. Gaining a commission as a colonel, Hughes fought at the Battle of Wilson's Creek, Missouri, on August 10, 1861, and at the Battle of Pea Ridge (Elkhorn Tavern), Arkansas, on March 7–8, 1862. He was killed in action in a skirmish near Independence, Missouri, on August 11, 1862.

Hughes's book, however, lived on after him, as other reprints of *Doniphan's Expedition* were published during the twentieth century. Many years after its original publication, his memoir came out in a special edition, compiled and published by William E. Connelley in 1907, titled *Doniphan's Expedition and the Conquest of New Mexico and California.* Connelley, a historian in Topeka, Kansas, decided to bolster Hughes's account by adding numerous letters, documents, lengthy notes about persons and events associated with Doniphan's March, and rosters of the volunteer companies comprising the units on the expedition. Connelley's edition expanded Hughes's work from 407 pages to a total of 670 pages. A later issue by Rio Grande Press of the original volume (minus photographs of Doniphan and Col. Sterling Price) appeared in 1962 under the title *Doniphan's Expedition, an Account of the U.S. Army Operations in the Great American Southwest* and lacking even a brief introduction.

The present volume of the Hughes memoir is a reprinting of the 1914 U.S. Government Printing Office version, which was published as part of the congressional serial set, officially *Senate Document No. 698*, serial 6589, 63d Congress, 2d session. In order to print it more efficiently, the Printing Office reset the memoir, changing its length from 407 to 202 pages. This version also deleted the photographs of Doniphan and Price but kept the attractive woodcuts while placing them at different locations in the book.

In his memoir of military service, Hughes mentioned several persons without always giving much information about them. His book is about his year as a soldier and, naturally, he had nothing to say about the veterans' postwar lives. The following alphabetical listing is included to help round out the descriptions of several key figures in *Doniphan's Expedition*.

MERIWETHER LEWIS CLARK, major commanding the volunteer artillery battalion from St. Louis attached to Doniphan's regiment, was the son of William Clark, of the famous Lewis and Clark Expedition. Meriwether Clark graduated from the U.S. Military Academy, class of 1830, and had served in the U.S. Army from 1830 to 1833. His half-sister married Col. Stephen W. Kearny. Resigning his commission, Clark went into business in St. Louis as an architect and civil engineer and served a term in the Missouri state legislature. Following the Mexican War, Clark was federal surveyor general of Missouri from 1848 to 1853. During the Civil War he supported the Confederacy and was first a colonel and later a brigadier general, serving with artillery units. After Appomattox he found a job as commandant of the Kentucky Military Institute. Clark died at Frankfort, Kentucky, in 1881.[13]

ALEXANDER W. DONIPHAN, enjoying the fame he won from his audacious march across Mexico, after the war resumed his law practice in Liberty, Missouri. He sought other business opportunities, including opening an insurance company. In 1849 Doniphan was one of the principal founders of William Jewell College, a small Baptist college in Liberty. His law practice prospered but did not make him wealthy. For various reasons Doniphan declined to run for office in the years immediately following the Mexican-American War, but he was elected to the Missouri state legislature in 1854. Although he was a slaveowner, Doniphan believed that the Union was more important than slavery or secession. In early 1861 he served as a delegate to the "Old Gentlemen's Convention" in Washington, D.C., a gathering of moderates from several states. They tried to hammer out a last-minute compromise that might defuse the crisis and pre-vent civil war, but the convention failed to determine a solution. Once the Civil War started in the spring of 1861, Doniphan refused to ac-cept a military commission from either side. In the late 1860s he moved his law practice to Richmond, Missouri, and opened a modest bank. Doniphan died at Richmond in 1887.[14]

WILLIAM GILPIN, major of Doniphan's regiment, was born in Pennsylvania and graduated from the University of Pennsylvania in 1833. He then attended the U.S. Military Academy (1834–35) but did not graduate. Working through political contacts, Gilpin managed to obtain a commission in the U.S. Regular Army and served in the Sec-ond Regiment of Dragoons from 1836 to 1838. He resigned his com-mission, moved to Missouri, engaged in business, including operating a newspaper, and traveled down the Santa Fe Trail in 1843. After Doniphan's March, Gilpin recruited his own battalion and patrolled the Santa Fe Trail during the last year of the Mexican-American War. He later served as governor of Colorado Territory (1861–62). Writing books and magazine articles, Gilpin tirelessly promoted the idea of settling the Trans-Mississippi West and speculated in land deals in Colorado. He died in Denver in 1894.[15]

WILLARD P. HALL, a private in Company C from Clay County, settled in Missouri from western Virginia in 1840, after graduating from Yale College in 1839. Although he and Doniphan had opposed each other in politics—the colonel was a Whig and the private a Demo-crat—Hall's cordial personality and skill as a lawyer prompted Gen-eral Kearny to choose him to help Doniphan write the so-called Kearny Code in Santa Fe. In 1846, before the expedition moved south, Hall was elected to the U.S. House of Representatives, but rather than go back to Missouri immediately, he decided to accompany American troops marching to California. Hall was reelected twice to Congress, but failed to win election to the U.S. Senate in 1856. During the se-cession crisis of 1861 he helped to hold Missouri for the Union and subsequently served as lieutenant governor (1862–63) and governor (1864–65) of the state. Hall worked as a successful attorney after the Civil War. He died at St. Joseph, Missouri, in 1882.[16]

THOMAS B. HUDSON, dashing captain of the Leclede Rang-ers, a volunteer cavalry company from St. Louis, was born in Tennes-see and arrived in St. Louis in 1835. He promptly entered politics, holding a seat on the city council, serving as city attorney, and win-ning an election to the state legislature in 1842. Hudson resumed his law practice in St. Louis after the war and was also president of a small railroad company. He died at his residence near St. Louis, 1867.[17]

STEPHEN W. KEARNY, brigadier general, U.S. Army, was born at Newark, New Jersey, in 1794. He entered the army in 1812 as a lieutenant and began establishing an excellent record. Receiving sev-eral promotions, he eventually rose to colonel of the First Dragoons in 1836. After commanding the Army of the West, Kearny led U.S. forces in the conquest of California in 1847. He contracted yellow fever at Veracruz, Mexico, and took leave to St. Louis. In 1848 he died at the home of his wife's brother, Major Meriwether Lewis Clark.[18]

JAMES KIRKER, civilian scout who joined the Doniphan Expedition outside El Paso del Norte, continued his activities as scout, fur trapper, and mountain man in the Southwest and northern Mexico after the war. He died in California in 1853.[19]

DAVID D. MITCHELL, lieutenant colonel of Col. Sterling Price's Second Regiment of Missouri Mounted Volunteers, was born in Virginia in 1806, and had made his way to Missouri, working for the American Fur Company and as federal superintendent of Indian affairs in St. Louis in the early 1840s. Mitchell served on detached duty with Doniphan through the Chihuahua campaign. He later regained his post as superintendent of Indian affairs at St. Louis (1849–53) and was president of the Missouri and California Overland Mail Company until his death in 1861.[20]

OLIVER P. MOSS, captain of Clay County's Company C, was one of Colonel Doniphan's life-long friends. Like Doniphan, Moss moved to Missouri from Kentucky. They married sisters and arranged to have their weddings performed on the same day in 1837. During his postwar career, Moss supported William Jewell College in Liberty and served as sheriff of Clay County.[21]

MOSBY M. PARSONS, captain of Doniphan's Company F, from Cole County, moved to Missouri from Virginia in 1835. He practiced law in Jefferson City. Receiving public acclaim for his service in the Mexican War, he won elections to the Missouri General Assembly, holding seats in both the state house and senate in the 1850s. In 1861 Parsons devoted himself to the Confederacy, eventually becoming a major general in the Southern armies during the Civil War. Afterwards he was one of several former Confederate officers who fled to Mexico and served with Maximilian's French forces there. Anti-French Mexicans killed Parsons in 1865.[22]

STERLING PRICE, Doniphan's military and political rival in Missouri, was born in 1809 in Virginia and arrived in Missouri in 1830. As a Democrat, he held seats in the Missouri state legislature (1840–44) and the U.S. House of Representatives (1845–46) before his service as a volunteer colonel. Price led his Second Regiment of Missouri Mounted Volunteers on a superfluous campaign following the same path as Doniphan's March, recapturing Chihuahua City in March 1848. Price was elected governor of Missouri (1853–57). During the secession crisis he decided to support secession and was made a major general in the Confederate army. Price fought in campaigns in Arkansas and Mississippi and led a raid into Missouri in 1864. He sought refuge in Mexico after the Civil War but returned home to St. Louis, where he died in 1867.[23]

JOHN W. REID, commander of Company D, from Saline County, was another native Virginian who had settled in Missouri, arriving in the state in 1840. By 1844 he had passed the bar and was practicing law in Jefferson City. Reid later sought political office, holding a seat in the Missouri legislature (1854–56) and winning election to the U.S. Congress in 1860. He resigned in 1861, took the side of the Confederacy, and served for a time as an aide to Gen. Sterling Price.

He died at Lee's Summit, Missouri, in 1881, after maintaining his law practice there.[24]

CHARLES L. RUFF, lieutenant colonel of Doniphan's regiment, obtained an appointment to West Point from his home state of Pennsylvania in 1834 and graduated in 1838. He served in the dragoons until 1842, when he resigned from the army and settled in Missouri, opening a law office in Liberty. Before the battle at Brazito, Ruff left the First Missouri after being commissioned as captain in the U.S. Army's Regiment of Mounted Rifles in 1846. He fought in the major battles around Mexico City during 1847 and was seriously wounded. Continuing his army career, Ruff served in several western states and territories from 1848 to 1861 and was a recruiting officer for the Union army during the Civil War. He died in Philadelphia, Pennsylvania, in 1885.[25]

JOHN D. STEVENSON, commander of Company E, from Franklin County, arrived in Missouri from Virginia about 1842. He practiced law in Union, in Franklin County. His reputation as a bold combat officer helped him in politics, and he was elected to both houses of the Missouri legislature during the 1850s. In contrast to several fellow veterans of Doniphan's regiment, Stevenson remained loyal to the Union and was commissioned in the Federal army. He served in a variety of assignments and finished the Civil War as brigadier general of volunteers. Stevenson applied and gained a commission as colonel of the Thirtieth Infantry Regiment in the U.S. Regular Army and served until 1870, when he resigned and returned to St. Louis to practice law. He died there in 1897.[26]

DAVID WALDO, commander of Company A, from Jackson County, hailed from western Virginia and had settled in Missouri in 1826. He attended Transylvania College in Lexington, Kentucky. Having made a major contribution to the expedition by helping Doniphan and Hall write the Kearny Code, Waldo served with the First Missouri Regiment for the remainder of Doniphan's March into Mexico. Returning to Missouri with the rest of the veterans, Waldo engaged in a freight-hauling business. He died at Independence in 1878.[27]

RICHARD H. WEIGHTMAN, captain of one of the artillery batteries in Clark's battalion of St. Louis volunteers, was a native of the District of Columbia, a graduate of the University of Virginia, and a cadet at the U.S. Military Academy from 1835–37 but did not graduate. He moved to St. Louis in the 1840s. After the Mexican War he settled in Santa Fe, where he opened a law office and managed a newspaper. Running for office as a Democrat, Weightman served as New Mexico's territorial delegate to the U.S. Congress from 1851 to 1853. Following a gunfight in New Mexico, in which he killed a man, he moved back to Missouri. At the outbreak of the Civil War Weightman gained a commission as colonel in the Confederate forces and was killed in action at the battle of Wilson's Creek, Missouri, in August 1861.[28]

NOTES

1. Frederick Merk, *Manifest Destiny and Mission in American History: A Reinterpretation* (New York: Alfred A. Knopf, 1963), 24–28, 34–39, passim.

2. Paul H. Bergeron, *The Presidency of James K. Polk* (Lawrence: Univ. of Kansas Press, 1987), 15–20; David M. Pletcher, *The Diplomacy of Annexation: Texas, Oregon, and the Mexican War* (Columbia: Univ. of Missouri Press, 1973), passim; Andre P. Duchateau, "Missouri Colossus: Alexander William Doniphan, 1808–1887" (Ed.D. diss., Oklahoma State Univ., 1973), 89–90.

3. Gene M. Brack, *Mexico Views Manifest Destiny, 1821–1846: An Essay on the Origins of the Mexican War* (Albuquerque: Univ. of New Mexico Press, 1975); Josefina Zoraida Váquez, "The Texas Question in Mexican Politics, 1836–1845," *Southwestern Historical Quarterly* 89 (January 1986): 309–44; Pedro Santoni, *Mexicans at Arms: Puro Federalists and the Politics of War, 1845–1848* (Fort Worth: Texas Christian Univ. Press, 1996), 27–31, 38–39, passim.

4. K. Jack Bauer, *The Mexican War* (New York: Macmillan, 1974), 48, 68.

5. Ibid., 69–72; Richard Bruce Winders, "Mr. Polk's Army: Politics, Patronage, and the American Military in the Mexican War" (Ph.D. diss., Texas Christian Univ., 1994), 31, passim.

6. Roger D. Launius, "Alexander W. Doniphan, Missouri's Forgotten Leader," in F. Mark McKiernan and Roger D. Launius, eds., *Missouri Folk Heroes of the 19th Century* (Independence, Mo.: Independence Press, 1989), 63–65; Duchateau, "Missouri Colossus," 7–11.

7. Launius, "Alexander Doniphan," 65–72; Duchateau, "Missouri Colossus," 16–91.

8. Joseph G. Dawson III, "'Zealous for Annexation': Volunteer Soldiering, Military Government, and the Service of Colonel Alexander Doniphan in the Mexican-American War," *Journal of Strategic Studies* 19 (December 1996): 11–13.

9. Ibid.

10. Joseph G. Dawson III, "American Xenophon, American Hero: Alexander Doniphan's Homecoming from the Mexican-American War as Hallmark of Patriotic Fervor," *Military History of the West* 27 (spring 1997): 1–31.

11. Ibid., 20–26.

12. Information on Hughes can be found in William E. Connelley, *Doniphan's Expedition* (Topeka, Kans.: by the author, 1907), 46–58. Other volunteer soldiers' accounts include Frank S. Edwards, *A Campaign in New Mexico with Colonel Doniphan* (Philadelphia, Pa.: Carey and Hart, 1847; Ann Arbor, Mich., Univ. Microfilms, 1966; reprint, Albuquerque: Univ. of New Mexico Press, 1996); William H. Richardson, *Journal of William H. Richardson, A Private Soldier in Col. Doniphan's Command* (Baltimore, Md.: J. W. Woods, 1848); Richard S. Elliott, *Notes Taken in Sixty Years* (St. Louis, Mo.: R. P. Studley and Co., 1883); Isaac George, *Heroes and Incidents of the Mexican War* (Greensburg, Pa.: Review Publishing Co., 1903); Jacob S. Robinson, *A Journal of the Santa Fe Expedition under Col. Doniphan*, ed. Carl L. Cannon (Princeton, N.J.: Princeton Univ. Press, 1932; reprint, New York: Da Capo, 1972); George R. Gibson, *Journal of a Soldier under Kearny and Doniphan*, ed. Ralph P. Bieber (Glendale, Calif.: Arthur H. Clark Co., 1935); Abraham S. Johnston, Marcellus B. Edwards, and Philip G. Ferguson, *Marching with the Army of the West*, ed. Ralph P. Bieber (Glendale, Calif.: Arthur H. Clark Co., 1936) (Johnston was a lieutenant in the regular army); William C. Kennerly, *Persimmon Hill: A Narrative of Old St. Louis and the Far West* (Norman, Okla.: Univ. of Oklahoma Press, 1948).

13. Bruce S. Allardice, *More Generals in Gray* (Baton Rouge: Louisiana State Univ. Press, 1995), 61–62.

14. Launius, "Alexander Doniphan," 77–81.

15. Thomas L. Karnes, *William Gilpin, Western Nationalist* (Austin: Univ. of Texas Press, 1970).

16. *Biographical Directory of the American Congress* (Washington, D.C.: Government Printing Office, 1928), 1049.

17. J. Thomas Scharf, *History of St. Louis City and County*, 2 vols. (Philadelphia, Pa.: Events and Co., 1883), 2:1487.

18. Dwight Clarke, *Stephen Watts Kearny, Soldier of the West* (Norman: Univ. of Oklahoma Press, 1961).

19. William C. McGaw, *Savage Scene: The Life and Times of James Kirker* (New York: Hastings House, 1972).

20. Ray H. Hattison, "David Dawson Mitchell," in LeRoy R. Hafen, ed., *The Mountain Men and the Fur Trade*, 10 vols. (Glendale, Calif.: Arthur H. Clark Co., 1965–71), 2:241–46.

21. William M. Paxton, *Annals of Platte County, Missouri* (Kansas City, Mo.: Hudson-Kimberly, 1897), 549–51; Connelley, *Doniphan's Expedition*, 134–35.

22. Ezra J. Warner, *Generals in Gray* (Baton Rouge: Louisiana State Univ. Press, 1959), 228–29.

23. Robert E. Shalhope, *Sterling Price, Portrait of a Southerner* (Columbia: Univ. of Missouri Press, 1971).

24. *Biographical Directory of the American Congress*, 1452.

25. George W. Cullum, *Biographical Register of the U.S. Military Academy*, 3d ed., 3 vols. (Boston: Houghton Mifflin, 1891), 1:728–29.

26. Ezra J. Warner, *Generals in Blue* (Baton Rouge: Louisiana State Univ. Press, 1964), 476–77.

27. Connelley, *Doniphan's Expedition*, 133–34.

28. *Biographical Register of the American Congress*, 1679.

THE VOLUNTEER.

The above cut was originally drawn to represent J. W. Patton, immediately after his first
fire, at the Battle of Brazito, but is here given as a sample of Col. Doniphan's command.

| 63D CONGRESS
2d Session | SENATE | DOCUMENT
No. 608 |

DONIPHAN'S EXPEDITION

ACCOUNT

OF THE

CONQUEST OF NEW MEXICO

GENERAL KEARNEY'S OVERLAND EXPEDITION TO
CALIFORNIA; DONIPHAN'S CAMPAIGN AGAINST THE
NAVAJOS; HIS UNPARALLELED MARCH UPON CHIHUA-
HUA AND DURANGO; AND THE OPERATIONS
OF GENERAL PRICE AT SANTA FE

PRESENTED BY MR. STONE

MAY 26, 1914.—Referred to the Committee on Printing

WASHINGTON
GOVERNMENT PRINTING OFFICE
1914

REPORTED BY MR. CHILTON.

IN THE SENATE OF THE UNITED STATES,
October 21, 1914.

Resolved, That the pamphlet submitted by Mr. Stone on May 26, 1914, entitled "Doniphan's Expedition, Containing an Account of the Conquest of New Mexico," by John T. Hughes, of the First Regiment of Missouri Cavalry, be printed as a Senate document, with accompanying illustrations.

Attest:

JAMES M. BAKER,
Secretary.

By PETER M. WILSON,
Chief Clerk.

II

DONIPHAN'S
EXPEDITION;

CONTAINING AN ACCOUNT OF THE

CONQUEST OF NEW MEXICO;

GENERAL KEARNEY'S OVERLAND EXPEDITION TO CALIFORNIA;
DONIPHAN'S CAMPAIGN AGAINST THE NAVAJOS; HIS
UNPARALLELED MARCH UPON CHIHUAHUA AND
DURANGO; AND THE OPERATIONS OF
GENERAL PRICE AT SANTA FE:

WITH

A SKETCH OF THE LIFE OF COL. DONIPHAN.

ILLUSTRATED WITH PLANS OF BATTLE FIELDS AND FINE ENGRAVINGS.

BY JOHN T. HUGHES, A. B.,
OF THE FIRST REGIMENT OF MISSOURI CAVALRY.

"Cut the rope, or pull up the picket."

CINCINNATI:
U. P. JAMES, No. 167 WALNUT STREET,
BETWEEN FOURTH AND FIFTH.

2

PREFACE.

The author is well apprised that any new publication, at this time, must either possess a high degree of literary merit, or treat of events in which all feel a lively interest, to recommend it to the favorable consideration of the reading public. For the success of this work he relies chiefly on the latter circumstance.

Mexico has recently been the theater of many thrilling events. The presses of the country are teeming with books written on Mexico, the Mexican war, and Mexican manners and customs. Descriptions of camps, marches, battles, capitulations, and victories, have almost sated the public mind. But these have all, or nearly all, had reference to the central or southern wings of our Army. Little has been said, or written, in regard to the "Army of the West." The object of the following pages is to supply this deficiency, and to do justice to the men, whose courage and conduct have accomplished the most wonderful military achievement of modern times. For, what can be more wonderful than the march of a single regiment of undisciplined troops through five populous States of the Mexican Republic—almost annihilating a powerful army—and finally returning home, after a march of near 6,000 miles, graced with the trophies of victory?

To the kindness and courtesy of Cols. Doniphan and Price, Lieut. Col. Jackson and Maj. Gilpin, Capts. Waldo and Reid, Montgomery, Leintz, and Dudley H. Cooper, the author is indebted for much valuable information. He also desires to express the obligations under which he feels himself to the late lamented Capt. Johnston, aid-de-camp to Gen. Kearney, whose notes were recently published, and to the Hon. Willard P. Hall, of Missouri, for an account of the march of Lieut. Col. Cooke to California, and of the subsequent operations of Gen. Kearney in that country.

His acknowledgments are also due to his valued and esteemed friend, L. A. Maclean, of the Missouri Horse Guards, who generously and gratuitously furnished most of the designs which embellish this work. These sketches were engraved by H. C. Grosvenor, of Cincinnati.

Except for the long-established custom of prefacing books, the reader would scarcely demand of the author an explanation of his motives in attempting to publish to the world a full and faithful account of the western expedition, embracing the conquest of New Mexico; the treaty with the Navajo Indians; Gen. Kearney's overland march to California; Col. Doniphan's invasion and capture of Chihuahua; his triumphant march through the States of Durango and Coahuila; his junction with Gens. Wool and Taylor; his return to New Orleans by way of the Mexican Gulf, and his subsequent cordial reception by the citizens of St. Louis and Missouri generally; together

3

with the brilliant achievements of the Army under Col. Price at Santa Fe. These are subjects of great historical interest to every American citizen.

The author was an eyewitness of, and an actor in, many of the scenes which he essays to describe, having been present at the capture of Santa Fe and in the Battles of Brazito, Sacramento, and El Poso. The narrative has been prepared with a conscientious regard for truth—the beauty of all history. He, therefore, trusts that his labors may meet with a favorable reception by an enlightened and generous public.

THE AUTHOR.

CONTENTS.

8 CONTENTS.

Chapter XXII.

Chapter XXIII.

Chapter XXIV.

LIST OF EMBELLISHMENTS.

9

MEMOIR

OF

COL. A. W. DONIPHAN.

Alexander William Doniphan, whose history is so thoroughly identified with that of Missouri, and who has acted so conspicuous a part in the recent War with Mexico as the leader of the unexampled expedition against Chihuahua, was born of respectable parentage on the 9th of July, 1808, in Mason County, Ky. He first breathed the air of that chivalrous State. There his tender years were spent and his youthful mind received its first impressions. Amidst Kentucky's wild, romantic mountain scenery his young faculties were first begun to be developed, unfolded, expanded. Here also from maternal lips—the lips of a kind, patient, persevering, and intelligent mother—he first learned sentiments of honor, honesty, and patriotism. His mind from the very earliest age was fired with an admiration of the ancient orators and sages. He no less admired the patriots of the Revolution, ever regarding them as bright examples and worthy of imitation. Possessed of a brilliant mind, he formed his life from the best models. Such is the influence which an affectionate and intelligent mother is capable of exerting over the destiny of her offspring.

His father, Joseph Doniphan, emigrated from Virginia to Kentucky amongst the earliest pioneers, having accompanied Daniel Boone, the great adventurer, toward the far distant West on one of his early visits to the "dark and bloody ground," then covered by unbroken forests and impervious canebrakes. Pleased with the country, he returned to Virginia, married, removed, and settled in Mason County. Here he established his fortunes and for many years enjoyed uninterrupted peace and prosperity, except occasional disturbance with the Indians. At length, being seized by an indisposition, he died, devolving thereby the care of providing and educating his children upon his widow. The responsible duty was faithfully and cheerfully discharged.

Alexander's father dying when he was only 6 years of age, left him in charge of his mother. He was the object of her first and most especial regard. His education was to her a matter of the highest importance. Alexander being the youngest child, his mother discontinued the management of her farm when he had attained an age to be sent to a better school than the vicinity in which they lived then afforded, having herself gone to live with a married daughter. Having attained his ninth year, he was placed under the guardianship of his elder brother, George Doniphan, of Augusta, Ky., to whose care and kind attention Col. Doniphan acknowledges himself indebted for all his attainments and whatever distinction he may have acquired in the world. The elder brother therefore enjoys the

11

enviable satisfaction of knowing his efforts contributed to rear and give destiny to one of the great minds of the age. Indeed, Col. Doniphan's name and fame are familiar to every American citizen. Not only so—the world regards him with admiration, and justly, for he towers amongst men as the stately oak amongst his compeers of the forest.

Five years after Alexander was removed to Augusta the conferences of Ohio and Kentucky determined to locate a college at some point on the Ohio River convenient to the citizens of each State, to be under the control of the Methodist Episcopal Church. It was located at Augusta. At this institution Alexander graduated with high honors in 1827, in the nineteenth year of his age. He then read history, with great advantage, for six months, and in the spring of 1828 commenced the study of the law, under the supervision of that learned, profound, and able lawyer, Martin Marshall, of Augusta. He obtained a license to practice as an attorney before the courts in the fall of 1829; and having spent the winter of that year in traveling over the southwestern and western States, determined to locate himself at Lexington, Mo. Here he remained and enjoyed a lucrative practice for three years, during which he obtained considerable celebrity as an able and eloquent lawyer and established his reputation as an intelligent and useful citizen. In 1833 he removed to Liberty, in upper Missouri, more from its healthful situation and its salubrity than from any other cause. He still resides in this romantic and pleasant village.[1]

From this period of his history his success at the bar has been almost unexampled in Missouri. Immediately upon his locating in Liberty, a heavy business flowed into his hands. The fame which he had previously acquired as an able advocate and a sound lawyer gave him advantages that but few can enjoy. Never did Pericles gain a more complete ascendant over the minds of the Athenians than Col. Doniphan, by his courteous conduct as a citizen, his capacity as a lawyer, his talent as a legislator, and his powers as an orator, has attained over the people of upper Missouri. Although a majority of the people of Missouri are politically opposed to him, no one man enjoys more of their confidence and esteem as a patriot and a citizen.

About this period of his life he was united in marriage to the amiable and intelligent daughter of Col. John Thornton, of Clay County. He has two little cherub boys, whose correct training and proper education appear to be matter of the highest concern and of first-rate importance with him. Therefore, instead of grasping after political preferment, for the purpose of satisfying a selfish and sordid ambition, we see him endeavoring to accomplish the noblest of earthly objects—the proper training and instruction of his children. To this end he is often seen in the district schools, as well as the high

---

[1] When anyone inquires of Col. Doniphan why he does not choose to live in a more considerable town than Liberty, he gives them Plutarch's reply: " If I should remove hence, the place would be of still less note than it now is."

Like Epaminondas, the great Bœotian, Col. Doniphan has mostly lived in a house neither splendidly furnished, nor painted, nor whitewashed, but plain as the rest of his neighbors.

While commanding the Army, Col. Doniphan rarely wore any military dress, so he could not be distinguished by a stranger from one of the men whom he commanded. He fared as the soldiers and often prepared his own meals. Any private man in his camp might approach him with the greatest freedom and converse on whatever topics it pleased him, for he was always rejoiced to gain information from anyone, though a common soldier. Whoever had business might approach his tent and wake him when asleep, for he neither had a bodyguard nor persons to transact his business for him.

school of the town, encouraging by his presence the young developing minds and pointing them to the high rewards of industry and perseverance. The hero of Sacramento is now a trustee of the school in his own village.

He has long and honorably held the office of brigadier general in the militia of Missouri. In 1838 Gov. Boggs ordered a strong military force to proceed to far West, the headquarters of the Mormon sect, and quell the disturbances and insurrectionary movements which had been excited by their great prophet, Jo Smith. This fanaticism and insubordination threatened to embroil the whole country. In a short time troops were in motion from all parts of the State. Military preparations were being actively pushed forward by the prophet to meet the emergency. A sanguinary slaughter was expected to ensue. Gen. Doniphan, with his brigade (belonging to the division of Maj. Gen. Lucas), rendered important service in overawing the insurgent forces and quelling the disturbances without bloodshed. This was Gen. Doniphan's first campaign.

In all the relations of social and private life, where a man's true character is best known, and where, lamentable to tell, most of our ostensibly great men are most sadly deficient, Col. Doniphan's conduct is most exemplary. Here his virtues shine brightest. As a husband, he is affectionate; as a father, he rules his household with reason and decision. A just and wise economy marks the administration of his family affairs. As a neighbor, he is sociable and pleasant; as a citizen, benevolent and extensively useful. In all his dealings with mankind he is just and honorable. He is interesting and fluent in conversation. His manner and whole deportment are prepossessing, and one rarely makes his acquaintance without forming a lasting attachment for him. As an orator he possesses great and shining powers. His address is of the most agreeable nature, his air commanding, his language full and flowing, his gestures graceful, his enunciation distinct, his voice shrill and sonorous, his arguments convincing, his mind comprehensive and clear, his figures and illustrations happy and natural, his fancy not only brilliant but dazzlingly vivid; finally, when excited, the tide of his eloquence is almost irresistible. He is the very fullness of physical and intellectual vigor and possesses in an eminent degree the original elements of greatness. His best speeches have always been delivered extemporaneously, much of the fire and pathos being lost in the attempt to commit them to paper. He is not a member of any church, society, or fraternity, but in his views is tolerant of all and is the devoted friend of universal education. In stature, Col. Doniphan is upward of 6 feet tall, well proportioned, altogether dignified in his appearance and gentlemanly in his manners. His features are bold, his bright hazel eye dazzlingly keen and expressive, and his massive forehead is of the finest and most classic mold.

Unambitious of political advancement, he has never sought that unsubstantial, popular applause which sometimes elevates men to stations far above their abilities and merits and as often consigns them to useless obscurity, ever regarding fame as valuable and lasting only when based on virtue and substantial worth. For many years, having assiduously devoted his time and talent to his profession as a lawyer, he has acquired not only an enviable distinction amongst men, but has raised himself to ease and affluence. He commenced the world without fortune and without the aid of powerful friends to relieve him from those embarrassments which every man is destined to encounter who relies upon his own energy for success. But by dint of perseverance and a clear and well-balanced judgment he has arrived at both fame and fortune.

Never having been desirous of engaging permanently in political life, he has constantly refused to become a candidate for office, except on two occasions, notwithstanding he considers the public service to be the most honorable and exalted, and worthy to command the very best talent the country can afford. In 1836 he represented his county by an almost unanimous vote, although there was then a small majority in the county politically opposed to him. His success in this election was owing to his personal popularity and his great weight of character. In 1840, during that exciting political contest between Gen. Harrison and Mr. Van Buren, his political friends, in view of his great abilities as a stump orator, almost forced him to take the field as a candidate once more—it being looked to as a test race to decide the political complexion of the country. He was again elected by a large majority. While in the legislature he distinguished himself for his boldness, independence, liberality of sentiment, and faithfulness as a representative. From this period he has pertinaciously refused to become a candidate for any office whatever, frequently declaring in his public addresses that he neither expects nor desires ever to be a candidate again.[1] He has made these declarations, not that he feels a contempt for the public service (for no one better comprehends the value of liberty or regards the prosperity of the country with more interest than Col. Doniphan), but through a modest willingness to see the high functions of the Government discharged by others who have made these things the study of their whole lives.

In 1846, when hostilities were declared to exist between the United States and Mexico, and the Executive proposed to send an invading army across the plains to the Province of New Mexico, Gen. Doniphan actively interested himself in raising the requisite number of men to accompany the expedition. This expedition was to be under command of Col. Kearney. To hasten the preparations for the departure of the expedition, Gen. Doniphan visited many of the counties in upper Missouri, harangued the people, and in a very short space of time the complement was raised. They assembled at Fort Leavenworth and were mustered into service. Gen. Doniphan had volunteered as a private in the company from his own county, commanded by his brother-in-law, Capt. O. P. Moss. On the 18th of June, 1846, he was elected colonel of the First Regiment of Missouri Cavalry, over his opponent, Gen. J. W. Price, by a respectable majority. No fitter man could have been chosen; for his sagacity planned, his judgment conducted, and his energy, together with that of his officers and men, accomplished the most wonderful campaign of any age or country. This was done without an outfit, without money, and almost without ammunition, by the citizen commander of citizen soldiers. The history of this expedition will be Col. Doniphan's most lasting monument. His deeds will ever live to praise him.

---

[1] In his speech at Independence, on the 29th of July, 1847, he declared he had not been a candidate for office for "seven years," and did not expect to be for the next "seventy-seven" to come.

DONIPHAN'S EXPEDITION.

CHAPTER I.

Origin of the War with Mexico—Hostilities begun—Act of Congress to raise troops—Plan of invasion—Causes which justify the war—Army of the West—Gov. Edwards's requisition—Troops rendezvous at Fort Leavenworth—Drill exercises—Election of field officers—Strength of the expedition—Ladies visit the fort—Presentation of flags—Two squadrons dispatched in pursuit of Seyres and Armijo—Departure of the expedition—March conducted by detachments—Scene at the Stranger—The Kansas—Shawnees—Bewilderment—Bluff Hill—Santa Fe trail—Fiery steeds—Description of troops composing the Army of the West.

The passage, by the American Congress, of the resolutions of annexation, by which the Republic of Texas was incorporated into the Union as one of the States, having merged her sovereignty into that of our own Government, was the prime cause which led to the recent war with Mexico. However, the more immediate cause of the war may be traced to the occupation, by the American Army, of the strip of disputed territory lying between the Nueces and the Rio Grande. Bigoted and insulting Mexico, always prompt to manifest her hostility toward this Government, sought the earliest plausible pretext for declaring war against the United States. This declaration of war by the Mexican Government (which bore date in Apr., 1846) was quickly and spiritedly followed by a manifesto from our Congress at Washington, announcing that " a state of war exists between Mexico and the United States." Soon after this counter declaration the Mexicans crossed the Rio Grande, in strong force, headed by the famous generals, Arista and Ampudia. This force, as is well known, was defeated at Palo Alto on the 8th, and at Resaca de la Palma on the 9th of May, 1846, by the troops under command of Maj. Gen. Taylor, and repulsed with great slaughter. The whole Union was soon in a state of intense excitement. Gen. Taylor's recent glorious victories were the constant theme of universal admiratiton. The war had actually begun, and that, too, in a manner which demanded immediate and decisive action. The United States Congress passed an act, about the middle of May, 1846, authorizing the President to call into the field 50,000 volunteer troops, designed to operate against Mexico at three distinct points, namely, the southern wing or "Army of Occupation," commanded by Maj. Gen. Taylor, to penetrate directly into the heart of the country; the column under Brig. Gen. Wool, or the "Army of the Center," to operate against the city of Chihuahua; and the expedition under the command of Col. (now Brig. Gen.) Kearney, known as the "Army of the West," to direct its march upon the city of Santa Fe. This was the original plan of operation against Mexico. But subsequently the plan was changed; Maj. Gen. Scott, with a well-appointed army, was sent to Vera Cruz; Gen. Wool effected a junction with Gen. Taylor at Saltillo, and Gen.

Kearney divided his force into three separate commands; the first he led in person to the distant shores of the Pacific; a detachment of near 1,000 Missouri volunteers, under command of Col. A. W. Doniphan, was ordered to make a descent upon the State of Chihuahua, expecting to join Gen. Wool's division at the capital, while the greater part was left as a garrison at Santa Fe, under command of Col. Sterling Price. The greatest eagerness was manifested by the citizens of the United States to engage in the war; to redress our wrongs; to repel an insulting foe; and to vindicate our national honor and the honor of our oft-insulted flag. The call of the President was promptly responded to; but of the 50,000 volunteers at first authorized to be raised, the services of only about 17,000 were required.

The cruel and inhuman butchery of Col. Fannin and his men, all Americans; the subsequent and indiscriminate murder of all Texans who unfortunately fell into Mexican hands; the repeated acts of cruelty and injustice perpetrated upon the persons and property of American citizens residing in the northern Mexican provinces; the imprisonment of American merchants without the semblance of a trial by jury, and the forcible seizure and confiscation of their goods; the robbing of American travelers and tourists in the Mexican country of their passports and other means of safety, whereby in certain instances they were deprived of their liberty; the forcible detention of American citizens, sometimes in prison and at other times in free custody; the recent blockade of the Mexican ports against the United States trade; the repeated insults offered our national flag; the contemptuous ill-treatment of our ministers, some of whom were spurned with their credentials; the supercilious and menacing air uniformly manifested toward this Government, which with characteristic forbearance and courtesy, has endeavored to maintain a friendly understanding; her hasty and unprovoked declaration of war against the United States; her army's unceremonious passage of the Rio Grande in strong force and with hostile intention; her refusal to pay indemnities; and a complication of less evils, all of which have been perpetrated by the Mexican authorities or by unauthorized Mexican citizens in a manner which clearly evinced the determination on the part of Mexico, to terminate the amicable relations hitherto existing between the two countries are the causes which justify the war. Are not these sufficient? Or should we have forborne until the catalogue of offenses was still deeper dyed with infamous crimes, and until the blood of our brothers, friends, and consanguinity, like that of the murdered Abel, should cry to us from the ground? Who that has the spirit, the feelings, and the pride of an American would willingly see his country submit to such a complication of injury and insult? In truth, the only cause of regret is that the war was not prosecuted with more vigor, energy, and promptitude from the commencement. This, perhaps, would have prevented the effusion of so much blood and the expenditure of so much treasure.

It is the "Army of the West" that commands our immediate attention. About the middle of May Gov. Edwards, of Missouri, made a requisition on the State for volunteers to join the expedition to Santa Fe. This expedition was conducted by Col. Stephen W. Kearney, of the First Dragoons, United States Army, a very able and skilled officer. The troops designed for this service were required to rendezvous at

Fort Leavenworth, situated on the right bank of the Missouri River, 22 miles above the mouth of the Kansas, which was the place of outfit and departure for the western army. The "St. Louis Legion,"[1] commanded by Col. Easton, had already taken its departure for the Army of Occupation. Corps of mounted volunteers were speedily organized in various counties throughout the State in conformity to the governor's requisition, and company officers elected. By the 5th of June the companies began to arrive at the fort and were mustered into the service of the United States, and lettered in the order of their arrival. The process of mustering the men into the United States service, and of valuing their horses, was intrusted to the late lamented Capt. Allen, of the First Dragoons. Gen. Kearney had discretionary orders from the War Department as to the number of men which should compose his division and what proportion of them should be Cavalry and what Infantry. Owing to the great distance across the plains, Cavalry was deemed the better description of troops, and accordingly the whole western army, with the exception of one separate battalion, consisted of mounted men. For the space of 20 days, during which time portions of the volunteers remained at the fort, rigid drill twice per day, once before and after noon, was required to be performed by them, in order to render their services the more efficient. These martial exercises, upon a small prairie adjacent to the fort, appropriately styled by the volunteers "Campus Martis," consisting of the march by sections of four, the saber exercises, the charge, the rally, and other cavalry tactics doubtless proved subsequently to be of the most essential service. It is due to the officers of the Regular Army, by whom the volunteers were principally carried through the drill exercises, to state that their instructions were always communicated in the kindest and most gentlemanly manner.

The election of field officers for the First Regiment Missouri Mounted Volunteers, was justly regarded as a matter of very great importance; as in the event of Gen. Kearney's death or disability, the colonel of that regiment would be entitled to the command of the expedition. On the 18th of June, the full complement of companies having arrived, which were to compose the First Regiment, an election was holden, superintended by Gen. Ward, of Platte, which resulted in the selection of Alexander William Doniphan, a private in the company from Clay County, an eminent lawyer, a man who had distinguished himself as a brigadier general in the campaign of 1838, against the Mormons at Far West, and who had honorably served his countrymen as a legislator, for colonel of the regiment. C. F. Ruff was chosen lieutenant colonel, and William Gilpin, major. Lieut. Col. Ruff and Maj. Gilpin had both volunteered as privates, the former in the company from Clay, and the latter in that from Jackson County.

The First Regiment of Missouri Mounted Volunteers was composed of eight companies, A, B, C, D, E, F, G, and H, respectively from the counties of Jackson, Lafayette, Clay, Saline, Franklin, Cole, Howard, and Calaway, commanded by Capts. Waldo, Walton, Moss, Reid, Stephenson, Parsons, Jackson, and Rodgers, numbering

---

[1] This corps was discharged at the expiration of 6 months.

856 men. The battalion of Light Artillery consisted of two companies from St. Louis under Capts. Weightman and Fischer, numbering near 250 men, with Maj. Clark as its field officer. The battalion of infantry from the counties of Cole and Platte, respectively commanded by Capts. Angney and Murphy, the former being the senior officer, numbered 145 men. The Laclede Rangers from St. Louis, under command of Capt. Hudson, 107 in number, attached to the First Dragoons, whose strength was 300, composed the entire force of Col. Kearney. Thus it will appear that the advance of the Western Army under the immediate command of Col. Kearney consisted of 1,658 men, and 16 pieces of ordnance, twelve 6-pounders, and four 12-pound howitzers.

When this column was on the eve of departure for the different borders of New Mexico, the people of upper Missouri collected in crowds at the fort to bid their sons, brothers, and relatives adieu before they launched upon the boundless plains of the West. The ushering of an army upon the green bosom of the great prairies, with pennons gaily streaming in the breeze, is a sight no less interesting in its nature, and there can be no less solicitude felt for its safety than is manifested at the departure of a fleet for some distant land, when, with spreading sails, the vessels launch upon the restless, heaving deep. Before the expedition set out, the patriotic ladies from the adjacent counties on several occasions came to the fort (on board the steamboats which were then almost daily arriving and departing) to present their countrymen with flags wrought by their own hands— at once the token of their regard and the star-lighted emblem of their country's liberty. On the presentation of these flags the ladies usually delivered addresses which seemed to inspire every heart with courage, and nerve every arm for the dangers of the campaign. On the 23d day of June, a large deputation of ladies from Clay arrived at the fort on the *Missouri Mail* with the finest flag, perhaps, of which the expedition could boast, and presented it to Capt. O. P. Moss of their county, accompanied by the following patriotic address, delivered by Mrs. Cunningham:

The ladies of Liberty and its vicinity have deputed me as one of their number, to present this flag to the volunteers from Clay County, commanded by Capt. Oliver Perry Moss, and I now in their name present it to you as a token of their esteem for the manly and patriotic manner in which you have shown your willingness to sustain the honor of our common country, and to redress the indignities offered to its flag.

In presenting to you this token of our regard and esteem, we wish you to remember that some of us have sons, some brothers, and all of us either friends or relatives among you, and that we would rather hear of your failing in honorable warfare than to see you return sullied with crime or disgraced by cowardice. We trust, then, that your conduct in all circumstances will be worthy the noble, intelligent, and patriotic nation whose cause you have so generously volunteered to defend; your deportment will be such as will secure to you the highest praise and the warmest gratitude of the American people; in a word, let your motto be, "Death before dishonor." And to the gracious protection of Him who rules the destinies of nations, we fervently commend you.

The captain modestly received the flag in a brief and pathetic response. Its motto was: "The love of country is the love of God."

The above specimen is given as illustrative of the enthusiastic and uncalculating spirit of the western people when the country calls them to vindicate her national honor. Without counting the cost, either of treasure or blood, they fly to arms, impelled by patriotism, and act upon the principle "we are for our country, right or wrong."

About this time, Capts. Waldo and Reid of the volunteers, and Capts. Moore and Burgwin of the First Dragoons, United States Army, were dispatched by Col. Kearney with their respective companies upon the route to Santa Fe, with orders to pursue with all possible vigor and capture the trains of Messrs. Speyers and Armijo of the trading caravan, who were far in advance of the other merchants, and who, it was understood, were furnished with British and Mexican passports, and were endeavoring to supply the enemy with munitions of war. The pursuit was vain, however, as the sequel will develop.

The organization of the expedition was completed by the appointment to office of the following gentlemen, viz: Capt. Riche to be sutler to the dragoons; C. A. Perry to be sutler, G. M. Butler, adjutant, Dr. Geo. Penn, principal surgeon, and T. M. Morton and J. Vaughan, assistant surgeons of the First Regiment.

About 100 wagons, loaded with provisions for the Army, having already been sent forward upon the road, and other means of transportation being furnished for whatever was thought necessary upon the expedition by McKissack, quartermaster, on the 26th day of June, 1846, the main body of the Western Army commenced its march over the great prairies or plains, which extend from the western border of Missouri to the confines of New Mexico, a distance of near 1,000 miles. The annual caravan or merchant train of 414 wagons, heavily laden with dry goods for the markets of Santa Fe and Chihuahua, lined the road for miles. Independence was the point of departure for this army of merchants. Col. Kearney and the rear, consisting partly of volunteers and partly of the First Dragoons, soon followed, having left the fort on the 29th of the same month.

The march of the "Army of the West," as it entered upon the great prairies, presented a scene of the most intense and thrilling interest. Such a scene was indeed worthy the pencil of the ablest artist or the most graphic pen of the historian. The boundless plains, lying in wavy green not unlike the ocean, seemed to unite with the heavens in the distant horizon. As far as vision could penetrate, the long files of cavalry, the gay fluttering of banners, and the canvas-covered wagons of the merchant train glistening like banks of snow in the distance might be seen winding their tortuous way over the undulating surface of the prairies. In thus witnessing the march of an army over the regions of uncultivated nature, which had been the pasture of the buffalo and the hunting ground of the wily savage, and where the eagle and the Stars and Stripes never before greeted the breeze, the heart could but swell with sentiments of honest pride, mingled with the most lively emotions.[1]

There are many obstacles which impede the progress of an army. There was no road, nor even a path leading from Fort Leavenworth into the regular Santa Fe Trail. The Army therefore steered its

---

[1] In a letter addressed by the author to the editor of the Tribune, a paper published in Liberty, about the time the expedition set forward, the following language was employed: " There is a novelty in this anabasis or invasion of Cols. Kearney and Doniphan. For the first time since the creation, the Starred and Striped Banner of a free people is being borne over almost 1,000 miles of trackless waste, and the principles of republicanism and civil liberty are about to be proclamed to a nation fast sinking in slavery's arms; and fast closing her eyes upon the last expiring lights of religion, science, and liberty."

course southwesterly with the view of intersecting the main Santa Fe Trail at or near the Narrows 65 miles west of Independence. In accomplishing this many deep ravines and creeks with high and rugged banks were to be encountered. The banks must be dug down, the asperities leveled, bridges built, and roads constructed before the wagons could pass. All this required time and labor. The heat was often excessive, the grass was tall and rank, and the earth in many places so soft that the heavily loaded wagons would sink almost up to the axle upon the level prairie. The men were frequently compelled to dismount and drag them from the mire with their hands. The mules and other animals being mostly unused to the harness often became refractory and balky. Numbers of wagons daily broke down. Time was required to make repairs. Hence the march was of necessity both slow and tedious.

On the 28th, the advanced battalion under command of Lieut. Col. Ruff, arrived upon the banks of Stranger Creek, where it remained until the 30th. Here also was presented a scene of some interest. Some of the men were reclining at ease in their tents, beguiling time with a novelette of a newspaper; some were engaged in scouring and whetting their sabers, as if they already anticipated an attack from the Mexicans; others again were bathing their bodies in the limpid stream, or drawing the scaly fish to the shore. The Stranger is a branch of the Kansas, and drains one of the most fertile and picturesque districts of country over which the Army passed.

About noon on the 30th, we arrived upon the banks of the Kansas River. This is a deep, rapid, yet beautiful stream, 350 yards wide, and more than 500 miles in length. It is no doubt navigable by steamboats of the smaller class, for a considerable distance above its mouth, without difficulty. We crossed the river in boats without loss or accident, and encamped for the night on the west bank, among the friendly Shawnees. Some of the Shawnees have large farms, and as fine fields of corn as are to be met with in the States. They also have plenty of poultry, domestic animals, fine gardens, and many of the luxuries of civilized life. Here we obtained milk and butter; also peas, beans, potatoes, and other vegetables. The country between Fort Leavenworth and the Kansas, is very fine; the soil is exceedingly fertile,—vegetation is exuberant; and in many places the timber is tall and stately. Bold, fresh running springs gush from the ledges of limestone rock, and every river and creek is literally alive with the "finny tribe." It is destined perhaps at no distant day to sustain a dense and intelligent population. What a cheering reflection, that these beautiful ridges and outstretched plains will ere long be dotted with the cities, villages, and habitations of civilized life— that cultivated fields, surcharged with rich grains, will soon succeed to the seas of waving verdure which now luxuriously cover the earth, and that where now is heard the scream of the wild panther and the startling yell of the savage will soon become the busy scene of industry and domestic happiness!

On the 1st of July, the battalion continued its march in a southwesterly direction, to intersect the road leading from Independence to Santa Fe. After a toilsome march of near 15 miles, without a guide, through the tall prairie grass and matted pea vines, over hill and dale, mound and mountain, in our bewilderment, sometimes directing our course to the southward, sometimes to the westward, we at length struck upon the old Santa Fe trace, and encamped for the night near the blackjack grove or the Narrows. In our progress to-day, we encountered a formidable, precipitous, and almost impassable hill or bluff, consisting of a solid ledge of limestone, which we were compelled to surmount, as it was impossible to avoid it by turning either to the right or the left. The ascent was steep, rugged, and at least 200 feet in height, being the projecting spur of the high table-land which divides the waters of the Kansas from those of the Osage. The wagons were principally drawn up this abrupt precipice by the power of hand, ropes being attached to them on both sides. More than 100 men were often employed at once in drawing a heavily loaded Government wagon to the summit of the hill. The heat was excessive.

It may be proper here to observe, that for the sake of convenience in procuring supplies of fuel and water, which can only be obtained at certain points, in crossing the Great Plains, Col. Kearney very prudently adopted the plan of conducting the march by separate detachments. These detachments (for convenience in traveling) generally consisted of a squadron of two or three companies, or of an entire battalion. The companies of volunteers were generally composed of 114 men each, including commissioned officers. Thus the march was chiefly conducted to the borders of New Mexico, or the boundary line which separates between Mexico and the United States.

Col. Doniphan and Maj. Gilpin, with the second battalion, and Col. Kearney, with the battalion of artillery, the corps of field and topographical engineers, and a small squadron of volunteers and dragoons, followed closely in our rear; nothing of historical moment having occurred up to this time, since their departure from Fort Leavenworth. Numerous trains of Government wagons continued to be dispatched from the Fort upon the road to Santa Fe. Fort Bent, on the Arkansas, nearly 600 miles west of Independence, was, however, looked forward to as the first point of general rendezvous for all the different detachments, and for the Government trains. This post was subsequently converted into a provision depot for the United States Government.

The practicability of marching a large army over the waste, uncultivated, uninhabited prairie regions of the West was universally regarded as problematical. But the matter has been tested. The experiment proved completely successful. Provisions (chiefly breadstuffs, salt, etc.) were conveyed in wagons, and beef cattle driven along for the use of the men. The animals subsisted entirely by grazing. To secure them from straying off at night, they were either driven into corrals formed of the wagons or tethered to an iron picket driven into the ground about 15 inches.

At the outset of the expedition many laughable scenes took place. Our horses were generally wild, fiery, and ungovernable, wholly unused to military trappings and equipments. Amid the fluttering of banners, the sounding of bugles, the rattling of artillery, the clattering of sabers and cooking utensils, some of the horses took fright and scampered pell-mell, with rider and arms, over the wide prairie. Rider, arms, and accouterments, saddlebags, tin cups, and coffeepots were sometimes left far behind in the chase. No very serious or fatal accident, however, occurred from this cause. All was right again as soon as the affrighted animals were recovered.

The "Army of the West" was, perhaps, composed of as fine material as any other body of troops then in the field. The volunteer corps consisted almost entirely of the young men of the country; generally of the very first families of the State. All parties were united in one common cause for the vindication of the national honor. Every calling and profession contributed its share. There might be seen under arms, in the ranks, the lawyer, the doctor, the professor, the student, the legislator, the farmer, the mechanic, and artisians of every description, all united as a band of brothers to defend the rights and honor of their country, to redress her wrongs and avenge her insults. This blooming host of young life, the elite of Missouri, was full of ardor, full of spirit, full of generous enthusiasm, burning for the battle field and panting for the rewards of honorable victory. They were prompted to this gallant discharge of duty, and prepared to breast every storm of adversity, by the remembrance of the dear pledges of affection they left behind them; their mothers, their sisters, their young brides, their aged fathers, who, they knew would receive them with outstretched arms, if they returned triumphant from many a well-contested field with the laurels of victory; but who, they were equally certain, would frown with indignation upon him who, in the hour of battle, would desert the flag of his country. Their chivalry failed them not.

CHAPTER II.

All was now fairly upon the great Santa Fe Road which led to the
enemy's country. At break of day on the 2d of July, the reveille was
sounded. The army was on the march ere the first beams of the morning sun had kissed the glittering dewdrops from the prairie grass,
bearing aloft their streaming flags to the breeze, with their " broad
stripes and bright stars," and " E Pluribus Unum." As the troops
moved off majestically over the green prairie, they presented the
most martial and animating sight. The long lines stretched over miles
of level plain, or wound serpentinely over the beautifully undulating
hills, with guns and sabers glittering in the sheen of the rising sun,
while the American eagle seemed to spread his broad pinions and
westward bear the principles of republican government.

The following interesting phenomenon was related to the author
by one who declares that he was an eyewitness of the fact, and that
28 others will testify to the truth of his declaration:

Early in the spring of 1846, before it was known, or even conjectured, that
a state of war would be declared to exist between this Government and Mexico,
29 traders, on their way from Santa Fe to Independence, beheld, just after a
storm and a little while before sunset, a perfectly distinct image of the " bird
of liberty," the American eagle, on the disc of the sun. When they beheld the
interesting sight they simultaneously and almost involuntarily exclaimed that
in less than 12 months the eagle of liberty would spread his broad pinions
over the plains of the West, and that the flag of our country would wave over
the cities of New Mexico and Chihuahua.

The prediction has been literally and strikingly verified, although
the story is, doubtless, more beautiful than true. Quite as much
credit is due to it, however, as to the wonderful story about the
chariots of fire, which the Romans are said to have seen in the
heavens after the assassination of Caesar by Brutus and Cassius in
the Roman senate.

A march over the great plains is attended with a recurrence of
pretty much the same scenes from day to day. The same boundless
green—the emerald prairies—seems to spread out before you; the
same bright heavens are above; the same solid earth of uniform surface beneath; or if the monotony be at all broken, it is by the gradual
change of the broad prairie into a succession of gently rolling hills,
as if when the unruffled bosom of the ocean is heaved into waves
by the storm. Occasionally the dull scene is relieved by the appear-

23

ance of a rill or brook, winding among the undulations of the prairie, skirted by clumps and groves of trees, or by the wild sunflower, pink, or rose, which seem to blossom only to cheer with their mellifluous odors the waste around them. Some witty remark, or lively song, will often create a hearty laugh; the feeling will perhaps be communicated from one end of the line to the other. In this way the greatest good humor and most cheerful flow of spirits are kept up continually on the march. An army is always cheerful and frolicsome.

On the plains our horses were the objects of our most especial attention. Whoever was so unfortunate as to lose his charger was necessitated to continue the march on foot, or drive a wagon, both of which were unpleasant to the volunteer soldier, to say nothing of the chagrin of losing his place in his company as a cavalier. We therefore secured our horses with all possible care at night, to guard against escapes. Great prudence was also necessary in riding cautiously, and grazing carefully, to prevent the stock from failing on the road. Chasing deer, antelope, and buffalo on the plain will ruin a horse, and speedily unfit him for military service. When a soldier by ill luck happened to lose his horse he would purchase another at almost any cost, if there chanced to be a surplus one in camp. His situation enabled him fully to appreciate the force of the expression which Shakespeare puts into the mouth King Richard, "A kingdom for a horse!" No wonder, then, that Alexander wept when Bucephalus died.

The Fourth of July, independence day, seemed to inspire the troops with new life and cheerfulness; although upon the wide prairies of the West, we could not forget to commemorate the annual return of the hallowed day that gave birth to our national liberty. Though on the march all day, and in the midst of a boundless solitude, with nothing for the eye to rest upon save the heaven above or the solid earth beneath, and none of the lovely objects of home around us, and none of the festivities spread before us, which usually greeted us on the anniversary of our liberty, yet our bosoms swelled with the same noble impulses and the same quenchless love of freedom which animated the breast of our ancestors of Seventy-six, and caught inspiration from the memory of their achievements. Ever and anon the enthusiastic shout, the loud huzza, and the animating Yankee Doodle were heard in honor of independence day. After a toilsome march of 27 miles upon the green, boundless plain, exposed to the heated rays of an almost vertical sun, we pitched our tents at sunset on the banks of Bluff Creek, where we found plenty of cool spring water and an abundant supply of grass and fuel. The greatest good humor prevailed in camp.

A march of 12 miles on the 5th brought us to the famous Council Grove, a place remarkable in the history of the Santa Fe trade, and distinguished above all others as being the point of general rendezvous for traders, trappers, mountaineers, and others of border life. Here timbers for repairing wagons which may fail on the road across the great plains are generally procured, this being the last grove where good timber can be obtained on the route. In this pleasant and romantic valley the Army was detained two days for this purpose. The Council Grove is nothing more than a forest of timber about one mile in width, skirting a beautiful meandering stream, the head branch of the Neosho River, fed by innumerable rills and springs of the finest and most delicious water, although some writers have attempted to invest it with a sort of romantic interest, and dignify it with a name calculated to induce the belief that the various wild tribes of the plains once met annually upon this consecrated spot " to smoke the calumet of peace." This grove, where the prairie traveler often takes a pleasant siesta, and where a few houses and a blacksmith shop have recently been erected for the use of the Government, is situated about 150 miles west of the western frontier of Missouri.

Advancing about 16 miles further, over high, rolling prairies, we encamped near the Diamond Springs. The heat was oppressive. The most enchanting spots ever depicted by the pen of the eastern romancer possess not more charms for the youthful imagination than do the groves and the fine, gushing, transparent Diamond Springs for the thirsty, wayworn traveler on the plains. These crystal fountains derive their name from the limpidness of their waters. Travelers across the plains are compelled to stop at certain places for water, wood, and rest. These places for convenience are mostly dignified with appropriate names, though in the midst of solitary wastes where there never existed, and perhaps never will exist, a human habitation, or the least vestige of civilization.

Our provisions becoming scant, on the 7th, Lieut. S. Jackson, of Howard, with four men, was sent forward seven or eight days' march in advance of the command, with orders to halt a train of provision wagons at the Pawnee Fork of the Arkansas. This order was promptly executed. It may not be improper in this connection to observe that the Government trains, which were fitted up at Fort Leavenworth, were despatched upon the road in companies of 25 or 30 wagons, irrespective of the marches of the different detachments of troops. It therefore often happened that some portions of the Army, for short periods of time, were destitute of supplies upon the road. Each of these trains of wagons had a superintendent general, or wagon master, and the wagoners were well armed, so that there was no need of an escort or guard, as these brave and hardy teamsters were at all times prepared to fight their own battles against the Indians who beset the roads for plunder. Had the wagoners employed in Gen. Taylor's division of the Army been equally well furnished with arms, perhaps so many of them would not have fallen a sacrifice to the Mexican guerrillas.

After a progress of 29 miles,[1] over a level, smooth surface, covered with tall, rank grass, waving in green ridges before the sporting breeze, we arrived upon the banks of the Cottonwood Fork of the Neosho. On these elevated prairies an interesting phenomenon is presented, worthy of the consideration of the philosopher. A zigzag strip of grass of more luxuriant growth than the rest, resembling the forky course of lightning, may often be distinctly traced by the eye. The proposition then arises, may not the lightning, in its course, thus have touched and marked the earth, communicating to the soil a degree of fertility which manifests itself in the exuberant produc-

---

[1] The distance of each day's march was generally reported by Capt. Emory, of the Field and Topographical Engineers, and also the latitude and longitude of all places of importance on the route.

tion alluded to? And may not barren countries and sterile lands be reclaimed by conducting the electric fluid into the bosom of the earth by means of lightning rods or an iron forest? Surely these propositions are of some magnitude.

A march of 15 miles brought us to Turkey Creek, where we found a tolerable supply of grass and water, but not a stick of timber—not even a twig as large as a pipestem. This was the first time the men were necessitated to broil their meat and boil their coffee on a smouldering heap of the dried ordure of the buffalo, which lay scattered in great profusion upon the prairie. This " prairie fuel," as the volunteers termed it, is a tolerable substitute for wood in dry, but is worse than useless in wet, weather. It was our chief reliance, however, as we advanced further upon the great plains.

On the 9th, after a hurried march of 25 miles, we arrived upon the banks of the Little Arkansas, about 10 miles above its confluence with the main Arkansas River. Here the mosquitoes, and their allies, the black gnat, in swarms, attacked us in the most heroic manner, and annoyed us as much if not more than the Mexican lancers did at a subsequent period. While at this camp an express arrived from the two detachments immediately under command of Cols. Doniphan and Kearney, representing them as being in a starving condition, and calling upon Lieut. Col. Ruff to furnish them with such portion of his provisions as could be spared. Lieut. Col. Ruff, being destitute himself, and having, as already noticed, sent an express to Pawnee Fork for supplies, directed the expressmen from Col. Kearney to proceed thither and bring to a halt such a number of provision wagons as would be sufficient for the three detachments. One of these expressmen, A. E. Hughes, in attempting to swim the Pawnee River, at that time very much swollen by the recent freshets, was drowned. His corpse was afterwards found floating in the stream, and was taken and buried with appropriate military honors.[1]

On the morning of the 10th a heavy drenching rain was descending. Twenty or thirty men were sick and comfortably sheltered by their tents from the driving storm. An order was given, however, to take up the line of march. Some of the captains at first refused to strike tents, not wishing to expose their sick men unnecessarily to the inclement weather. The order was regarded as ill timed and highly improper. An altercation took place between Capt. Jackson and Lieut. Col. Ruff, commanding the detachment, the result of which, however, was less serious than was at first anticipated. At length all struck their tents and were ready for the march. We left at this camping place for the detachment with Col. Doniphan the only provisions we had to spare, consisting of two barrels of flour, two of pork, and one of salt. This relieved the colonel considerably, as he had with him only two companies, numbering about 220 men. Col. Kearney was still in the rear of Col. Doniphan, about one day's march, with five companies, very scant of provisions, pushing forward with the utmost vigor. The two companies under Capts. Reid and Waldo were in our advance some three days' march, and still further on was the detachment of dragoons under Capts. Moore, Burgwin, and Lieut. Noble.

---

[1] Mr. Innman, a merchant of Lexington, was drowned in the Missouri, at Fort Leavenworth, just before the expedition set forward. He was the first man lost. His interment took place at the fort.

Col. Doniphan, having quickened his pace, overhauled the first battalion under command of Lieut. Col. Ruff, on the evening of the 11th, encamped on Cow Creek. This was the first time we had seen Col. Doniphin since leaving Fort Leavenworth, a distance of 250 miles. Uniting the two detachments, his force was now swelled to near 700 men. It was on this creek that Don Antonio Jose Chavez, a New Mexican trader, was robbed and murdered in the spring of 1843 by a marauding party of 15 men, headed by Capt. John McDaniel, of Liberty, pretending to hold a commission under the government of Texas. This unfortunate Mexican had with him five servants, and about $10,000, principally in gold bullion. The perpetrators of this bloody deed were promptly arrested and brought to justice. The captain and one of his comrades being convicted of murder before the United States court at St. Louis, were executed according to law. The rest who were concerned in the robbery were sentenced to fine and imprisonment. A few escaped.

Early on the morning of the 12th the command left Cow Creek and after a march of 26 miles encamped for the night at Walnut Creek, near its junction with the Arkansas. The day was excessively hot. The thermometer, though exposed to the breeze, stood at 95° F. The earth was literally parched to a crust and the grass in many cases crisped by the heat of the sun. In the distant horizon upon the green plains might be seen ephemeral rivers and lakes, inviting you to drink of their seemingly delicious waters. It is all, however, a tantalizing illusion, for as you approach the enchanting spot the waters recede. This deceptive mirage which so much resembles lakes and rivers of water may perhaps be produced by the rays of the sun being reflected from the glossy green surface of the prairies, and also by their suffering some dispersion in their passage through the atmosphere, which, in that open and elevated country, is in constant motion. These false ponds and rivers appear to be at the distance of about 1 mile from the spectator. In approaching the Arkansas a landscape of the most imposing and picturesque nature makes its appearance, while the green, glossy undulations of the prairie to the right seem to spread out in infinite succession, like waves subsiding after a storm, covered with herds of gamboling buffalo; on the left, towering to the height of 75 to 100 feet, rise the yellow, golden sun-gilt summits of the sand hills, among which winds the broad majestic river, "bespeckled with verdant islets thickly set with cottonwood timber." The sand hills in shape resemble heaps of driven snow.

The march had now been continued nearly all the day without water. The men and animals were growing faint with thirst, but the waters of the big Arkansas, rolling silently and majestically through its own wide savannahs, suddenly appearing, reinvigorated them. Horse and man ran involuntarily into the river and simultaneously slaked their burning thirst. The Arkansas here is a broad, sandy, shallow stream, with low banks, fordable at almost any point, and is skirted on either side by clumps of elm, oak, walnut, cottonwood, and other trees. The principal growth, however, is to be found on the islands, which chequer with green spots the broad course of the river. At Walnut Creek we overtook 15 merchant wagons belonging to the Santa Fe trade. Henceforward they continued with the Army for the protection it afforded.

By the dawn of day on the 13th we were on the march. Innumerable herds of buffalo presented themselves in all directions. The whole plain was literally alive with them as far as the eye could reach. These huge animals, whose flesh is esteemed the greatest delicacy on the plains, present a sight of no ordinary interest to an army of hungry men whose palates, more than their eyes or curiosity, need to be satisfied. Great numbers of them were killed, and the Army feasted upon them most sumptuously. A march of 15 miles brought us to the noted Pawnee Rock, of which Mr. Josiah Gregg, in his "Commerce on the Prairies," thus speaks: "This rock is situated at the projecting point of a ridge, and upon its surface are furrowed, in uncouth but legible characters, numerous dates, and the names of various travelers who have chanced to pass that way." A great battle, as the legend goes, was once fought near this rock, which appears conspicuous above the prairies at the distance of 15 miles, between the Pawnees and their mortal enemies, the Cheyennes, whence the name. Digressing to the left and proceeding from this point southwardly 4 or 5 miles, for wood and water, we encamped on the east bank of the Arkansas. Here the men forded the river and killed plenty of buffalo, elk, antelope, and deer, and brought in quantities of the grape plum, ripe and of excellent flavor. Here also fish were caught in abundance. The night was therefore consumed in feasting and merriment.

Early on the morning of the 14th the Army was put in motion, Capt. Congreve Jackson and his company being left to pay the last honors to the remains of young N. Carson, who died suddenly the previous night. His burial took place near the Pawnee Rock, a decent grave being prepared to receive the corpse, wrapped in a blanket instead of a coffin and shroud. A tombstone was raised to mark the spot where he reposes, with his name, age, and the date of his decease engraved in large capitals. He slumbers in the wild Pawnee's land. This is but a sample of the interment of hundreds whose recent graves mark the march of the Western Army. A progress of 14 miles brought us to the Pawnee Fork, where, to our great relief, we found Lieut. Jackson, who had been sent forward from the Diamond Springs with 25 commissary wagons. To guard this provision train against the treacherous and wily Pawnees, who constantly beset the road for murder and plunder, Capt. Waldo had left Lieut. Reed with 36 men.

On the 15th Col. Kearney, with the rear of the Army, consisting of five companies, two of Volunteer Infantry, two of Volunteer Light Artillery, one of Mounted Volunteers, and a small number of the First Dragoons, overhauled Col. Doniphan, forming a junction of their forces at the Pawnee Fork. Mr. Riche, sutler to the First Dragoons, and post master on the expedition, brought up the mail to our encampment. This mail brought us the first and only intelligence we had received from the States since our departure from Fort Leavenworth, although we had advanced upon the road 300 miles. No one can so fully appreciate the value of a newspaper or a letter as he who is cast abroad on the solitary plains and cut off by intervening deserts from all the enjoyments of society. Everything in the shape of news was devoured with the utmost eagerness. The river, swollen by recent showers, was impassable. Col. Kearney, however, with his accustomed energy, determined not to delay. He therefore caused trees to be felled across the deep, rapid current. This was the labor of a day. On the trunks of these trees the men passed over, carrying with them their sick, arms, accoutrements, tents, and baggage. In this manner the principal loading of the wagons was also transported. Our animals were forced to swim the stream. The wagons, the bodies being made fast to the running gear, were next floated across by means of ropes attached to them and hauled up the hill by manual power. This immense labor having been accomplished without serious accident or loss, on the 17th Col. Kearney put his whole column in motion. The sick were conveyed in the baggage wagons. This was a miserable arrangement. Spring carriages, for the use of the medical department, should have been fitted out by the Government to accompany the expedition. Had this been done many valuable lives might have been saved.

The companies of infantry kept pace with the mounted men. Their feet were blistered by their long and almost incredible marches. The ground was often marked with blood in their footprints; yet with Roman fortitude they endured the toils of the campaign. Their courage could neither be abated by distance, nor their resolution relaxed by difficulties, nor their spirits subdued by privations, nor their ardor cooled by length of time. Diverging from the main Santa Fe road, we followed the Arkansas. Having performed a toilsome march of 27 miles, over a level, sandy, bottom prairie, darkened by herds of lowing buffalo, and abounding with numerous insects and reptiles, we encamped for the night, and pitched our tents on the verge of that broad and beautiful stream. Our encampment, laid off in military order, resembled a small city, and seemed as though it had sprung up by enchantment. This river has some singular features: Its banks are seldom elevated more than 2 feet above the surface of the water in the channel, which is remarkably broad and shallow. The current is swift. Consequently, under the agency of the wind and the heat of the sun, evaporation takes place rapidly. This is a wise provision of nature for furnishing moisture to the adjacent plains, which otherwise must have remained barren and parched, as but little rain falls during the year in this region. To-day Maj. Howard returned from Santa Fe, whither he had been dispatched by Col. Kearney, to ascertain the disposition of the New Mexicans in reference to submitting to the Government of the United States. He failed, however, to accomplish fully the purpose of his mission; reporting that the common people, or plebeians, were inclined to favor the conditions of peace proposed by Col. Kearney, to wit, that if they would lay down their arms and take the oath of allegiance to the Government of the United States they should, to all intents and purposes, become citizens of the same Republic, receiving the protection and enjoying the liberties guaranteed to other American citizens; but that the patrician classes, who held the offices and ruled the country, were hostile and were making warlike preparations. He added further that 2,300 men were already armed for the defense of the capital and that others were assembling at Taos. This report produced quite a sensation in our camp. It was now expected that Col. Kearney's entrance into Santa Fe would be obstinately disputed.

On the 20th, after a march of near 30 miles over a surface covered with friable, calcareous limestone, we arrived at the crossing of the

Arkansas, where we found an abundant supply of grass, wood, and water. During our progress to-day we enjoyed a very fine view of a buffalo chase. Nothing except a charge upon the Mexicans could have animated the men more, or produced more thrilling sensations. The broad plain spread its green bosom before us; our bannered column extended for miles along its level surface. Suddenly a band of 400 buffalo, emerging from the Arkansas, broke through our ranks, when our men charged upon them with guns, pistols, and drawn sabers. A scene of beautiful confusion ensued. Pell-mell they went scampering and thundering along the plain, exhibiting just such a tumult as perhaps the solitudes never before witnessesd. Several of these huge animals paid the forfeit of their lives for their temerity.

Early on the morning of the 21st we continued our march, winding along the north margin of the river, leaving the main Santa Fe Road by the Cimarron at the crossing. This part of the country abounds in serpents, cameleons, prairie lizards, horned frogs, dry-land turtles, and the whole tribe of the entomologist. Grasshoppers are as numerous as were the locusts sent by the afflicting hand of Providence in swarms upon the land of Egypt. To cheer the solitude and break the monotony of the plains, in many places a rich variety of flowers blossom and brush "waste their sweetness on the desert air." The prairie pink or yamper is an exquisite flower of a rich purple color. The root of this plant is bulbous and esculent. When dried the Indians use it for bread. The blue lily of the bottom prairie, the white poppy, and the mimic morning-glory are interesting specimens of prairie flowers, and would do honor to the finest gardens in Missouri. After a progress of 27 miles, we encamped on the river bank, in a rich bottom prairie. At this time we had on the sick list 100 men.

Wednesday, 22d, we vigorously pushed forward, rarely ever losing sight of that broad, bright zone of water, the Arkansas, which was our only dependence for quenching thirst. In many places scattering clumps of cottonwood trees border each of its banks, and on every island (which is guarded by the stream from the sweeping, annual prairie conflagrations) invite into their umbrageous bowers the sun-burnt, way-worn soldier. A few hours' rest refits him for the march. To-day we passed Pawnee Fort, an old decayed stockade, and a few crumbling cabins on an island, where many years ago, as tradition says, a great battle was fought between the Pawnees and their besiegers, the Cheyennes. The face of the country is uniformly level. A great variety of pleasing and interesting flowers made their appearance; prairie dog villas abound. These wide solitary domains of the prairies, although they can never be occupied by civilized man, are nevertheless tenanted by very interesting little villagers. These little prairie dogs, or squirrels, which have attracted the attention of the traveler and the tourist, are queer creatures. They would sit perched on their domiciles and bark like a terrier at the whole Army. A march of 18 miles brought us to our camp on the river bank, where we obtained excellent water by sinking barrels 2 or 3 feet in the sand; the river water being rendered unpleasant by the excessive heat of the sun. The Arkansas is one of the finest streams in the world for bathing purposes. The water is generally two or three feet deep, swiftly rolling over a bed of yellow sand no less beautiful than the golden sands of the fabled Pactolus. Of an evening I have witnessed more than 500 men enjoying this reinvigorating luxury at one time, splashing and plunging about in the waves.

The march was continued on the 23d, without the occurrence of any event worthy of historical record. Mr. Augustus Leesley, an intelligent young man of the Cole company, died of a chronic affection on 22d, and his corpse was decently interred to-day on the roadside in a desolate tract of country, 4 miles above Pawnee Fort; 12 rounds were fired over his grave, and a rude stone was placed to mark the spot where he rests. The Army again becoming scant of provisions Lieut. Sublette with four men was sent in advance to bring to a halt a train of commissary wagons. This order was promptly put into execution by Lieut. Sublette, notwithstanding the wagons were much farther upon the road than was anticipated. Taking with him but two days' rations and being out seven, he and his party were compelled to travel night and day to escape starvation.

On the 24th we marched 12 miles and nooned in a rich bottom prairie, where the grass was abundant and of good quality. The wild, spontaneous pumpkin vines made the prairie resemble the cultivated fields of Missouri. Limestone and sandstone were here found promiscuously arranged, the latter predominating in the vicinity of the mountains. Eight miles further brought us to our camp on the river margin, densely covered with tall grass, pea vines, and rushes. Many of our horses had by this time failed and had been abandoned to their fate on the great prairies. A man 600 miles from the nearest civilized settlements in a desert country feels a kind of friendship and sympathy for his horse when he abandons him on the plains to be devoured by wolves or captured by Comanches that almost makes him shed tears. He feels as though he were abandoning his best friend to perish in a desolate land.

The march was continued with the utmost vigor on the 25th, 26th, and 27th, following the course of the river, at an average of about 27 miles per day, over a heavy, sandy road. Lieut. Col. Ruff, with the First Battalion, being now some 4 or 5 miles in advance of the main Army, halted and ordered drill until Col. Kearney should come up. This ill-timed order for drill, where Apollo's shafts fell thick and heavy, and where every breeze that swept across the parched and heated plain felt as withering as the breath of the Sahara, produced an excitement in his command which came near resulting in a total disregard of the order. In consequence of this and certain other strict orders subsequently issued, Lieut. Col. Ruff's popularity with his men began to wane. We were now passing beyond the region frequented by the buffalo, the most interesting and by far the most useful tenant of the plains, and entering upon the confines of a still more desolate tract. The earth was covered with a salinous incrustation, and the parched grass was stiffened by salt crystallizations. The pulverized earth resembled smoldering embers.

On the morning of the 28th the whole Army moved off, exhibiting a fine appearance, with streaming penons and glittering arms, as they wound around the hills or stretched along the level plain. The shrill notes of the clarion animated every heart. There are moments of pride in the history of every man's life; so there are crises of more than ordinary interest in the march of every army. This was one of them. Every bosom heaved with emotion; for we could now see, though we could not, like the ancient herald, hurl a spear, into the enemy's country. The earth was covered with pebbles washed by the rains, and worn by the winds as smooth as glass, and heated by the sun to such a degree that they would scorch the naked foot to a blister. The plain here is intersected by high ridges of hard sandstone, striped with blue and red, somewhat resembling the gaudy colors of the rainbow. This is a segment of the great American Sahara. Excepting in the Arkansas bottom, there is little or no vegetation. For many months in the year neither dew nor rain falls upon the thirsty desert.

Continuing the march on the 29th, we met Fitzpatrick, the mountaineer, on express from Fort Bent to Col. Kearney, with the following information from Santa Fe: "That Gov. Armijo had called the chief men of counsel together to deliberate on the best means of defending the city of Santa Fe; that hostile preparations were rapidly going on in all parts of New Mexico; and that Col. Kearney's movements would be vigorously opposed." Three Mexicans were taken prisoners near Fort Bent, supposed to be spies, with blank letters upon their persons addressed to Col. Kearney. This piece of ingenuity was resorted to no doubt, to avoid detection by American residents and traders at Bents Fort. These Mexicans were conducted, by order of Col. Kearney, through our camp and shown our artillery, then peaceably allowed to retire to Santa Fe and report what they had seen.

The future was pregnant with consequences of the greatest moment. An uncertain destiny awaited us. Some anticipated victory; others apprehended disaster. Twenty days were to determine our fate. We were already encamped in the enemy's territory. Were we to be defeated and completely overthrown, or were we to enter triumphantly into the capital and plant the flag of our country on its adobe walls? These were questions in the minds of all, which time alone could solve. The sequel, however, will develop the manner in which the principles of our republican Government were established in that benighted and priest-governed land, without the anticipated effusion of blood.

CHAPTER III.

Having on the 29th crossed the Arkansas and encamped in the Mexican territory, about 8 miles below Bents Fort, a greater degree of vigilance became necessary, to guard against the cunning of those Ishmaelites of the desert, the Comanches, whose country we had unceremoniously invaded, as well as to prevent surprise by the Mexicans themselves. Our encampment was therefore laid out with the most scrupulous regard to military exactness. A strong picket and also camp guard were detailed and posted. Our animals being much fatigued by long marches, it was deemed advisable to rest and recruit them some two or three days. They were, by order of the colonel, turned loose upon the prairie to graze, under a strong guard, a few of them only being tethered. At first a few of them took fright at an Indian, or perhaps a gang of prowling wolves, which by degrees was communicated to others, until the whole caballada took a general estampeda, and scampered over the plain in the most furious manner. This was a scene of the wildest and most terrible confusion. A thousand horses were dashing over the prairie without riders, enraged and driven to madness and desperation by the iron pickets and the lariats which goaded and lashed them at every step. After great labor most of them were recovered, some of them 30 and some of them 50 miles from camp. About 65 of the best of them were irrecoverably lost.

Fort Bent[1] is situated on the north bank of the Arkansas, 650 miles west of Fort Leavenworth, in latitude 38° 2' north and longitude 103° 3' west from Greenwich. The exterior walls of this fort, whose figure is that of an oblong square, are 15 feet high and 4 feet thick. It is 180 feet long and 135 feet wide and is divided into various compartments, the whole built of adobes, or sun-dried brick. It has been converted into a Government depot. Here a great many of the Government wagons were unloaded and sent back to Fort Leavenworth for additional supplies. Here also the caravans of traders awaited the arrival of the Army, thenceforward to move under the wing of its protection.

While in this encampment on the 30th Capts. Reid and Waldo, of the Volunteers, and Capts. Moore and Burgwin and Lieut. Noble, of the First Dragoons, with their respective commands, rejoined the Army, having vainly pursued Speyers and Armijo, who it was supposed were endeavoring to supply the enemy with ammunition and arms. About this time Lieut. De Courcy was dispatched with 20

---

[1] See p. 45.

men with orders to proceed directly through the mountains to the valley of Taos, and having ascertained the intentions and disposition of the people, to report to Col. Kearney on the road to Santa Fe as soon as practicable. Having received his instructions, this pacificator set forward on the 31st, prepared for either of the alternatives, peace or war.[1]

Here it was that the chief of the Arapaho Tribe of Indians visited our camp to see the American commander and look at his " big guns." With astonishment he expressed his admiration of the Americans, signifying that the New Mexicans would not stand a moment before such terrible instruments of death, but would escape to the mountains with the utmost dispatch.

August 1 we moved up the river and encamped near Fort Bent. Here, by order of the colonel commanding, Dr. Vaughan, of Howard, assistant surgeon, was left in charge of 21 sick men who were unable to proceed further and had been pronounced physically unfit for service. Of this number some died,[2] some were discharged and returned to Missouri, and others, having recovered, came on and rejoined the Army at Santa Fe.

The march upon Santa Fe was resumed August 2, 1846, after a respite of three days in the neighborhood of Fort Bent. As we passed the fort the American flag was raised in compliment to our troops, and in concert with our own streamed most animatingly in the gale that swept from the desert, while the tops of the houses were crowded with Mexican girls and Indian squaws intently beholding the American Army. After a march of 24 miles, following the course of the river, we pitched our tents on a perfectly bare sand beach, with scarcely a shrub or spear of grass for our almost famishing animals. The gale from the inhospitable desert, which extended southwardly to the Raton Mountains and southeastwardly to the borders of Texas, and over which the next day we were to commence our march, furiously drove the sand like pelting hail upon us. A few patches of the prickly pear, the wild sage, the spiral or screw bush, and a mimic arbor vitæ are the only green shrubs that can vegetate in this arid and parched waste.

After spending a comfortless night on the banks of the Arkansas, the water of which is very cool and refreshing so near the mountains, on the morning of the 3d we struck off at right angles with the river from a point a few miles above the mouth of the Timpa, pursuing our course up that stream on account of water. The Army was now upon the Great American Desert. The wind and driven sand continued to annoy both man and beast. The parched earth appeared as though it had not been refreshed by a shower since the days of

---

[1] The following interesting anecdote was related by the lieutenant who conducted this pioneer party :

" We took three pack mules laden with provisions ; and as we did not expect to be long absent, the men took no extra clothing.

" Three days after we left the column our mules fell down, and neither gentle means nor the points of sabers had the least effect in inducing them to rise. Their term of service with Uncle Sam was out. ' What's to be done? ' said the sergeant. ' Dismount ! ' said I, ' Off with your shirts and drawers, men ! tie up the sleeves and legs, and each man bag one-twentieth part of the flour ! ' Having done this, the bacon was distributed to the men and tied to the cruppers of their saddles. Thus loaded, we pushed on without the slightest fear of our provision train being ' cut off.' "

[2] William Duncan and Fugitt, the former of Clay and the latter of Jackson County, were among those who died. Four others died ; names not known.

Besides these 21 volunteers, there was a number of dragoons and teamsters left sick under the care of Asst. Surg. Vaughan. The whole amounted to about 60.

Noah's flood. The wagons moved heavily, the wheels uniformly sinking over the fellies in the sand or pulverized earth. A toilsome march of 25 miles brought us to our camp on a bare sand bank totally destitute of green grass or other vegetation for our animals. The water was scarce, muddy, bitter, filthy, and just such as Horace in his Brundusium letter pronounced "vilissima rerum."

The American desert is, perhaps, no less sterile, sandy, parched, and destitute of water and every green herb and living thing than the African Sahara. In the course of a long day's march we could scarcely find a pool of water to quench the thirst, a patch of grass to prevent our animals perishing, or an oasis to relieve the weary mind. Dreary, sultry, desolate, boundless solitude reigned as far as the eye could reach and seemed to bound the distant horizon. We suffered much with the heat and thirst, and the driven sand—which filled our eyes and nostrils and mouths almost to suffocation. Many of our animals perished on the desert. A Mexican hare or an antelope skimming over the ground with the utmost velocity, was the only living creature seen upon this plain. The Roman Army under Metellus, on its march through the deserts of Africa, never encountered more serious opposition from the elements than did our Army in its passage over this American Sahara.

The march was continued on the 4th with little or no alteration. The wind still drove the sand furiously in our faces, the heat was oppressive, and the sand was deep and heavy. After a progress of 27 miles we again encamped on the vile, filthy Timpa, the water of which was still bitter and nauseating. Our animals perished daily.

Vigorously pushing forward on the 5th, having made 28 miles during the day, we passed out of the desert, crossed the river Purgatoire, and encamped on its southern bank. This lovely, clear, cool, rippling mountain stream was not less grateful to our Army after four days' unparalleled marching on the desert than was that stream to the Israelitish army, which gushed from the rock when struck by the rod of the prophet. The lofty Cimarron and Spanish peaks were distinctly visible to the south and west, towering in awful grandeur far above the clouds, their summits capped with eternal snow.

After supper W. P. Hall,[1] R. W. Fleming, M. Ringo, the author, and others whose names are not remembered, led by a spirit of adventure as well as by a desire to recruit their horses, which had now been famishing for four days, determined to pass over the Purgatoire near to the base of the mountains toward the northwest, where there was plenty of good grass, and let them graze during the night. We went about 2 miles up the river before we ventured to cross. By this time it was dark. The valley for 3 miles in extent was covered with undergrowth and matted together so thickly with vines that it was almost impervious. After hours of labor and bewilderment among the brush we finally got into the stream. On the opposite side the black locusts and willows grew so densely that it was impossible to penetrate further. Our progress was thus impeded. There were only two alternatives, either to cut our way through or return to camp. We chose the former. So we went to work with

---

[1] Mr. W. P. Hall was chosen as a Representative to Congress while a private soldier in Col. Doniphan's regiment. He was an inmate of the same tent with the author.

our bowie knives, chopping the brush in the dark and leading our horses in the space thus cleared. In this manner we made our way through that inexpressibly dismal brake which lines the margin of the Purgatoire. About midnight we got through into the open plain close under the mountains, which towered high in the heavens to the westward. Our horses fared well; but we ourselves returned the next morning entirely satisfied ever afterwards to remain in camp during the night.

On the 6th we advanced about 7 miles and encamped on a spring branch issuing from the base of the Cimarron peak.[1]. Here several of the men ascended to the summit of this lofty mountain, elevated many thousand feet above the plains and valleys below. The scene was truly grand and magnificent. The Spanish peaks, twin brothers in the midst of desolation, rose still above us to the westward, lifting high into the heavens their basaltic pillars and spurs, girt with clouds, and glistening with perennial snow; while towering still above these rose the grander and loftier summits of the Cordilleras like blue, amethystine clouds in the distant southwestern horizon. Thus surrounded by the grandest scenery the world can furnish the author read with double enthusiasm the first canto of Campbell's Pleasures of Hope.

On the 7th, at an early hour, the advance was sounded. Our route led up a narrow defile through the mountains between the Cimarron and the Spanish peaks, called the Raton Pass. This day's march was extremely arduous and severe on our teams. Rough roads and rocky hills obstructed our progress. The wagons were often hauled up the abrupt and declivitous spurs of the mountains by means of ropes, and in the same manner let down on the opposite side. Progressing a distance of 18 miles up this chasm or pass, with mountains precipitously rising on both sides, we arrived at a point where they suddenly diverge on either hand, and several miles beyond as suddenly contract, thus forming an amphitheater on the grandest scale sufficiently spacious to accommodate the whole human race in an area so situated that one man might stand on the Cimarron peak and behold them all. The great amphitheater of Statilius Taurus, with its 70,000 seats rising in circular tiers one above another would have been nought in the comparison. The knobs and peaks of basalt and granite, projecting into the region of the clouds, present a scene of true sublimity. This display of the Almighty's power is sufficient to extort reverence from the lips of an infidel. Surely the "undevout astronomer is mad." Near this romantic spot we encamped for the night. The grass was abundant and of excellent quality; the water cool and refreshing.

On the 8th[2] the Army vigorously set forward and crossed the grand ridge which divides the waters of the Purgatoire, the Cimarron, and the Rio Colorado.[3] This elevated range of mountains is adorned by forests of pines and cedars. After an advance of 18 miles over the most difficult road we encamped on the banks of the Colorado.

---

[1] The Cimarron peak is estimated to be 13,000 feet above the Gulf of Mexico.
[2] This morning Henry Moore, of Saline County, died, and was interred in the Raton Pass. Also one of the infantry, belonging to Capt. Angney's company, was found in the road in an almost lifeless state. The dragoons took care of him and brought him up to camp. He afterwards died.
[3] The Rio Colorado is the head branch of the Canadian Fork of the Arkansas.

In consequence of the great fatigue in crossing the Cimarron Ridge of Mountains the command was permitted a respite of one day, as there was here a fine supply of wood, water, and grass—three things not only convenient but almost essential to an army. This was the Sabbath, and the only Sabbath's rest we had enjoyed since our departure from Missouri. Here we shaved and dressed, not to attend church, not to visit friends, not in deference to the conventional rules of society, but in remembrance of these privileges and requirements. Neither was this a day of feasting with us, for it was on this day that our rations, which had never been full, were cut down to one-half.[1] From this time on to Santa Fe we were actually compelled to subsist on about one-third rations. While the rays of the sun fell with unusual power in the valley a heavy shower was refreshing the sides of the mountains, and as the cloud retreated a brilliant rainbow "spanned with bright arch" their basaltic summits.

After several hours of drill out upon the level prairie, the volunteer regiment returned to camp to partake of their scanty allowance, not having eaten a bite that morning or the previous evening. But we were determined to make the best of a hard case, and trust Uncle Sam for his future good conduct. Therefore, all cheerfully submitted to the unavoidable privation. While encamped here, on the night of the 9th, Capt. Jackson's company lost about 20 horses in an estampeda, most of which, after an arduous search of one or two days in the mountains, were recovered.

After a forward movement of 22 miles on the 10th, with the gray tops of the mountains projecting above us on the right and the gently sloping valley of the Colorado on the left, we pitched our tents on the green banks of the Bermejo, more seriously annoyed by the half-ration experiment than the dread of Mexican armies. It is but natural that those who have been reared in opulence, when they first experience hardships and privations, should look back with regret upon the luxuries and pleasures of life, which they have but recently exchanged for the toils of a long and arduous campaign. Our men, like good soldiers, however, bore the evils of the march with Roman fortitude, accommodating themselves to the actual circumstances which surrounded them. They never afterwards, during the campaign, had regular and ample supplies.

About noon on the 11th we were rejoined by the detachment under Lieut. De Courcy, near the Poni, returning from their excursion to Taos. They had with them 14 Mexicans, prisoners, whom they had picked up in various places. These prisoners, in true Mexican style, reported "that the Pueblos, Yutas, and other Indian tribes, to the number of 5,000, had combined with the New Mexicans to oppose our march, and that they would annoy our lines every day from San Miguel to Santa Fe.." We soon learned how much credit was due to Mexican reports.[2] Having progressed 17 miles, we encamped on the Reyado, a cool mountain stream, where there was neither grass nor fuel.

---

[1] About one-third as much as the law contemplates as the daily ration of a soldier.

[2] *Punica fides* was the reproach of the ancient Carthaginians. *Fides Mexicana* is now a term of synonymous import, when applied to the Mexican people. Treachery is their national characteristic.

Early on the morning of the 12th we passed the newly made grave of some unfortunate soldier,[3] who had died the previous day, and was buried, perhaps without ceremony, on the roadside, Col. Kearney being now some distance in advance of Col. Doniphan, with near 500 men. Thus were our numbers diminished, not by the sword, but by disease. Almost every day some dragoon or volunteer, trader, teamster, or amateur, who had set out upon the expedition buoyant with life and flattered with hopes of future usefulness, actuated by a laudable desire to serve his country, found a grave on the solitary plains. To die in honorable warfare; to be struck down in the strife of battle; to perish in the field of honor; to sacrifice life for victory is no hardship to the fallen brave, is no source of regret to surviving friends; for the remembrance of the noble deeds of the slain sweetens the cup of sorrow. But to see the gallant, the patriotic, the devoted soldier, sinking and wasting his energies under the slow, sure progress of disease, which finally freezes the current of life, fills the heart with melancholy. Such cases claim our sympathy and merit our remembrance.

A march of 20 miles, mostly through the gorges of the mountains, over a rocky, flinty road, brought us to the Ocate, a limpid stream of fresh water, where we halted for the night. The nearest timber was 2½ miles distant. Of an evening when the Army would halt for the purpose of selecting a camp ground, and the order was given to dismount, a busy scene ensued. Every man was his own servant. Some were scrambling after the scattering sticks of wood or dry brush, some busy in pitching their tents and arranging them in order, some tethering the animals, and some bringing water for cooking purposes. At length, "all is set." The coffee is made, the meat broiled, and the bread prepared as it may be, when the several messes, gathering round their respective fires, seated upon the ground with appetites sharpened by a long day's march, dispatch, in "double-quick time," their scanty fare. Supper over, the men next see after their horses, picket them on fresh grasses, return to camp, spread their blankets upon the earth, wrap up in them, and unceremoniously fall asleep, leaving the spies and guard to take care of the enemy.

Here Col. Doniphan assembled his soldiers on the green and briefly addressed them. He concluded by reproving them for their indiscretion in wasting their ammunition upon game, assuring them that there were only 15 rounds of cartridge in camp; that there was every reason to apprehend an engagement with the enemy in a short time; that strict discipline and prompt obedience were essential to the safety of the expedition; that their own honor, and the reputation of their State, demanded the cheerful performance of duty; that to retreat or surrender was a proposition that could not be considered; and that we must conquer or die, for defeat was annihilation.

After a drive of 19 miles, along a rugged road, through narrow defiles between the spurs of the mountains, we encamped on a ravine, bordered by a strip of fine grass, near the Santa Clara Spring, Col. Kearney having advanced 6 miles farther, and taken his position on the River Mora.

Having advanced, on the 14th, to the Mora, we rejoined Col. Kearney. We were now on the verge of the Mexican settlements.

---

[3] This was probably a dragoon. The initials E. M. were marked on the rude slab that designated his final resting place.

The country was becoming fit for cultivation. Droves of swine, herds of cattle, and flocks of sheep and goats were feeding in the valleys and grassy glades. The hills and upland were adorned with comely groves of cedars and pines. Ranchos with their cornfields and gardens were making their appearance, and every thing began to wear the semblance of civilization. After a vigorous march of 25 miles, we encamped on the Gallinas Creek, near the small town Las Bagas, the first Mexican village on the road. Strict orders were given the soldiers not to molest the inhabitants, and also to respect the lives and property of such Mexican citizens as remained peaceable and neutral.

At dawn of day on the morning of the 15th, the spies, Messrs. Bent and Estis, who had been sent out the previous evening to reconnoiter, and ascertain the position of the enemy, and learn if it was his intention to make battle, returned and reported to Col. Kearney that 2,000 Mexicans were encamped at a place about 6 miles from Las Bagas, called the canyon or Pass, and that they intended there to give us battle. Maj. Swords had just arived from Fort Leavenworth, with the United States mail, bringing intelligence of the appointment by the President of Col. Kearney to be a brigadier general in the United States Army. Other important documents were received besides Col. Kearney's commission as a brigadier general, but now there was no time for reading letters and newspapers.

Gen. Kearney immediately formed the line of battle. The dragoons, with the St. Louis mounted volunteers, were stationed in front; Maj. Clark, with the battalion of volunteer light artillery, in the center; and Col. Doniphan's regiment of mounted volunteers in the rear. The two companies of volunteer infantry were deployed on each side of the line of march as flankers. The baggage and merchant trains were next in order, with Capt. Walton's mounted company (B) as a rear guard. There was also a strong advance guard. The cartridges were hastily distributed; the cannons swabbed and rigged; the portfires burning; and every rifle charged. The advance was sounded by martial trumpet and horn. The banners streamed in every direction. The officers dashed along the lines—the high-toned chivalry of the American character beamed from every eye—in every countenance was expressed the settled determination to win—every heart was stout—every lip quivered with resolution, and every arm was nerved for the conflict.

In passing this little town, Las Bagas, the general halted the Army, and on the top of a large flat-roofed building assembled the alcalde or magistrate and other men of distinction among the Mexicans, and there, on the holy cross, administered to them the oath of allegiance to the laws and Government of the United States. This done, the Army hurried on to the canyon in high spirits and hope, being confident of victory. When we arrived, however, at the place where we expected to engage with the enemy, to our great disappointment the Mexicans had dispersed, and there was no one to oppose our march. It is perhaps better thus to have gained a bloodless victory by the terror of our arms than to have purchased it with blood and loss of life.

About noon we passed the small village Tecolate, the inhabitants of which willingly received us, and cheerfully took the oath of allegiance to our Government, administered to them by Gen. Kearney as at Las Bagas. Our men were covered with sweat and dust, from the exercise and excitement through which they had gone, so completely that it was impossible to tell one man from another. Having marched 20 miles, we encamped within about 6 miles of San Miguel, near a small rancho, where we found plenty of water, wood, and fine grass for our animals.

On the 16th, after a progress of 6 miles, we arrived at San Miguel, situated on the river Pecos, and famous as being the place near which the Texan Army under command of Gen. McLeod fell into the hands of Gen. Salezar and Gov. Armijo, in 1841. Here again Gen. Kearney, assembling the citizens of the place, as usual, on the terraced roof of some spacious building, delivered to them a stern, sententious speech, absolving them from any further allegiance to the Mexican Government. When the general was about to compel them to swear fealty to our Government on the sacred cross the alcalde and priest objected. The general inquired the grounds of their objection. They replied, that the oath he required them to take would virtually render them traitors to their country, a sin of which they disdained to be guilty. Gen. Kearney having promised protection to their persons and property, as to other citizens of the United States, and also having threatened to subvert the town unless they should submit, they were at length induced to take the oath.

The Army having proceeded about 10 miles farther, encamped on the Pecos, near San Jose. Here the water was excellent, but the grass was indifferent. Bold springs of delicious water gush from the rocks.

During the night of the 16th, while we were encamped at San Jose, the picket guard placed out by Col. Doniphan took the son of the Mexican general, Salezar, prisoner. He was a spy, and was held in custody until our arrival at Santa Fe, where he was afterwards set at liberty. This prisoner's father, Gen. Salezar, is the same detestable wretch who captured the Texans near Anton Chico and San Miguel, and treated them with such wanton cruelty and inhumanity. It was by his order that G. Wilkins Kendall was robbed of his passports; it was his influence that procured the execution of the brave Howland, Rosenbury, and Baker, all American citizens. Young Salezar was taken by James Chorn and Thomas McCarty, of the Clay company. Also, two other Mexican soldiers were made prisoners the same night.

On the morning of the 17th, these last mentioned prisoners were, by order of Gen. Kearney, conducted through our camps and shown our cannon. They were then suffered to depart, and tell their own people what they had seen. To color and exaggerate accounts is a truly Mexican characteristic. They therefore returned to their comrades in arms, representing our numbers at 5,000 men, and declaring we had so many pieces of cannon that they could not count them. This highly colored account of our strength no doubt spread dismay through their ranks, and increased the desertions from Armijo's standard, which were already going on to an extent well calculated to alarm him.

After a march of 10 miles, we came to the Pecos village, now in ruins. This village was formerly the seat of a flourishing and powerful tribe, claiming to be the lineal descendants of the great Montezuma. "A tradition was prevalent among them," observes Mr. Gregg "that Montezuma had kindled a holy fire, and enjoined their ances tors not to suffer it to be extinguished until he should return to deliver his people from the yoke of the Spaniards. In pursuance of these commands, a constant watch had been maintained for ages to prevent the fire from going out; and, as tradition further informed them, that Montezuma would appear with the sun, the deluded Indians were to be seen every clear morning upon the terraced roofs of their houses attentively watching for the appearance of the 'king of light,' in hopes of seeing him 'check by jowl' with their immortal sovereign. Some say that they never lost hope in the final coming of Montezuma until, by some accident or other, or a lack of a sufficiency of warriors to watch it, the fire became extinguished, and that it was this catastrophe that induced them to abandon their villages."

The spacious temple, on whose altar the sacred Montezumian or vestal fire was kept alive for so many successive ages, was built of sun-dried bricks, as the tradition proceeds, more than 300 years ago. This building appears to be of Mexican architecture and is of the following dimensions: Its length is 191 feet, breadth 35 feet, and 50 feet to the ceiling; the walls are 6 feet thick. The interior of the temple, the division into compartments, the subterranean cells, the decorations of the altar, and the stone cisterns and tanks, display some taste, although the edifice is but the wreck of what it has been, the turrets having tumbled to the ground. The entire village appears to have been originally surrounded by a stone wall 8 feet in height and 4 in thickness.

Most of the Pueblos of New Mexico have similar traditions among them respecting their great sovereign, Montezuma, and to this day look for him to come from the East to deliver his people from Mexican bondage. After our arrival in Santa Fe, an intelligent New Mexican declared to me "that the Pueblo Indians could not be induced to unite their forces with the Mexicans in opposing the Americans, in consequence of an ancient and long-cherished tradition among them, that at a certain period of time succor would come from the East to deliver them from their Spanish oppressors and to restore to them the kingdom of Montezuma, and that they hailed the American Army as the long-promised succor."

Gold is emphatically the god of the Mexicans. They have no motives but those of profit; no springs of action but those of self-love; no desires but those of gain; and no restraints but those of force. The eternal jingle of cash is music to their ears. Virtue, honesty, honor, piety, religion, patriotism, generosity, and reputation are to them pompous and unmeaning terms, and he whose conduct is shaped by principles of fair dealing is regarded as incomparably stupid. Vice, fraud, deceit, treachery, theft, plunder, murder, and assassination stalk abroad in open daylight and set order, law, and justice at defiance. The virtue of females is bought and sold. Such is the moral and social system in Mexico.

As our Army passed by the villages and other settlements in New Mexico, the men, women, boys, and girls, in great numbers, would come out to the road, bringing with them vegetables, bread, milk, eggs, cheese, fruits, pepper, chickens, and other eatables, and with the utmost importunity, following along the lines, would seek a purchaser of their valuable stores. In this manner these traffickers drained most of the specie from the purses of the American soldiers. Proceeding 3 miles beyond the Pecos Ruin, we encamped for the last time on the Pecos River, the water of which is exceedingly beautiful and transparent. The earth in many places is carpeted with fine grass and adorned with shadowing pines and cedars.

When Gov. Don Manuel Armijo learned more certainly that we were approaching Santa Fe, the capital of New Mexico and seat of his official residence, he assembled by proclamation 7,000 troops, 2,000 of whom were well armed and the rest more indifferently armed, and marched them out to meet us at the canyon or pass of the Galisteo, about 15 miles from Santa Fe, intending there to give us battle. He had written a note to Gen. Kearney the day previous, stating that he would meet him somewhere that day or the day following. The letter was very politely dictated and so ambiguous in its expressions that it was impossible to know whether it was the governor's intention to meet Gen. Kearney in council or in conflict. The general, however, hastened on and arrived at the canyon about noon on the 18th with his whole Army in battle array. Here, again, no enemy appeared to dispute our passage. The Mexicans had dispersed and fled to the mountains.[1] This canyon is nothing more than a deep fissure or chasm through the ridge of the mountains which divides the waters of the Pecos from those of the Rio Del Norte. Here the Mexicans had commenced fortifying against our approach by chopping away the timber so their artillery could play to better advantage upon our lines, and throwing up temporary breastworks; but they lacked either courage or unanimity to defend a position apparently so well chosen.

It is stated upon good authority that Gov. Armijo, Gen. Salezar, and other generals in the Mexican Army, disputed for the supreme command, and that the common people being peaceably disposed toward the Americans, readily seized upon the dissention of their leaders as a pretext for abandoning the army. Thus Gov. Armijo was left without soldiers to defend the pass. However this may be, one thing is certain, that an army of near 7,000 Mexicans, with 6 pieces of cannon, and vastly the advantage of the ground, permitted Gen. Kearney, with less than 2,000 Americans, to pass through the narrow defile and march right on to the capital of the State.[2]

Thus, on the 18th day of August, 1846, after a tiresome march of near 900 miles in less than 50 days, Gen. Kearney with his whole command entered Santa Fe, the capital of the Province of New Mexico, and took peaceable and undisputed possession of the country, without the loss of a single man or the shedding of one drop of blood, in the name of the Government of the United States, and planted the American flag in the public square, where the Stars and Stripes and the eagle still stream above the Palacio Grande, or stately residence of the ex-Gov. Armijo. When the American flag was raised a national salute of 28 guns was fired from the hill east of the town by Maj. Clark's two batteries of 6-pounders. At the same time the streets were filled with American cavalry, moving firmly

---

[1] Gov. Armijo, with near 200 dragoons, made his escape in the direction of El Paso del Norte. He was subsequently heard of in Durango and Guadalajara.
[2] The separate sovereignties which constitute the Mexican confederacy were formerly styled Departments. They are now called States.

and rapidly through the city, displaying their colors in the gayest and most gorgeous manner. This day we completed a march of 29 miles, partly over a slippery road (for a heavy rain had fallen the previous night) and partly over a ragged, rocky way through the mountain passes. After incredible exertions, and late at night, the baggage trains and the merchant wagons came into camp, a few of them having failed on the way or fallen behind, so rapid was the march of our army during the whole day. Gen. Kearney selected his camp ground on the hill commanding the town from the east, a bare, gravelly spot of earth, where neither wood nor grass was to be obtained. So constant was the army kept in motion that the men took no refreshments during the day, nor were the horses permitted to graze a moment. At night the men lay down to rest without eating or drinking, as they were almost overcome by fatigue; our animals, for want of forage, were become feeble and incapable of further exertion. Without a blade of grass or other food they stood tethered to their iron pickets or sank to the earth of exhaustion. Many of them had performed their last day's noble service. Gen. Kearney had taken up his headquarters in the govorner's palace and caused the American colors to be raised above it. Thus the city of Santa Fe was bloodlessly possessed by the American forces.

On the morning of the 19th Gen. Kearney assembled the citizens of the town near the Government building and spoke to them in this manner, Robedou being the interpreter:

New Mexicans, we have come amongst you to take possession of New Mexico, which we do in the name of the Government of the United States. We have come with peaceable intentions and kind feelings toward you all. We come as friends to better your condition and make you a part of the Republic of the United States. We mean not to murder you or rob you of your property. Your families shall be free from molestation; your women secure from violence. My soldiers will take nothing from you but what they pay you for. In taking possession of New Mexico we do not mean to take away your religion from you. Religion and Government have no connection in our country. There all religions are equal; one has no preference over another; the Catholic and Protestant are esteemed alike.

Every man has a right to serve God according to his heart. When a man dies he must render to his God an account of his acts here on earth, whether they be good or bad. In our Government all men are equal. We esteem the most peaceable man the best man. I advise you to attend to your domestic pursuits—cultivate industry—be peaceable and obedient to the laws. Do not resort to violent means to correct abuses. I do hereby proclaim that, being in possession of Santa Fe, I am therefore virtually in possession of all New Mexico. Armijo is no longer your governor. His power is departed, but he will return and be as one of you. When he shall return you are not to molest him. You are no longer Mexican subjects; you are now become American citizens, subject only to the laws of the United States. A change of government has taken place in New Mexico, and you no longer owe allegiance to the Mexican Government. I do hereby proclaim my intention to establish in this department a civil government on a republican basis similar to those of our own States. It is my intention also to continue in office those by whom you have been governed, except the governor and such other persons as I shall appoint to office by virtue of the authority vested in me. I am your governor—henceforward look to me for protection.

The general next proceeded to inquire if they were willing to take the oath of allegiance to the United States Government, to which having given their consent, he then administered to the governor ad interim, the secretary of state, the prefecto, the alcalde, and other officers of state the following oath:

Do you swear in good faith that under all circumstances you will bear allegiance to the laws and Government of the United States, and that through good and evil you will demean yourselves as obedient and faithful citizens of the same, in the name of the Father, and of the Son, and of the Holy Spirit? Amen.

Here shouts and huzzahs were raised by the Mexicans for Gov. Kearney. A very aged Mexican embraced him and wept.

Gen. Kearney having administered a similar oath to various delegations from the different pueblos who came to offer submission, tranquillity and universal satisfaction seemed to prevail. Our commander next ordered a flagstaff 100 feet high to be erected in the public square, from the top of which the American flag now streams over the capital.

Gen. Kearney's army was not well provisioned; nor was it furnished, in all its parts, with stout, able, and efficient teams, such as the difficult nature of the country over which it had to pass required. The commissary and quartermaster departments were wretchedly managed. During much of the time. owing either to neglect or incompetency of the heads of these departments, the general found it necessary to subsist his men on half rations. It repeatedly happened that the wagons, particularly of the volunteer corps, were left so far behind during a day's march that they did not come into camp before midnight. Thus the men had to feast or famish by turns, owing to the gross and culpable neglect of Government agents. The volunteer troops were furnished with very sorry and indifferent wagons and teams, wholly inadequate for such an expedition, whilst the regulars were furnished in the very best manner. Owing to an unaccountable arrangement by the War Department, the volunteer regiment was not allowed a full staff of officers, and hence proceeded the ill-management of these affairs.

Rumor and exaggeration are two grand evils in an army. While on the march to New Mexico we were one day startled at the news that the Mexicans had driven all their cattle and sheep into the distant mountains, deserted their villages and ranchos, and burnt the grass [1] upon the road. Had this been the case our animals must inevitably have perished. On another we were perhaps told that a body of 8,000 or 10,000 Mexicans and Pueblo Indians combined were advancing upon the road to meet us and give us battle. We were thus constantly kept in uncertainty until experience brought the matter to a test. These pernicious rumors were generally spread through the camp by the Mexican prisoners that were daily picked up on the road. When we came to the Mexican ranchos or farm houses we found abundance of grass and thousands of horned cattle, and plenty of sheep and goats scattered upon the hills and mountains. These flocks had each of them its respective shepherd. We did not molest them. We took nothing, not even a melon, an ear of corn, a chicken, a goat, or a sheep, from those poor people for which we did not pay the money. This generous and Christian conduct on the part of the American Army completely secured the good will and

---

[1] Owing to the dryness of the climate in New Mexico the grass is parched and crisped at all seasons and will almost as readily take fire in August as in November.

friendship of the Mexicans, for they supposed, and were even taught by their priests and rulers to believe that they would be robbed, plundered, and murdered, and the whole country ravaged by the invading army. By this means the rulers hoped to stimulate the common people to oppose the Americans. Their appliances, however, failed of success. The kind treatment the Americans uniformly extended toward those people is worthy of the highest praise and will doubtless, before the tribunal of a community of men who can justly appreciate the moral force of such an example, do the command more credit than the gaining of 10 victories.

BENT'S FORT. See page **33**.

CHAPTER IV.

The next day after the capture of Santa Fe and its occupation by the American troops a heavy detail was made from the different companies to conduct the horses and other animals belonging to the command into the neighborhood of Galisteo, 27 miles southeasterly from the capital, for the purpose of grazing them, forage being scarce and extremely difficult to be procured near town. This grazing party to the command of which Lieut. Col. Ruff had been appointed—the detachment from each company being under a lieutenant—proceeded directly to the mountains and valleys of Galisteo Creek, where, finding grass and water abundant and of good quality, they made their encampment. This encampment, however, was afterwards changed from one place to another, according as the pasturage demanded. This party of men was at first most scandalously neglected by the subsistence department at Santa Fe, supplies being sent them very sparingly and irregularly. After much complaint, however, they were more liberally provisioned. The stock, which had been exhausted by want of forage and long marches, was soon in a thriving condition and again fit for service, so fine and nutritious is the grass in the hill country of New Mexico.

A few days previous to the Americans entering Santa Fe the American merchants and other Americans resident there were under continual apprehensions of being robbed, mobbed, and murdered by the enraged populace, whose supreme delight was best promoted by heaping reproaches on the "Texans" and "North American invaders," as they contemptuously styled us. The Americans, however locked their storerooms, barred up their houses, and resolved, if an attack were made upon them, to occupy a strong building and unitedly withstand a siege until relief could be sent them by Gen. Kearney. They were not, however, seriously molested, though frequently insulted.

On the morning of the 19th August a serious difficulty occurred between two volunteers, one of them—his name Herkins—being intoxicated. The affray took place in the plaza, under the eye of Gen. Kearney. Capt. Turner, Maj. Swords, and others were immediately ordered to arrest the rioter. Herkins, with drawn sword, resisted. After giving and receiving several slight wounds, he was taken and confined. By the sentence of a court-martial his wages were withheld and he was "drummed out of the service" of the country.

Gen. Kearney's next official act, as the civil and military governor of the Department of New Mexico, was the issuing of the following proclamation:

46

PROCLAMATION TO THE INHABITANTS OF NEW MEXICO, BY BRIG. GEN. S. W. KEARNEY, COMMANDING THE ARMY OF THE UNITED STATES IN THE SAME.

As by the act of the Republic of Mexico a state of war exists between that Government and the United States, and as the undersigned, at the head of his troops, on the 18th instant took possession of Santa Fe, the capital of the Department of New Mexico, he now announces his intention to hold the department with its original boundaries (on both sides of the Del Norte) as a part of the United States and under the name of the Territory of New Mexico.

The undersigned has come to New Mexico with a strong military force and an equally strong one is following close in his rear. He has more troops than necessary to put down any opposition that can possibly be brought against him, and therefore it would be folly and madness for any dissatisfied or discontented persons to think of resisting him.

The undersigned has instructions from his Government to respect the religious institutions of New Mexico, to protect the property of the church, to cause the worship of those belonging to it to be undisturbed, and their religious rights in the amplest manner preserved to them. Also to protect the persons and property of all quiet and peaceable inhabitants within its boundaries against their enemies, the Eutaws, Navajos, and others. And while he assures all that it will be his pleasure, as well as his duty, to comply with those instructions, he calls upon them to exert themselves in preserving order, in promoting concord, and in maintaining the authority and efficiency of the laws, and to require of those who have left their homes and taken up arms against the troops of the United States to return forthwith to them, or else they will be considered as enemies and traitors, subjecting their persons to punishment and their property to seizure and confiscation for the benefit of the Public Treasury. It is the wish and intention of the United States to provide for New Mexico a free government, with the least possible delay, similar to those in the United States, and the people of New Mexico will then be called on to exercise the rights of freemen in electing their own representatives to the Territorial legislature; but until this can be done the laws hitherto in existence will be continued until changed or modified by competent authority, and those persons holding office will continue in the same for the present, provided they will consider themselves good citizens and willing to take the oath of allegiance to the United States.

The undersigned hereby absolves all persons residing within the boundary of New Mexico from further allegiance to the Republic of Mexico, and hereby claims them as citizens of the United States. Those who remain quiet and peaceable will be considered as good citizens and receive protection. Those who are found in arms or instigating others against the United States will be considered as traitors and treated accordingly. Don Manuel Armijo, the late governor of this department, has fled from it. The undersigned has taken possession of it without firing a gun or shedding a drop of blood, in which he most truly rejoices, and for the present will be considered as governor of this Territory.

Given at Santa Fe, the capital of the Territory of New Mexico, this 22d day of August, 1846, and in the seventy-first year of the Independence of the United States.

By the governor:

S. W. KEARNEY, *Brigadier General.*

About this time Gen. Kearney came in possession of six pieces of artillery, understood to be the same that Gov. Armijo had at the Galisteo Pass on the 18th, which place he abandoned on our approach, and also a part of the ammunition carried out by Speyers and Armijo from Independence. These pieces of cannon were almost worthless, excepting one of them, a very fine Texan piece, inscribed with the name of Gen. Lamar, President of Texas, which was taken in 1841 by Gen. Salezar from Gen. McLeod near San Miguel. These pieces were temporarily added to Maj. Clark's two batteries. The New Mexicans made use of copper slugs instead of grape and cannister shot. They also had copper balls.

New Mexico, whose climate is generally bland and salubrious, embraces within its ample territorial limits more than 200,000 square

miles. Of this vast area, which includes a wilderness of bleak, desolate, unproductive snow-capped mountains, many of whose summits
are 13,000 feet above the level of the sea, only the valleys which are
susceptible of irrigation from constantly flowing streams can be cultivated with any degree of success. It is traversed by numerous elevated mountain ranges, the principal of which are the Sierra Madre,
or Cordilleras, and the Sierra Blanco. Between these spreads out
the magnificent basin-like valley of the Del Norte, coursed by a
broad, bright zone of water and dotted by towns, villages, ranches,
and farmhouses. This valley contains the principal wealth of the
State. Gardens richly blooming, orchards surcharged with ripened
fruit, vineyards bending under the clustering grape, fields of wheat
waving their golden harvests before the wind, shady groves of
alamos, all irrigated by canals of clear, pure, rippling water, strongly
contrast with the gigantic granite peaks which, blue as amethyst,
tower high into the heavens. These mountains, beyond doubt, contain inexhaustible stores of mineral wealth. Besides gold, silver,
lead, and copper, bituminous and anthracite coal, black oxides, brim-
stone in its pure state, salt, and vast quantities of gypsum, are known
to abound. Corn, wheat, rye, beans, pulse, pepper, and onions are
the staple productions of the country. Immense herds of cattle,
droves of horses and mules, and innumerable flocks of sheep and
goats feed upon the mountain pastures. The New Mexicans are emphatically a pastoral people. The bold, unfailing mountain streams,
with their foaming cascades and dashing cataracts, present fine facilities for manufacturing and seem to invite enterprise.

New Mexico contains, according to a census taken in 1844, a mixed
population of 160,000, of which number one-third are Pueblo Indians, the original proprietors of the soil, who submitted to the Spaniards in the early conquest of the country—profess the Romish faith—
have their churches and ecclesiastics, and yield an unforced obedience
to the laws of the State, but live in villages or pueblos, isolated from
other New Mexican settlements, and enjoy a social system of their
own, refusing for the most part to intermarry with their Mexican
neighbors. They still retain a rancorous hatred toward their conquerors. More recently, however, New Mexico, owing to her remote-
ness from the Central Government, has been subject to the desolating
incursions of the bordering tribes and prostrated by feuds and intes-
tine broils. Many bloody tragedies have been enacted there. Thus
distracted and unsupported, she fell an easy prey to the victorious
American arms.

Santa Fe, the capital of New Mexico, occupies the site of an ancient
pueblo and contains an estimated population of 6,000. It is situated
on Santa Fe Creek, a beautiful, clear stream, issuing out of the mountains toward the east, having its source in a lake. From this creek
various canals part above the town and lead through the fields, gardens, and orchards for the purposes of irrigation. Families use the
water of the canals. Their houses, generally flat roofed and one story
high, are built of sun-dried bricks, called adobes in the Spanish language. In the city there are six Catholic churches, but no public
schools, the business of education being intrusted to ecclesiastics.
The streets are crooked and narrow. The whole presents very much
the appearance of an extensive brickyard. The public square is about

90 yards from north to south and 100 from east to west. The governor's residence or palace is situated on the north side of the plaza. The architecture is of the rudest order.

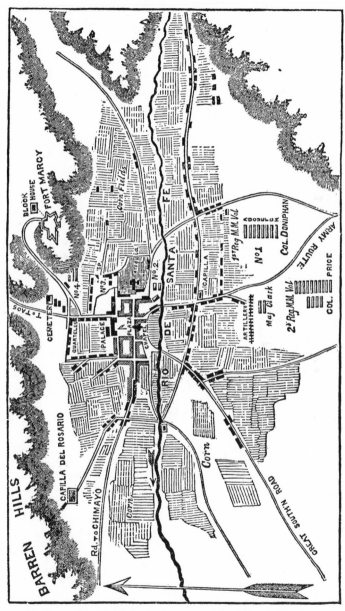

PLAN OF SANTA FE AND ITS ENVIRONS.

Note.—The numbers near the encampments show the regular order of the changes. No. 1 is the only instance in which the regiment was all together, being afterwards broken up into detachments and sent off into different parts of New Mexico. No. 2 shows the regiment decreased, etc. Distance from salient angle of Fort Marcy to the flagstaff in the center of the plaza, 664 yards.

The flag staff is 100 feet high; it was made and erected by the volunteers. Fort Marcy mounts 14 guns.

For many years Santa Fe has been the port of entry for American goods and the great emporium where the merchants of central Mexico annually meet the American caravans to purchase their stocks. It is a city of considerable trade.

The New Mexicans are generally under the medium size, and are of a swarthy, copper complexion, though every shade of color may sometimes be met with, from the fair Castilian to the darkest hue of the aborigines. They are hospitable, but ignorant and treacherous. The women, with few exceptions, are neither fair nor handsome, yet their dark, penetrating, lustrous, beaming eyes peer out most captivatingly from the folds of their rebozos,[1] and their black, glossy ringlets of hair, which, indeed constitutes their greatest beauty. They seem to possess more intelligence than the men and are infinitely their superiors in vivacity and gracefulness of demeanor.

MEXICAN GROUP.

The New Mexicans, both males and females, have a great fondness for jewelry, dress, and amusements. For amusement, the fandango appears to be the most fashionable place of resort, where every belle and beauty presents herself attired in the most costly manner, and displays her jewelry to the best advantage. To this place of recreation and pastime, which is generally a large, capacious saloon, or interior court, all descriptions of persons are allowed to come, free of charge, and without invitation. The fandango generally commences about 9 o'clock p. m.; and the tolling of the church bells is the signal for the ladies to make their appearance at the saloon; which they do almost simultaneously. The New Mexican ladies dress gaudily, but with little taste. They mostly wear dresses without bodies; having only a skirt, and a long, loose, flowing scarf or wrapper, dextrously thrown about the head and shoulders, so as to supersede both the use

---

[1] The rebozo is a long scarf or wrapper, used by the Mexican ladies to cover the head and shoulders.

of dress bodies and bonnets. There is but little order kept at these fandangoes, and still less attention paid the rules of etiquette.[1] A kind of swinging, gallopade waltz is their favorite dance—the cotillion is not much in vogue. Read Lord Byron's graphic description of the Dutch waltz, then stretch your imagination to its utmost tension, and you will perhaps have some faint conception of the Mexican fandango. Such familiarity of position would be repugnant to the refined rules of polite society, in our country; but among the New Mexicans, nothing is reckoned a greater accomplishment than that of being able to pass handsomely through all the mazes of the waltz.

There is one republican feature about these fandangoes. It is here that all classes, rich and poor, meet and intermingle, as did the ancient Romans at their Saturnalia, upon terms of equality. A sumptuous repast or collation is rarely ever prepared for the frolicsome coterie, but always an abundance of knicknacks, sweetmeats, and the exhilarating vino, or wine; and although it costs a man but little to attend the fandango and mingle in the gleeful throng, yet it very much resembles the descent of Æneas to the kingdom of Pluto—it is easy enough to get there, but to return—hic est labor.

Second Lieut. Jas. S. Oldham, of the company from Jackson County, was arrested on the 24th, upon a charge of "disobedience to orders," by Lieut. Col. Ruff, and court-martialed on the 26th. He was deprived of his command and dismissed from the service "with a disability to serve in the Armies of the United States for a period of 12 months." Not knowing all the circumstances of the case, and not having heard all the testimony before the court-martial, the author's opinion were better withheld than expressed. The head and front of his offending, however, was his persisting, contrary to order, in the determination to leave the grazing encampment near Galisteo and proceed to Santa Fe with the view of obtaining provisions for his men who were then in pressing want. It has already been observed that this grazing party was supplied with the utmost parsimony.

About this time, when all was quiet in the camp, and in the capital, and universal satisfaction seemed to prevail, both among the conquerors and the conquered, six dragoons and two volunteers, without any apparent cause, deserted the Army. The remembrance of the privations and hardships which they had suffered on the plains and the thoughts of the still greater perils and sufferings yet to be encountered perhaps determined them to sacrifice their honor and their usefulness, forgetting the duties which they owed to themselves, their friends, and country. Whether they went over to the enemy or returned to the States was never certainly known. Arms supposed to have been theirs were subsequently found in the city of El Paso.

The whole of New Mexico being thus in quiet possession of the American troops, while deputations from the various pueblos and villages were daily arriving at the capital, offering submission to the general and cheerfully taking the oath of allegiance to the United States Government, an express, borne by five men, three regular dragoons and two volunteers, was sent, on the 25th, from Santa Fe to Fort Leavenworth, to be forwarded thence to Washington, containing a full account of Gen. Kearney's conquest of New Mexico,

---

[1] The author speaks of the fashions which prevailed during the continuance of the American Army in that country.

and asking for further instructions from the War Department. The bearers of this express, having encountered the severest trials on the plains during the inclement winter season, returned to Santa Fe some time after Christmas.

Near this same time the priest of San Filipe and the curate of the churches in the Valley of Taos, came to acknowledge the authority of the conquerors, receive his commands, and ask protection for the churches and church property. The general having assured them that their temples of worship would be respected and their "religion in the amplest manner preserved to them," they returned home peaceably and favorably disposed toward the Americans, more subdued by kindness than by force of arms. They did not even forbear to speak in praise of the generous and magnanimous conduct of their conquerors.[1]

Also a young Pueblo chief, with a few of his warriors, came in to see the new governor. He said "he had heard of Gen. Kearney and had come to see him; that he desired to know what his intentions were; whether he intended to protect the Pueblo or murder them; that the priests had told him that the Americans would plunder and kill them, and take their wives and daughters away from them, and that such as they took prisoners they would brand on the face with a red-hot iron, and thus make them American citizens; that he now desired to know if such was the truth; that if it were so, he would go back to his people and encourage them to fight the Americans; that it was better to die honorably in defense of his people and country than to suffer these outrages." He also stated that "Gov. Armijo had visited Taos and pursuaded the Pueblo to join his army, but that the wise men of the Pueblo—old, venerable men who had great experience and great knowledge—told Armijo that it was useless to fight the Americans; that they were a numerous people; that if he whipped the Americans in one battle, or destroyed one army, others would keep on coming from the east as long as the sun continued to shine, and that finally they would kill all the Mexicans and then kill the Pueblo, their allies. Moreover, that Armijo would run when the fight came on and leave the Pueblo to be slaughtered by the enraged Americans; that they first desired to have an interview with the American commander, to learn the truth of these things before they would go to war." Gen. Kearney then asked him what other rumors he had heard, to which he replied that it was useless to tell a man of his information and knowledge about the tales that came like the wind and had no responsible source; that "reports were for women and children to listen to, not men." Gen. Kearney, pleased with the boldness and magnanimity of the young chief, gave him some money and other presents and dismissed him with the assurances of his friendship.

On the 29th Gen. Kearney, having occasion to transfer some public property into the hands of a public functionary, took up a bit of blank paper and commenced writing, when the alcalde, who happened to be present, remarked to the general that an instrument of writing was not legal unless it were drawn up on paper stamped with the government seal or coat of arms for the State of New Mexico.

---

[1] It was not long before these same faithless priests and leaders were detected in a conspiracy against the new government. O fides Mexicana.

He then stepped out and brought a few sheets of the government paper to Gen. Kearney, politely observing "that the government sold it at only $8 per sheet, a very moderate sum to pay for having an important document strictly legal." Without ceremony Gen. Kearney changed his purpose for the moment and wrote in substance as follows:

The use of the "stamp paper" by the government of New Mexico is hereby abolished. Done by the governor.

S. W. KEARNEY, *Brig. Gen.*

"I will now," continued he, "take it at its real value, just as other paper." The alcalde was astounded, for his prospects of further extortion were blasted. The common people who had been compelled to pay the exorbitant sum of $8 for a sheet of paper when an instrument of writing was wanted which required a seal rejoiced that they were now relieved of a burdensome tax. It is thus, by acts of tyranny on the part of the government, that New Mexico has been the abode of misery and slavery instead of happiness and liberty.

CHAPTER V.

In consequence of certain rumors which were almost daily brought to Gen. Kearney that the malcontents, principally the friends and adherents of the deposed Gov. Armijo, and some Pueblo Indians were rallying and concentrating a large armed force somewhere in the vicinity of Albuquerque with the view to make battle and recover the capital from the hands of the Americans, he determined to silence these reports and disperse these "rebels" against his authority by marching thither in person and at the head of the following detachments of troops: One hundred artillerymen, under Capts. Weightman and Fischer, forming an extra battalion, commanded by Maj. Clark, manning eight pieces of cannon; 45 dragoons, under Capt. Burgwin, and 55 of the St. Louis Volunteers (Laclede rangers), under Capt. Hudson, being attached to the dragoons, forming a squadron of 100 men, commanded by Burgwin, the oldest captain; and 500 Mounted Volunteers, under command of the following officers· The company from Jackson County furnished 68 men, under Lieut. Reed; the company from Lafayette 60, under Capt. Walton; the company from Clay 67, under Lieut. Sublette; the company from Saline 54, under Capt. Reid; the company from Franklin 68, under Capt. Stephenson; the company from Cole 60, under Capt. Parsons; the company from Howard 60, under Lieut. De Courcy; and that from Calaway 64, under Capt. Rodgers, with Lieut. Col. Ruff at the head of the regiment, Maj. Gilpin in command of the first battalion, and Walton, the senior captain, in command of the second. Gen. Kearney, with about 25 of his staff officers and body guard and generally 50 or 60 fawning, sycophantic Mexicans rode at the head of the column, which consisted of about 725 mounted men, exclusive of the general's volunteer Mexican escort.[1]

We left Santa Fe on the morning of the 2d of September, with all our banners gaily fluttering in the breeze, the men being in high spirits and possessing cheerful minds, as there was once again some faint prospect of an engagement with the enemy. Men, seeking that just

---

[1] Quite too much consideration and kindness has been bestowed upon the treacherous Mexicans by all the American generals. It was a common remark amongst the volunteers at Santa Fe that Gen. Kearney would punish a volunteer for an offense for which a Mexican would be excused; in other words, that he "treated the Mexicans better than he did his own soldiers." The same remark applies to the conduct of Gen. Wool while at Parras and to that of Gen. Worth while in command at La Puebla. However, the blame more justly rests on the War Department.

and laudable praise which is the reward of the brave, encountering perils with resolution, enduring privations with fortitude, traversing plains and deserts with patience, and surmounting obstacles of every nature with courage, feel disappointed when the fleeing enemy bears with him those trophies which ought to belong to the victors, and which they would, should a battle ensue, take home with them as the evidences of their valor. It is the returning soldier, decorated with the spoils of the foe, and graced with the trophies of victory, more than he that has spent his strength in marches and pursuits, that receives the applause of his countrymen.

We took the main Chihuahua road leading directly south with the view of striking the Rio Grande del Norte at the nearest point on account of water, as the country between Santa Fe and the Del Norte (which is about 35 miles following the road) is remarkably dry and barren. The stream that waters the town of Santa Fe, and which furnishes abundant water power for grist and saw mills, entirely disappears in the sand about 5 miles below the city. This day's march was over an undulating, sterile country, intersected by numerous deep, dry gullies, impassable by cavalry. The creeks were destitute of water; the surface of the earth was in some spots sandy and in others rocky, mostly covered with wild sage in the low lands and with clumps of dwarf cedar on the sides of the hills and mountains. There were few flowers or other vegetable productions worthy of note, the earth being almost entirely bare. This part of New Mexico possesses considerable mineral wealth, which can and no doubt will be fully developed whenever the Government becomes settled so as to afford security and protection to such scientific chemists as may desire to embark in a golden enterprise.

A progress of near 25 miles brought us to our encampment on the Galisteo Creek, at Del Gardo, about 15 miles from the gold mines in the Galisteo mountains, commonly known by the appellative El Placer. Here there was water in sufficient quantities for men and animals, but wood and grass could not be obtained without much labor.

On the morning of the 3d the sun rose brightly and beautifully, beaming over the lofty ridges of mountains to the eastward, and seemed to promise more than his usual quantum of heat during the day. There was no possibility of procuring any water between our encampment and the Rio del Norte, a distance of nearly 15 miles. We prepared for an early start, put up our baggage, and filled our canteens with water. Much to the surprise and inconvenience of the volunteers, just as they were about moving off upon the march, Gen. Kearney rode round among the troops, and seeing many of the men carelessly habited on account of the oppressive heat of the day, gave orders for "every man to put on his coat or he would dismiss him from the service of the country." This order came like a clap of thunder in a clear sky, as the heat was very great, and the reason and philosophy of the order did not so readily appear to the volunteers who were accustomed to think for themselves and consult their own convenience and comfort in matters of dress. However, after some hesitation they obeyed the order, sacrificing their comfort to the general's taste, upon the principle that they had better concede a portion of their liberty than assert their rights under the circumstances of the case, notwithstanding their opinions of law and propriety differed widely from the general's. The men thus reasoned one with another: If we suffer this man to act the tyrant in things of small moment, where is the security that he will not tighten the reins of his authority over us until we shall finally become his slaves and no longer be the servants of the public, whose interest we believe we can promote as well, and whose cause we can serve as faithfully in one apparel as in another? Is our service, then, to be less valued because we choose to appear on parade in citizen's dress in preference to the soldier's uniform? But, on the contrary, if we contend one with another and our strength becomes divided, we shall presently fall a prey to the enemy, and instead of gaining the applause of our countrymen, after performing so many hard marches and suffering so many days with heat and thirst and hunger and sickness, we shall return home the most dishonored of men. Therefore let us make choice of the less of two evils. When the general came to where Capt. Reid had drawn up his men in wait for marching orders, observing them also attired carelessly, and feeling enraged that the captain had not enforced stricter discipline in regard to military dress, he said, "Captain, have your men no jackets?" to which the captain replied, "Some of them have and some of them have not." The general continued, "Make your men, Capt. Reid, put on their jackets or I will dismiss them from the service. The Government has paid them commutation for clothing and expects every man to dress in a manner wholesome for military discipline." The captain rejoined, "My men, sir, came here not to dress but to fight the enemies of their country, and they are ever ready to be of service to you and the country in that way. As to the commutation which you say the Government has paid my men for clothing, I must inform you that you misapprehend the truth. My men have never received one dime since they entered the service, and what money they brought from their homes with them they have already expended for bread while on half rations, owing to the neglect of your chief commissary. As to being dismissed from the service, sir, we do not fight for wages. If there is no place for us in the Army, we will furnish ourselves and fight the enemy wherever we may find him. Acting thus, we shall not lose the respect of our countrymen." Gen. Kearney bit his lips and rode off, giving orders for the march to commence.

When volunteers, actuated by patriotic motives, leave their homes and friends, sacrifice pecuniary considerations, lay aside their peaceful pursuits and professions, throw down their implements of husbandry, and abandon their workshops they have the right to "equip and clothe" themselves as to them shall seem fit and proper, and no officer can legally strip them of that right. When they obey all reasonable orders from higher authority in a prompt and cheerful manner they perform their whole duty to the country as citizen soldiers. There never was perhaps better material in an army than that which composed the Army of the West. Never did a set of men, never did veteran soldiers more cheerfully and resolutely perform their duty or show themselves more submissive to order and law. Would to God they had been governed in every respect in a manner more worthy of their obedience, their spirit, and their country. Many of the officers had performed their duty up to this period with signal ability, and it is a much more pleasing task to add than detract from their just amount of praise, to bear testimony of their worth than censure their conduct, to defend than to despoil their reputation. Gen. Kearney is a skillful, able, and sagacious officer, well fitted for the command of veteran troops, and his commission as a brigadier general commanding the Army of the West was regarded with general satisfaction. An officer should not be condemned for a few faults only unless they be of great magnitude. Gen. Kearney's greatest error consisted in an effort to reduce the volunteers to the same discipline and treat them with the same rigid austerity and dissociability which he was wont to exercise over the regular troops under his command. This is wrong. The former are bred to freedom, the latter trained to obedience. Patriotism makes those soldiers—these, the study of arms. Peace is the pursuit of the one, war the profession of the other. In battle, feeling, principle, honor fire the one, science, experience, discipline guide the other. They are equally brave.

This is an error very common to officers of the Regular Army when commanding volunteer corps. It was a great error with Gen. Kearney, because three-fourths of his army consisted of Volunteers—whose talent and good behavior entitled them to a respectful consideration, both at home and in the service of the country, and upon whose conduct and courage mainly depended the success and safety of the expedition. Conciliation, not force, was therefore proper to be employed by the commander to retain the affections and undivided services of his troops. To make Regulars of Volunteers—to cramp their freedom and move them as the magician moves his automata— is at once to extinguish that pride and spirit, that feeling of liberty, that chivalric patriotism, which renders them efficient troops and which ought to make an officer of Gen. Kearney's standing proud to command them. The historian ever feels more inclined to extenuate than to magnify the faults of men high in power; yet justice and impartiality and the cause of truth require that he should unsparingly chastise the vices, as well as extol the virtues, of those whose acts he essays to record.

We pursued our way down the Galisteo, high spurs of mountains towering in wavy ridges toward the eastern bank of the Del Norte, and the huge masses of the Sierra de los Mimbres lying embedded in the blue mists to the westward. On leaving the Galisteo, by the left bank and at the distance of 4 miles from it, the road forks. Here Gen. Kearney and the dragoons took the right, which bears westward to the Indian town, Santo Domingo, a small pueblo having 300 inhabitants, while the main body of the army followed on the direct road to San Felipe, on the Del Norte. The chief, or alcalde of Santo Domingo, at the head of about 70 dashing cavaliers, with a white flag, came out to escort the general into town by way of winning favor and also thereby intending him a compliment. They made a sham charge upon the general and performed several evolutions about him, displaying consummate horsemanship and brandishing their pointed lances, as if to show what they were capable of doing had their intentions not been peaceable and friendly. The whole of their movements were plainly beheld by the Volunteers from an eminence 2 or 3 miles distant. At first we were impressed with the belief that a skirmish was taking place between the forces of the alcalde and the general; but as we did not see the flash of their guns or hear of the roar of the cannon, and after some time saw the Indians and the general's troops all move off together toward the village, we were satisfied of the sham and concluded the general might drink his wine and puff his cigaritos without our aid, so we moved onward.

We were now at no great distance from the Rio Grande del Norte, which all were very anxious to see, both on account of water, as we were very thirsty, and because we regarded it as the western limit of our present campaign. From the lofty bluffs on the eastern side, looking over the ledge of dry, rocky, treeless hills intervening, we could distinctly see the water in the channel of the river, 3 miles distant. We hastened forward and were soon on the banks of the noted stream, at the foot of a conical-shaped mound resembling the frustum of a pyramid. San Felipe is situated on the western bank of the river, contains a population of about 600, and has a Catholic church. The place submitted to the Americans without opposition. These people were friendly disposed and sold our men such things as they desired to purchase. In a beautiful cottonwood grove, 2 miles below San Felipe, offering a delightful retreat, we encamped for the night and enjoyed the luxury of washing, bathing, and slaking our thirst in the celebrated Rio Bravo del Norte. The Mexicans brought into our camp great quantities of the Oporto grape, finely flavored and most luscious, matured in the most delightful climate. They were sold to the soldiers. The Mexicans transport these grapes, when matured, to Santa Fe and other markets, stored up in small square boxes made of wickerwork and packed on mules and asses. The air in the river valley is at this season extremely bland and balmy.

On the 4th we continued our march down the river on the eastern bank. The valley of this river is generally about 6 to 10 miles wide and is perhaps the best fruit country in the department. The whole valley is finely irrigated by aqueducts which convey the water from the river above. It is done in this manner: A large canal leads the water out from the river generally along the base of the mountains or bluffs, encircling the entire area meant for tillage, while numerous smaller canals and ditches deriving their water from this pass through all the lands and irrigate the cornfields, gardens, vineyards, orchards, and villages. This valley is hedged in by lofty mountains on both sides, consisting of sand and flint stone intermixed with basalt, forming a lane or strait; so were you to attempt to pass in any other direction than along the valley your way would presently be barricaded, so steep and abrupt are the mountains. These people possess many rich vineyards, peach orchards, and groves of apricots, besides flocks of goats and sheep which feed in the mountains and on the hills. Also melons, onions, pepper, salsify, garlic, and other vegetables abound. New Mexico in places is singularly destitute of timber. With the exception of a few clumps of dwarfish, wind-riven cedar on the overhanging bluffs, and the occasional cottonwood groves in the bottoms, the country is woodless, verdureless.

The Rio del Norte is more than 2,000 miles in length and from 250 to 300 yards wide at this point, and is so shallow that it may be forded almost anywhere. The water is cool, clear, and palatable as it comes down from the mountains to the northward. This river is not navigable at this distance from the Gulf of Mexico.

After a march of 8 miles from our last encampment we came to the city of Algodones, containing 1,000 inhabitants. The place submit-

ted willingly and received us kindly and gratuitously offered us
fruits, melons, and bread. This is one of the handsomest towns in
New Mexico. The vineyards, yards, pleasure grounds, orchards, and
gardens are walled in neatly. The tops of the walls were bristling
with cactus, to prevent theft and robbery. Here hundreds of Mexicans voluntarily fell in with the line of march, welcomed us, and
would often exclaim, by way of complimenting us and testifying
their respect and friendship, " Bueno Americano." They expressed
themselves well pleased with the change of government and the new
governor, and appeared to be proud of the idea of being considered
citizens of the great American Republic. In conversation with an
intelligent Mexican, who spoke some broken words of English, inquiry
was made what had become of the late governor, Armijo. He laugh-
ingly replied: "Armijo d—d rascal, gone to the d—l."

Twelve miles farther we came to Bernalilla, a small town containing a population of about 500. After a farther advance of 4 miles
we arrived at Sandia, of which the population is 300. These towns
are inhabited by a mixed race of Mexicans and Pueblo Indians. They
offered us no resistance. On both banks of the river, the towns,
villages and ranches or farmhouses cluster so thickly together that
it presents the appearance of one continued village from Algodones
to San Tome, a distance of nearly 60 miles, resembling in some
small degree that beautiful succession of stately mansions and farmhouses which line the St. Lawrence from Kingston to Montreal, except that the Mexican houses are built of adobes or sun-dried bricks,
having flat, parapetted roofs and small windows. The day's march
was 24 miles. Our camps for the night were commonly placed near
the river or an acequia [1] on account of water.

Albuquerque, the seat of the governor's private residence, his
native town, and the place at which we had some anticipations of
meeting him at the head of his troops, was reached after a march of
8 miles. Early in the morning (Sept. 5) the advance was sounded
by the bugles; the long files were soon moving down the river, followed by the artillery and baggage train. Our lines were arranged
in order, each company in its proper place, officers and men at their
respective posts, and our colors gallantly streaming above us as we
entered the town. On our approach a salute of 20 guns (escopetas)
was fired from the balustraded top of the Catholic church. This
dispelled our apprehensions, or rather put an end to our hopes of an
engagement with Col. Armijo.[2]

These people received us with demonstrations of friendship, and
submissively took the oath of allegiance to our Government. Melons,

---

[1] Acequia is the Mexican word for canal.

[2] In addition to the various intrigues by which Col. Armijo crept into power in New
Mexico, the following is confidently asserted to be true by one who has resided 13 years
in that country: In his early life Don Manuel Armijo was employed as a vaquero, or
herder of cattle, in the mountains east of Albuquerque. About this time three wealthy
citizens of New Mexico, Pino, Chavez, and one other, purchased 36,000 head of sheep and
started with them to the southern markets of Durango and Zacatecas. They spent one
night in Albuquerque, during which Armijo came to them and engaged to drive sheep as
one of their shepherds. He continued in this employment until they arrived in the great
jernada or desert intervening between El Paso and Laguna de los Patos, where he clan-
destinely took leave of them, disguising himself as an Apache chief, collecting 20 or 30
Apaches about him, and intercepted the flocks of his employers, killing some of the
shepherds and driving the rest back to El Paso. Having divided the booty, Armijo and
one Mexican accomplice, putting off their Indian disguise, drove their share of the flock
to Durango, sold them, pocketed the change, and returned to their former employments in
New Mexico. This trick and other similar intrigues furnished Armijo with means to
ingratiate himself into public favor.

grapes, apples, peaches, apricots, and pears were brought out to us by the inhabitants, which the soldiers purchased liberally. This town, numbering about 800 inhabitants, takes its name from the apricot groves in its vicinity, this fruit being called by the Mexicans alburquerque. Cranes, geese, ducks, brants, swans, and pelicans are found on the Del Norte. Very little dew or rain falls in this valley, although it rains or rather showers almost every day in the mountains.

The Army, after a march of 16 miles, encamped on the river 8 miles below Albuquerque.

This morning (6th) a deputation of some 30 well-dressed, intelligent-looking Mexicans came up from Peralta to offer submission to the general, whom they saluted as their new governor, assuring him that all was tranquil and orderly on the Rio Abajo, and that the people there desired to be our friends. They besought that their lives, families, and property might be protected; of which being assured they departed. The Army having progressed 8 miles, nooned at a beautiful cottonwood grove near the margin of the river, which, from its regularity, has the appearance of being artificial. Near the bluffs on the east side of the river are several large sand drifts or mounds of sand as fine and white almost as the driven snow. These ephemeral sand mountains continue to accumulate as long as the wind drives from the same point of the compass, but the current of the wind veering, they are swept away in less time than was required for their formation. At this place the grass was only moderate, wood scarce; blue pinks and other flowers were found. The flora of the Del Norte valley is rich, varied, and interesting. Here we pitched our camps to spend the day, as it was the Sabbath, and as we were much in need of rest.[1]

While we were marching down the valley of the great River of the North, feasting upon the fruits and melons of that sunny climate, it was impossible not to contrast our condition, as a triumphant army, with that of the wretched and ill-fated Texan prisoners who were captured near San Miguel, and conducted in chains and under guard down the same road, over the same ground, emaciated with hunger and ill usage, benumbed by the cold of winter, faint with sufferings, sinking under fatigues, and inhumanly butchered by order of that monster of cruelty, Gen. Salezar, when they became too feeble to endure the toils and hardships of the march. The remembrance of these outrages, practiced upon Texan and American citizens, so incensed the soldiers that they meditated wreaking their vengeance upon the heads of unoffending Mexicans. However, the more humane sentiment prevailed that the innocent ought not to suffer for the guilty—

---

[1] The night we lay at this grove the moon shone brightly. A small party of men, having passed the sentry, went down to Peralta, where we expected to amuse ourselves a few hours at a Mexican fandango. In this, however, we were disappointed, for only the homeliest women, such as we cared not to dance with, made their appearance at the saloon, the young and fair señoritas being shy of men who wore side arms. Returning in disgust soon after, we fell amongst the ditches and canals and, having climbed several walls, at length fell into a vineyard, surcharged with clusters of the most delicious grapes. This was a fortunate mishap ; for, drawing our sabers, we cut off the large, ripe, enticing clusters and carried an abundance of them to our companions in camp. These bunches were not, perhaps, as large as those the Hebrews hung upon a staff and upon the shoulders of two men, brought down from Eschol, but they were no doubt as luscious. Of course the sentinels must have their share as we returned to camp.

Another party, straggling about with similar motives, met with more difficulty ; for a part of them, carelessly scaling the walls of a vineyard in quest of grapes; jumped down on the inside, which was several feet lower than the ground on the outside. Having satisfied their appetites, they were unable to return. Their companions, who had remained without, were compelled to pull them over the walls by means of lariats.

that a magnanimous forbearance and forgiveness of injuries were more Christian and praiseworthy than the spirit of revenge. This reflection saved them.

Progressing on the 7th about 3 miles, we passed the small town Peralta, the population of which is about 300. This town is the place of residence of the Chavez family, the brothers and relations of the Chavez who was murdered by Capt. McDaniel's band of marauders on Cow Creek, a branch of the Little Arkansas. They are wealthy, and have chiefly educated their sons in the United States. They are friends to the Americans. The valley of the Del Norte heightens in interest and in the richness and variety of its grain and fruit productions as you descend toward the south, while the population gradually becomes more intelligent and less mixed with the Pueblo Indian races, speaking a language more nearly resembling the Castilian than the inhabitants in the more northern districts. At the distance of about 5 miles below Peralta we arrived at San Tome, a small town containing 800 inhabitants. This place was named in honor of one of the patron saints of the country. Here the people were assembled from all the neighboring villages and ranchos, to the number of 3,000, for the purpose of celebrating the anniversary of the holy vision, or the inception of the Virgin Mary. The occasion was rendered doubly grand when the inhabitants of the place were informed of the arrival of Gen. Kearney and his troops, as they were seemingly anxious both to testify their respect for the new governor, and also the more effectually to impress us with an idea of the pompous character of the church, to make a dazzling exhibition of its commemorative rites. They were ignorant of the fact, however, that we are plain republicans, and rather detested than admired their unmeaning pomp and senseless mockery of religion. It should be observed here that the doctrines of catholicism, or of the Romish faith, are neither understood nor practiced in their purity by the laity or clergy of New Mexico. Error has crept into the church. The worship has become encumbered by absurdities and the grossest ceremonies. The church is benighted. "Darkness has covered the earth and gross darkness the people." Hence their worship is little better than a caricature on the more enlightened worship of the Catholic Church in the United States and other Christian countries.

The general and his staff took up their quarters in town, while the volunteers and regulars encamped in the suburbs. About 8 o'clock at night the town was most brilliantly illuminated by the pine fagots that blazed from all the walls of the city and from the tops of the churches and the private houses. The general was saluted by the discharge of musketry and escopetas as he entered the town. For four hours an incessant discharge of firearms and the throwing of skyrockets and fireballs were kept up. The elements were lurid with long, zigzag streams of fire for 300 feet high. The catheron wheel made a circle of red light like a dizzy comet. These rockets would sometimes explode in the air and sometimes fall among the throng and explode, producing great confusion and tremendous shouts of laughter.

At the same time that all this was going on, in another part of the public square there were perhaps 1,500 persons, mostly women, boys, and girls, sitting on the ground listening to a comedy or some kind of theatrical exhibition which was being performed by several ladies and gentlemen on a stage erected in a large piazza fronting the square. Everything was said in the Spanish language, so that the Americans who were present (very few of whom could speak in that tongue) were unable to appreciate the merits of the play, or say whether it was original, or whether it was from Shakespeare or the Bible. The women were promiscuously intermingled with the men, and the music of instruments with the discharge of rockets, firearms, and the shouts of the throng. The whole made horrid discord. The pageant would have been imposing had it been attended with order and solemnity. Was this serving God in spirit and in truth"?

This strange performance attracted the attention of such of the men as were struck with its novelty. Some went, induced by curiosity, others that they might gain information of what was going on. When a goodly number of men had left camp and gone into town to witness what might be seen there, Lieut. Col. Ruff sent Lieut. Sublette, the officer of the guard that night, with a file of men, who, proceeding into town, picked up such of the soldiers as had left camp without permission, and having collected 70 or 80 in this way who offered no resistance, brought them to the lieutenant colonel's tent, who immediately ordered them to be detailed as an extra guard for the next day. Ruff, whose popularity had been constantly decreasing was now become odious to the men. They held meetings in the camp. Some advised that he should no longer be allowed to hold the command; others, that they should baptize him in a filthy lake hard by; while others again thought the best means of treating him would be to tie two asses together with a lariat and make one of them pass on one side of his tent and the other on a different side, and thus drag his tent down and roll him topsy-turvy in his sleep. "He would then rise," they said, "like Rip Van Winkle from 40 years of slumber." All these expedients failing, it is said that the door of his tent was thrown full of the entrails of the sheep which had been slaughtered for the use of the army. His bedding was therefore blooded and his tent filled with the stench.

On the next day this celebration was renewed. The church was crowded to overflowing, though ample enough to contain 2,000 persons. The altar was lighted up by 24 candles. Six priests officiated. Gen. Kearney and staff officers, and also some of the officers of the volunteer corps were present, and looked and no doubt felt supremely ridiculous, each one holding a long, greasy, tallow candle in his hand, which was to be blown out and relighted at certain intervals during the ceremonies. But it is a good maxim perhaps, "when you are in Rome do as Rome does." Every Mexican that entered the church bowed and worshipped the Holy Virgin, then the infant Savior in the manger, and then the crucified Savior on the cross. A very aged and decrepit lady came in much affected, bowed before the Savior and worshipped Him, and tremblingly wiped her falling tears on the robes with which the image was clad.

During the whole time singing, instrumental music, and the firing of musketry were strangely commingled. The same airs were played in the church gallery on the violin that were usually played at the Mexican fandangoes.

The padre walked about the plaza amongst the crowd after the conclusion of the ceremonies, while four men suspended over his head a gilded canopy. He was also preceded by a file of men firing their escopetas, and followed by a number of altar boys throwing rockets, which kept up a continual racket, making the heavens dizzy with streams of fire.

As already observed, the Mexicans are remarkably fond of gaming and other amusements. Accordingly, toward evening horse racing, dancing, and gambling occupied the attention of the throng. Great quantities of ripe fruit, grapes, melons, sweet cakes, and various other commodities were brought hither for sale by the market women upon asses and sumpter horses.

San Tome, which is about 100 miles from the capital, was the southern terminus of our campaign. We returned to Santa Fe, arriving here on the 13th, after an absence of 12 days; Maj. Gilpin being left with a detachment of men to take care of the stock in the neighborhood of Del Gardo.

This campaign, which was effected without bloodshed, was attended by some beneficial results. Gen. Kearney, in his proclamation of the 22d of August, had promised protection to such New Mexicans as should peaceably acquiesce in his government, both against the depredations of the Indians and from acts of violence on the part of their conquerors. He had engaged to defend their persons from harm and to preserve their rights and liberty in the amplest manner to them. He now visited the richest portion of the department that the people might see the conduct of his soldiers and have confidence in the efficiency of the protection he had promised. The civil behavior of the troops toward the inhabitants greatly conciliated those who were disaffected toward the American Government.

CHAPTER VI.

During Gen. Kearney's absence on his excursion to San Tome nothing of very great moment transpired at Santa Fe. Col. Doniphan remained in command of the troops which were left at the capital, attended to the administration of the laws as governor of the department, superintended the erection of Fort Marcy on the hill overlooking Santa Fe to the northward, and completed, by the aid of Willard P. Hall, the " Organic laws and constitution " for the government of the new territory.

The American flag, liberty's emblem, continued to stream bravely from the top of the tall staff erected for the purpose in the plaza. A civil government was established and put in motion. The constitution and laws for the government of the new Territory, which had been drawn up with much haste, were chiefly derived from the laws of Missouri and Texas and the Federal Constitution. The department of New Mexico was styled " the Territory of New Mexico in the United States."

In the capital was found, upon the arrival of Gen. Kearney at that place, a small printing press which was used for printing public laws, notices, proclamations, advertisements, manifestos, pronunciamentos, and other high-sounding Mexican documents in the form of pamphlets and hand bills. With this poor apology for a printing press and such worn type and indifferent ink, paper, and other materials as chanced to be about the establishment the constitution and laws of the Territory were published. As the Spanish language has no W, a difficulty presented itself in regard to the type, which was at length obviated by the substitution of two Vs for one W. In this manner were the constitution and laws printed, both in the Spanish and English languages in double column, placed in juxtaposition on each page. The arduous and difficult task of translating the laws into the Spanish was assigned to Capt. David Waldo, whose thorough acquaintance with the language and customs of the Mexicans as well as accomplished general scholarship, not only qualified him for the undertaking but rendered him eminently useful on several subsequent occasions during the campaign.

To the end that the machinery of this new government might be speedily put into operation, Gen. Kearney, acting under authority from the President, made the following appointments to office, viz: Charles Bent, to be governor of the Territory; Don Aduciano Virgil, secretary; Richard Dallan, marshal; Francis P. Blair, jr., United States district attorney; Eugene Leitensdoffer, auditor of public accounts; Joab Houghton, Antonio José Otero, and Charles Baubien, judges of the supreme court. Some of these men were Americans and others New Mexicans, the interests of both parties being consulted in the appointments. Thus was another star added to our constellation.

While the Army lay inactive at Santa Fe the men did not quarter in houses for this was impracticable, unless they first dispossessed Mexican families which they did not think proper to do, but pitched their tents on the bare earth—which was covered with sand and gravel—where they both slept and prepared and ate their food. Therefore by reason of exposure and the places of dissipation in the city, from which it was impossible to restrain them, very many of them took sick, many of them died, and others, lingering under a slow and wasting disease, soon became unfit for service and were discharged. Thus our numbers continually decreased, the hospitals being filled with invalids infected with various loathsome diseases.

On the 10th of September Dr. Vaughan, assistant surgeon, who had been left at Fort Bent in charge of the sick (about 60 in number), arrived at Santa Fe in company with Lieut. Ingalls, of the First Dragoons, commanding a small detachment, and Lieut. Abert, of the topographical corps, and such of those who had been sick as survived and were able to pursue on and rejoin the Army. Whether Dr. Vaughan treated the men with that attention and kindness which the condition of the sick requires (especially on a campaign where few comforts can be administered to them at best) was questioned by those who were under his direction. Their judgment, however, may have been the result of prejudice.

Fort Marcy, commanding the city from an eminence toward the north, was laid off by Lieut. Gilmer, of the topographic corps, and L. A. Maclean, a volunteer of Reid's company, and built by the volunteer troops, a certain number of men being detailed each day for the purpose. Those who labored 10 days or more consecutively received a compensation of 18 cents per day in addition to their regular allowance. The figure of this fort is that of an irregular tridecagon, and is sufficiently ample to mount a great number of cannon and accommodate 1,000 soldiers. Its walls are massive, thick, and strong, and are built of adobes 2 feet long, 1 foot broad, and 6 inches thick. It is a strong fortress and perpetuates the name of the present Secretary of War.

By this time such Mexican families as had fled to the fastnesses of the mountains upon the approach of the Americans were returning to their homes and gradually gaining confidence in the new Government. The administration of justice appeared to be conducted upon safer and broader principles than had hitherto been known in New Mexico. Industry, virtue, and honesty, and education, which is the parent of these, and which had been singularly neglected in that country, were encouraged and rewarded. Society seemed to be reforming and reestablishing upon a new and republican basis. Thefts, robberies, riots, and murders were punished with the utmost rigor. Thus law and order prevailed over anarchy and misrule—tranquillity was soon restored throughout the territory and general satisfaction reigned.[1]

On the 17th of September Lieut. Col. Ruff, of the First Regiment of Missouri Mounted Volunteers, in consequence of having received a captain's commission in the United States Army, and also feeling conscious that a large majority of the regiment were unwilling longer to suffer his government, and despised his efforts to extinguish in their bosoms that spirit of freedom and high-toned chivalry which make men proud of their country and of her service, resigned his command. The volunteers were ever ready to yield a willing and unforced obedience to his orders, for this was wholesome for discipline. But they were obstinate when driven. Col. Ruff, though ill qualified to govern volunteer troops, has some experience in military affairs, is well acquainted with tactics, and neither to "extenuate nor aught to set down in malice," is certainly a brave man and a good soldier.

At a subsequent period Mr. Ruff, as captain of a mounted rifle company, rendered some very important service in Gen. Scott's division of the Army. On the 29th of July, 1847, Capt. Ruff was dispatched by Gen. Smith with a squadron composed of one company of the Second Dragoons under Lieut. Hawes and his own company of mounted riflemen, in all 86 men, to attack the town of San Juan de los Llanos. Capt. Ruff, finding about 50 cavalry drawn up in front of the town, who retired upon his approach, divided his command into three parts and entered the town cautiously, toward the center of which the stone houses and churches were filled with armed men. Lieut. Hawes first received the enemy's fire, whereupon, dismounting and forming his men on foot, and being joined by Lieut. Walker of the mounted rifles, they very spiritedly returned the fire. The other party, under Capt. Ruff, advancing at the same time, drove the enemy from house to house with great slaughter until they reached the plaza. The fire of the riflemen was astonishingly destructive. Here two of the principal houses, one of them loop-holed, were defended with great obstinacy, but were finally carried. A party was now organized to assault the church, from the towers of which a continual fire had been kept up. But when the storming party began to advance a white flag was hung out. Hereupon the firing ceased and the Mexicans capitulated. In this engagement the Mexicans lost 43 killed and 54 wounded. Only one of the Americans was wounded—none killed.

It was this day that William Bray, a man belonging to Capt. Stephenson's company, became intoxicated and entirely incontrollable. After swearing and swaggering in a most unbecoming manner, resisting every effort which was made to pacify him, he seized his butcher knife and made threats against the life of his captain. The captain for some time carefully avoided him and endeavored to persuade him to his duty, but all in vain; he rushed furiously into the captain's tent with knife drawn and made an attempt upon his life. The captain in self-defense drew a pistol and shot Bray through the heart, who fell dead in an instant with his knife clenched in his hand. This occurrence was the more lamentable that Bray

---

[1] At a later period the New Mexicans grew weary of their conquerors and desired new rulers and a new government.

was 63 years of age and had been one of Jackson's soldiers at the Battle of New Orleans. On the morning of the 18th an election was ordered by Gen. Kearney to fill the vacancy occasioned by the resignation of Lieut. Col. Ruff, which resulted in the choice of Capt. Congreve Jackson over Maj. William Gilpin by a majority of 183 votes. Capt. Jackson's place was supplied by the election of H. H. Hughes to fill the vacancy, the same who commanded as major in Gentry's Missouri Regiment of Volunteers at the battle of Okechubee in Florida in 1837. He was chosen from the ranks.

During this day a squadron of two companies (Maldo's and Stephenson's) under command of Maj. Gilpin was dispatched to the little town of Abiquiu, on the Rio de Chana, to keep the Indians in check in that part of the Territory, and also a detachment of three companies (Parsons's, Reid's, and Hughes's), under Lieut. Col. Jackson, was ordered to proceed to the town of Ceballeta, on the Rio Puerco, about 120 miles southwesterly from the capital, for a like purpose. These detachments were to remain at their respective posts until Col. Doniphan took up the line of march for Chihuahua, when they were to rejoin him in that expedition. This expedition was to commence its march against the State and city of Chihuahua immediately upon the arrival of Col. Price's command at Santa Fe, in conformity to the following order, viz:

General Orders No. 30, sec. 2.

When all the companies of Col. Price's regiment shall have reached here, Col. Doniphan will proceed with his regiment to Chihuahua and report to Brigadier General Wool for duty.

By order of Brig. Gen.

S. W. KEARNEY.
(Signed)   H. S. TURNER,
Capt. A. A. A. Gen.

It was not even doubted for a moment by the most incredulous that Gen. Wool's division would have taken possession of Chihuahua long before Col. Doniphan could possibly reach that place, and the latter did not at first so much as anticipate the honor of cooperating with the general in the reduction of the stronghold of the northern Provinces and formerly the headquarters of the captains general of the vice regal Government of New Spain, for it was well known throughout the United States as well as in the Army of the West that Chihuahua was the unqualified destination of Gen. Wool's Army.

On the 20th a deputation of Eutaws, or more properly Yutas, was brought in by Maj. Gilpin to hold a council with the general, who made a speech to them through his interpreter and gave them much good advice. On their part they promised to be peaceable, orderly, to respect the lives and property of the Mexicans, and to be obedient to the laws of the United States which were now extended to the Territory of New Mexico. The general made them some trifling presents, which, however, were esteemed of great value among them, and they departed apparently well satisfied.

The same day an express arrived at the capital from Col. Price informing the general that he was short of provisions and asking fresh supplies. He was promptly furnished. This was the first and only reliable information we had received of the colonel and his forces since they left Fort Leavenworth. They were then at the Cimarron Springs, nearly 300 miles from Santa Fe, and were expected to arrive in 15 or 20 days. By this express information was also brought that W. P. Hall, a private volunteer soldier, was elected to Congress from one of the districts of Missouri by a large majority. Hall, Lucas, and myself were in one of the departments of the governor's house transcribing the new constitution and laws of the Territory when Col. Doniphan entered bringing the intelligence. Hall was not moved or elated, but behaved very calmly. It is especially creditable to Col. Doniphan that he should have been the first to announce to Mr. Hall the news of his success, when the latter and Col. Doniphan were strongly opposed in politics and had often met each other on the stump or rostrum during a heated political contest. But such is the magnanimous character of Col. Doniphan.

September 23 the chief of one branch of the Apaches, with about 30 of his tribe, came to hold a "grand council" with the governor general. The general made a long speech to them through an interpreter, encouraging them to industry and peaceful pursuits, and particularly to the cultivation of the soil, as the surest and best mode of procuring an honorable subsistence; "that they must desist from all robberies and the committing of all crimes against the laws of the territory; that if they did not he would send his soldiers among them and destroy them from the earth; but if they would be peaceable toward their white brethren he would protect and defend them as he would the New Mexicans, and make them all brothers to the white people and citizens of the same Republic, and children of the same father, the President, at Washington City."

To all these things the venerable sachem replied in a spirit worthy his tribe, setting forth the wishes of his people in a strain of bold, commanding eloquence, which has ever characterized the aboriginal orator. He said:

Father, you give good advice for me and my people; but I am now old and unable to work, and my tribe are unaccustomed to cultivating the soil for subsistence, The Apaches are poor; they have no clothes to protect them from the cold, and the game is fast disappearing from their hunting grounds. You must, therefore, if you wish us to be peaceable, speak a good word to the Comanches, the Yutas, the Navajos, and the Arapahoes, our enemies, that they will allow us to kill buffalo on the great plains. You are rich—you have a great nation to feed and clothe you—I am poor, and have to crawl on my belly, like a cat, to shoot deer and buffalo for my people. I am not a bad man; I do not rob and steal; I speak truth. The Great Spirit gave me an honest heart and a straight tongue. I have not two tongues that I should speak forked.

My skin is red, my head sunburnt, my eyes are dim with age, and I am a poor Indian, a dog, yet I am not guilty. There is no guilt there [putting his hand on his breast] no! I can look you in the face like a man. In the morning of my days my muscles were strong; my arm was stout; my eye was bright; my mind was clear; but now I am weak, shriveled up with age, yet my heart is big, my tongue is straight. I will take your counsel because I am weak and you are strong.

The general then gave them some blankets, butcher knives, beads, mirrors, and other presents for their squaws, and they departed under the promise that they would be good and faithful citizens of the United States.

On the 25th Gen. Kearney, with a very inadequate force for such an enterprise, set out from the capital for the distant shores of the Pacific, leaving Col. Doniphan in command of all the forces in New Mexico. The colonel was now actively employed in pushing forward preparations for his contemplated descent upon Chihuahua. Supplies were being procured for the men. Every soldier endeavored to mount himself upon a safe and durable animal, for the march was known to be long and perilous, passing through desert tracts of country. Wagons for the transportation of baggage and provisions were speedily being repaired. Harness and teams were put in readiness for the draught. It was the colonel's intention to begin his great march as soon as Col. Price should arrive at Santa Fe with his troops, and succeed him in the command at that place.

The author may perhaps be pardoned for adding, at the close of this chapter, a few brief remarks in commendation of the United States' troops, which will show the strong moral influence as well as the nationality of our republican institutions. He has observed his comrades in arms, after performing the severest toils during a long and fatiguing march of 900 miles, bearing with fortitude the burden and heat of the day, sometimes half faint of thirst and hunger, subsisting the greater part of the time upon half rations, refuse to pluck the ears of corn that grew thickly and invitingly around them. This exhibits a degree of moral firmness and a regard for the rights of property which is truly characteristic of the American people, is worthy of the highest praise, and is doubtless one of the happy results of our benign institutions. There was a national feeling in the Army of the West. Every soldier felt that he was a freeman; that he was a citizen of the model Republic; and that he ought to look upon the disgrace of American arms as individual dishonor. Hence their high moral sense and conscious superiority over the Mexican people. As the American soldier walked in the streets of the capital and met a group of Mexican ladies and gentlemen going to the plaza with marketables, or in more gaudy attire passing up the walks to the Catholic churches, he paid them the same complimentary marks of courtesy and civility with which he had been accustomed to greet his own fairer country women and men in the streets of St. Louis, Cincinnati, New York, or Philadelphia. This honorable feeling [1] was never once forgotten or lost sight of by the citizen soldier.

---

[1] This remark is intended to apply to the conduct of the men generally. Individual instances of bad conduct may have been witnessed.

CHAPTER VII.

In the previous chapters it has been briefly related how the war between the United States and Mexico took its origin, and in what manner the President proposed to conduct the war, invading the latter country at several distinct points. It has also been shown how the western expedition was fitted out and dispatched across the great solitudes which intervene between Fort Leavenworth and Santa Fe; by what means the men were able to subsist themselves upon the plains; and how, for greater convenience, the marches were conducted by separate companies, squadrons, and battalions. Finally, it has been related how the New Mexicans surrendered the capital into the hands of the Americans without resistance or bloodshed.

Lest the forces already dispatched under command of Gen. Kearney might not be able to accomplish the purposes of the expedition, or even to sustain themselves against the overwhelming numbers the enemy could bring into the field, it was deemed advisable by the President to send out a strong reinforcement. Sterling Price, a member of Congress from Missouri at the time, having resigned his membership early in the summer of 1846, and applied to President Polk, was appointed to the conduct of this new force. This reinforcement was to consist of one full mounted regiment, one mounted extra battalion, and one extra battalion of Mormon infantry, the whole to be filled up of volunteers.

After some delay the companies required rendezvoused at Fort Leavenworth, and were mustered into the service about the first of August. The companies from Boone, Benton, Carroll, Chariton, Lynn, Livingston, Monroe, Randolph, St. Genevieve, and St. Louis Counties, respectively, under command of Capts. McMillan, Hollaway, Williams, Holley, Barbeen, Slack, Giddings, H. Jackson, Horine, and Dent, composed the Second Regiment. Notwithstanding the President had designated Sterling Price as a suitable man to command the Second Regiment, the men thought he ought to be chosen by their free suffrages, or some other man in his stead. Accordingly they proceeded to hold an election that they might choose a commander. Sterling Price obtained the command. D. D. Mitchell was chosen lieutenant colonel, and Capt. Edmondson, major. The appointment of R. Walker to be adjutant, and Stewart, sergeant major, Dr. May, surgeon, and A. Wilson, sutler, completed the organization of the Second Regiment.

In the separate battalion, which was composed of the companies from the counties of Marion, Polk, Platte, and Ray, respectively, under command of Capts. Smith, Robinson, Morin, and Hendley, Willock was chosen lieutenant colonel. Thus the strength of Col. Price's command was about 1,200 men. Besides this cavalry force, he had a considerable number of heavy pieces of artillery, and artillerymen to manage them, commanded by officers of the regular service, and a great number of baggage and provision wagons. These trains of wagons, used to transport the baggage and provisions of the men, generally set out in advance of the army because, being heavily loaded they could not travel as fast as the cavalry, and that being wanted in the army, at any time it is easier for them to come to a halt than to make a forced march, and each wagon having a driver well armed, and each train of 30 or more wagons a captain of the teamsters, they did not need to be protected by any other guard against the Indians, but went as fast as it pleased them, and when attacked by these barbarians, they presently converted the wagons into a corral or breastwork, so as to defend themselves from harm; except the baggage wagons, which traveled with the army when they could keep pace along with it. With this force, thus furnished, Col. Price set out for Santa Fe,[1] marching by separate detachments over the plains, as Gen. Kearney and Col. Doniphan had ordered their captains to do before, about the middle of August.

Also, about this period Capt. Allen, of the First Dragoons, acting under instructions from the War Department, proceeded to the Council Bluffs, where the Mormons had been collecting for several months with the view to making a settlement, and there raised a body of 500 Mormons, all volunteer Infantry. This body of troops also rendezvoused at Fort Leavenworth, and, having been outfitted, commenced its march soon after the departure of Col. Price for the shores of the Pacific, a distance of 1,990 miles, where, having served to the expiration of one year, they were to be paid, discharged, and allowed to found settlements and bring their families. They were to proceed first to Santa Fe and thence to California, following the route of Gen. Kearney.

This Mormon Battalion consisted of five companies, lettered A, B, C, D, and E, respectively, under Capts. Hunt, Hunter, Brown, Higgins, and Davis, commanded by Lieut. Col. Allen, Dykes being adjutant and Glines being sergeant major. It was attended by 27 women, for laundresses, and was mustered into the service on the 16th of July. Lieut. Col. Allen, having delayed at the fort a short time after the companies began the march to forward some supplies, was suddenly taken ill and expired shortly afterwards, on the 22d of August.

Thus died Lieut. Col. Allen, of the First Dragoons, in the midst of a career of usefulness, under the favorite smiles of fortune, beloved while living and regretted after death by all who knew him both among the Volunteer and Regular troops. The Mormons were then conducted to Santa Fe by Lieut. Smith, of the First Dragoons. The manner in which the advance of the western army immediately under Gen. Kearney and Col. Doniphan conducted its

---

[1] It was the original intention of Col. Price to march his entire command to California by way of Santa Fe if Gen. Kearney were in a condition not to need his services at the latter place.

marches and the great success which attended them has been narrated in a previous chapter. Therefore, as this second force traveled over the same route and was from the nature of the country necessitated to perform nearly the same daily marches that it might obtain fuel, water, and forage (or grass, which is the only forage the plains can supply), and also as the management which was necessary to be used for the rapid progress of the reenforcing army was similar to that which had been adopted by the preceding forces, and the scenes and incidents occurring on this campaign, as well as the leading features of the country passed over, being such as have already been described, it is not deemed necessary to recapitulate them.

They were not molested at any time, or put to any serious inconvenience by the Indians who dwell upon the plains. Many horses died or failed during the march. Those which failed, being abandoned by their owners, were soon killed and devoured by the gangs of wolves which daily followed the army.

These barbarous tribes of Indians seldom have the courage or daring to oppose the march of any considerable number of men, but attack with the greatest fury small parties of men who chance to fall in their way, and when they have captured them they never suffer them to escape but uniformly torture and put them to death in the most cruel manner. Col. Price's forces, feeling entirely secure against these hordes by reason of their numbers, placed out no picket guards, as the other command had done, and sometimes had no sentinels about the camps at night. At a later period, however, the Indians infested the Santa Fe road with more boldness, and in several instances succeeded in killing Americans and capturing provision wagons and large droves of mules, oxen, and other stock belonging to the United States Government.

The troops composing this command when they arrived at the crossing of the Arkansas took the route by the Cimarron River, except two or three companies which proceeded by way of Fort Bent and the Raton Pass to Santa Fe. The Cimarron route is perhaps 100 miles the shorter way, but is not so well supplied with water or forage as the other. While the Army lay encamped somewhere on the Arkansas a general estampede occurred among the horses. Wildly and madly they plunged over the plain, near a thousand head, stung and galled by the lariats and iron pickets which they dragged after them. After great labor the majority of them were recovered; the rest either went wild on the prairies or were captured by the Comanches, who are excellent in horsemanship.

From the Cimarron Springs Col. Price sent forward an express to Santa Fe representing to Gen. Kearney that his command was without supplies and that his marches must of necessity be slow unless he could furnish him. This express reached Santa Fe on the 20th of September and provisions were forthwith dispatched upon the road to meet him. Meanwhile the colonel advanced upon the march as vigorously as the condition of his men and animals would permit. Thompson and Campbell, contractors to supply the Army with beef, were on the road with 1,400 beef cattle, but were too far behind to be of any service in the present exigency.

Col. Price, in a very feeble state of health, arrived at the capital in company with a few of his staff officers on the 28th of September, three days after Gen. Kearney's departure for California. The different detachments and companies of his command continued to come in almost daily. The greater part of them, however, together with the Mormon Battalion, arrived on the 9th, 10th, 11th, and 12th days of October. They quartered out on the ground as Col. Doniphan's men were doing, there being no more houses in Santa Fe than barely enough to shelter the inhabitants from the inclement weather.

The capital was now literally alive with artillery, baggage wagons, commissary teams, beef cattle, and a promiscuous throng of American soldiers, traders, visitors, stragglers, trappers, amateurs, mountaineers, Mexicans, Pueblo Indians, women, and children, numbering perhaps not less than 14,000 souls. The aggregate effective force of the American Army in New Mexico at this time was about 3,500 men.

Col. Price's command during its long and toilsome march to Santa Fe, which was completed in about 53 days in midsummer, was attended with most singular good fortune, having lost only three soldiers on the way—one by accident, the other two by sickness.[1]

About the 10th of August another requisition was made upon the governor of Missouri for 1,000 additional volunteers to join Gen. Kearney in New Mexico. This new force, the Third Regiment of Missouri Volunteers, was to consist entirely of Infantry and was to rendezvous also at Fort Leavenworth, where it was to be fitted out and be ready to march close in rear of Col. Price's command. In an incredibly short space of time the requisite number of troops was raised and company officers chosen. Forthwith they repaired to the fort and reported for service. Maj. Daugherty, of Clay County, was elected to the command of this regiment, and while actively engaged in hastening preparations for the arduous march over the plains he received orders from the President requiring him to desist from the enterprise and disband his force. This was accordingly done. The men, disappointed, returned to their homes. Thus those brave men, who had generously volunteered to serve the country on foot in a Cavalry expedition, were denied a share in the toils and honors of the campaign.

There being more troops in the capital after the arrival of the recruits under the command of Col. Price than were necessary to preserve order and tranquillity in the city, Col. Doniphan disposed of them in this manner: The three remaining companies of the First Regiment were sent out to the grazing encampment, which for better pasturage had been moved from Galisteo to the mountains or dividing hills between the river Pecos and the Del Norte, about 50 miles from Santa Fe and 20 from San Miguel. On this tableland the grass was very fine and nourishing, and there was a beautiful lake of fresh water near the camp ground abundantly sufficient for both men and horses. This glassy lake was situated in the edge of a glade several hundred yards wide and skirted by the handsomest groves of pines and cedars ever verdant; while the tall " gramma," resembling a rich meadow, carpeted its margin, as well as covered the beautiful succession of hills and dales which lay spread out to view. In this truly romantic spot of country the animals were soon refitted for service. A squadron of two companies under Maj. Ed-

---

[1] These were Blount and Willhoit. They were both interred at Fort Marcy.

mondson was ordered to relieve Lieut. Col. Jackson at Cebolleta and a detachment was sent to relieve Maj. Gilpin at Abiquiu; Jackson and Gilpin were severally to await at these places further orders. Also, one or two companies were sent back to forage or graze on the Mora, near the Santa Clara Springs, to prevent the Mexicans and Indians driving off the mules and beef cattle belonging to the army that were grazing there. The remainder of the Cavalry, together with all the Artillery, was retained at Santa Fe.

Things being in this posture, on the 11th an express reached Santa Fe from California by the hands of Fitzpatrick, the old mountaineer and pilot to Gen. Kearney. This express was from Commodore Stockton and Lieut.-Col. Fremont. It met Gen. Kearney on his road to California, about 150 miles from Santa Fe, by the hand of Lieut. Kit Carson, one of Lieut. Col. Fremont's men direct from Monterey. The express brought this intelligence:

The Pacific Squadron, Commodore Stockton, has taken possession of California, and the American flag is now proudly streaming above the walls of Monterey, the capital of the country. Lieut. Col. Fremont was on the Rio Sacramento when the squadron arrived off the coast and was not present when the capital surrendered. Five men-of-war were anchored in the bay when the express left Monterey. The inhabitants submitted without a struggle. Lieut. Col. Fremont had probably been appointed temporary governor of California.

Kit Carson returned to California as pilot to Gen. Kearney, while Fitzpatrick, his former guide, was entrusted with the bearing of the ditpatches to Fort Leavenworth, whence they were transmitted to Washington.

A great number of provision wagons was now coming in and filling up the streets of the city. The commissary and quartermaster departments were extremely busy in receiving and storing provisions and taking care of Government stock. At the head of these departments were Maj. Swords and Capt. McKissack. There were also a great number of assistant commissaries and quartermasters[1] and a tribe of clerks. Every exertion was now being used to provide a good outfit for Col. Doniphan's intended expedition against Chihuahua, which was looked upon as being both an arduous and a hazardous enterprise. The battalion of Mormons, to the future conduct of which Capt. Cooke, of the First Dragoons, had been appointed, were waiting for a new outfit for transportation across the mountains to the Californias. Also Capt. Hudson, of St. Louis, having given up his command of the Laclede Rangers to his first lieutenant, Elliot, and acting under the permission of Gen. Kearney, had raised a new company of volunteers, 100 strong, from the several corps at Santa Fe, designed for the California service. This company, denominated the California Rangers,[2] must also be provided with means of transportation over the mountains. Besides this pressing current of business, large deputations of Indians, headed by their respective chiefs, were constantly coming in to hold a "big talk" or "grand council" with Col. Doniphan, who as yet was looked upon as commander of all the forces in New Mexico and governor of the department. Such, then, at this time was the posture of affairs in Santa Fe.

---

[1] Lieuts. Pope Gordon and James Lea were appointed assistant commissary and quartermaster to the First Regiment—both active, energetic men.

[2] This company was dissolved by Col. Doniphan as soon as he learned that California was in the hands of the Americans.

CHAPTER VIII.

Doniphan ordered against the Navajos—Plan of the march—Condition of the troops—They take with them neither baggage, provision wagons, nor tents—Arrived at Albuquerque—A squadron sent to Valverde—Death of Adjt. Butler—War dance at Isleta—Express from the merchants—Valverde.

The express which reached Santa Fe on the 11th day of October, as already noticed, brought a communication from Gen. Kearney to Col. Doniphan, instructing him to delay for a time his contemplated movement upon Chihuahua, and desiring him to proceed with his regiment forthwith into the country inhabited by the Navajos, a large and powerful tribe of semicivilized Indians, and chastise them for the depredations they have recently committed on the western frontiers of New Mexico, as also for having refused to come in to the capital when sent for to offer submission to the conqueror and acknowledge his Government. This is a copy of the order:

HEADQUARTERS ARMY OF THE WEST,
Camp on the Rio del Norte near La Joya, Oct. 2, 1846.

I. As the chiefs of the Navajos have been invited to Santa Fe by the commanding general for the purpose of holding a council and making a peace between them and the inhabitants of New Mexico (now forming a part and under the protection of the United States), and as they have promised to come, but have failed doing so, and instead thereof continue killing the people and committing depredations upon their property, it becomes necessary to send a military expedition into the country of these Indians, to secure a peace and better conduct from them in future.

II. For the reasons set forth in the foregoing paragraph, Col. Doniphan, of the First Regiment Missouri Mounted Volunteers, previous to complying with paragraph II of orders No. 36, dated September 23d, will march with his regiment into the Navajo country. He will cause all the prisoners and all the property they hold, which may have been stolen from the inhabitants of the Territory of New Mexico, to be given up—and he will require of them such security for their future good conduct as he may think ample and sufficient by taking hostages or otherwise.

III. After Col. Doniphan has fully complied with these instruction he will proceed with his regiment to report to Brig. Gen. Wool, as directed in order No. 30.

By order of Brigadier General.

S. W. KEARNEY.

H. S. TURNER, Capt., A. A. A. Gen.

This order was founded upon the fact that the New Mexicans represented to Gen. Kearney as he passed near Socorro on his route to California, " that a party of Navajo Indians had recently crossed the mountains and made a sudden irruption into the settlements (which Gen. Kearney had promised to protect), killing seven or eight men, taking as may more women and children captives and driving off 10,000 head of sheep, cattle, and mules."

As the winter was now fast approaching and the mountains would soon be impassable by reason of the great quantity of snow which falls in that elevated region early in the season, and also on account of the great difficulty of procuring forage for horses and mules at such a time, Col. Doniphan determined to execute the order with all possible 'expedition. Accordingly, having dispatched directions to Maj. Gilpin at Albiquiu, and Lieut. Col. Jackson at Cebolleta, thence to penetrate into the heart of the Navajo district by different routes through the mountains, chastising the Navajos wherever they appeared hostile, and taking their chiefs as hostages for their future good behavior wherever they were disposed to be peaceable, at last forming a junction of their forces at a noted place called the Ojo Oso or Bear Spring, he himself set out, taking with him the three companies he had called in from the grazing encampment near San Miguel, intending to take a medium course through the hills and sierras, having Gilpin on his right and Jackson on his left, and thus to unite with them at the Bear Spring; Col. Price being left in command of the entire force at Santa Fe and the grazing grounds.

The three companies from the grazing grounds near San Miguel, having collected their stock together, commenced the march on the 26th of October, proceeded by way of Galisteo and Del Gardo to Santo Domingo, where Col. Doniphan and staff, with his baggage and provision wagons, were in wait for them. Four months' pay was now due the soldiers, and many of them would soon be destitute of comfortable clothing. Yet Col. Doniphan had neither a military chest, nor a paymaster, nor a dollar of Government funds to silence the just complaints or satisfy the reasonable wants of his men. They looked upon it as a hardship, and with reason, that they were ordered against the Indians without pay and with little else than their summer clothing to protect them from the cold in a country where they would be compelled to climb over the tallest mountains, and often encamp in the midst of snow, and ice, and rocks, and where it was impossible to procure either wood for fire, water to drink, or forage for horses and mules.

Now, besides these difficulties, the nature of the country is such that it is impracticable for artillery, baggage, or provision wagons, or even for the lightest carriages, so steep and abrupt are the rocks, hills, and mountains. Only pack mules and sumpter horses can be used with advantage. For this reason Maj. Gilpin sent all his baggage wagons back from Abiquiu into the Del Norte Valley; Lieut. Col. Jackson did the same thing from Cebolleta; and Col. Doniphan the same. They also threw away their tents, that, being light armed and unembarrassed, they might make their marches with greater expedition amongst the rocks, ravines, and steeps of the mountains. Moreover, the soldiers thought, as they had been previously ordered against Chihuahua, that some portion of the troops which were idle at Santa Fe might have been sent on this service; that after having spent three or four months in pursuit of the Indians amongst the gorges and chasms and fastnesses of the Cordilleras they would then be marched off on the Chihuahua expedition without being allowed one day to recuperate their wasted energies or to rest their jaded animals; and that so much delay would give Gen. Wool time to anticipate them in his movement upon Chihuahua, thereby robbing them of their share of the honor, or if it did not, that it would give the Mexicans ample time to learn of our intentions and make preparations to defend themselves and the city of Chihuahua to the best advantage, rendering it hazardous in the extreme for so small a force to venture thither as Col. Doniphan had at his command. This latter surmise proved true.

The detachment now with Col. Doniphan marched on the 30th of October down the country, keeping the river Del Norte on the right and the mountains and craggy hills on the left; and arriving about sunset at the village Sandia the men stayed there during the night, encamping on the ground without much system, but wherever each soldier preferred to lie, for now there was no danger and the men were tired of marchings and watchings and mounting guard. That night much rain fell and the men endured it all, for by this time few of them had any tents, and some of those who had did not take pains to pitch them. It was here that a Mexican came into camp and reported "that Gen. Wool had taken possession of Chihuahua with 6,000 men and much heavy artillery, and that the Mexicans made but a feeble resistance." This did not prove true.

The next day the march was continued down the river, the men encamping on a "brazo" during the night. There was now plenty of provisions in the camp for the soldiers, but wood was so scarce that it was a difficult task for them to prepare anything to eat at supper. Some of them collected together a few little bunches of dry brush, while others as they could picked up withered grass and weeds and dry ordure from the cattle, and with these made a fire and broiled their meat and boiled their coffee. About this time an election was ordered in the companies that they might each make choice of an additional second lieutenant, with the same rank and pay of the other lieutenants, so that there were now four commissioned officers to each company, one captain and three lieutenants. This order was made agreeably to an arrangement of the War Department, by which companies of 100 men or more were entitled to four commissioned officers.

Early the next day the detachment arrived at the town of Albuquerque, where such of the men as were able and desired it purchased wine and beer and mescal, which is made of the maguey and of which the Mexicans are very fond; also bread, fresh meat, eggs, and poultry. Lieut. Noble, with about 30 of the First Dragoons, was at this place recruiting the condition of his men and animals, some of the former being sick. Here the colonel crossed the river, his men following, and after them the provision and baggage trains. The river here is broad and shallow, not being above the hubs of the wagons; the bottom is so sandy, however, that if a wagon stops but a few minutes in the current it will presently be buried in the water and sand. On this account, many of the teams coming to a halt that they might drink of the cold water, some of wagons had to be drawn out by hand, the men wading into the water, rolling at the wheels, and pulling by ropes attached to the standards. This heavy work completed, the march was resumed, continuing down on the west bank of the river. That night the men encamped in a level bottom where there was a moderate supply of forage, but no kind of fuel. Some of the men collected tufts of dry grass and weeds together, and setting fire to them held their meat in the blaze until it was partially roasted. Thus they prepared their suppers.

It was here that the colonel received information from the caravan or merchant trains, which had advanced as far down the valley of the Del Norte as the ruins of Valverde for the purpose of grazing their mules and other animals to better advantage, that they apprehended an attack from the Mexicans almost daily, who were said be be advancing, 700 strong, with the view of plundering the merchant wagons. In this perplexity Col. Doniphan, that he might accomplish all his purposes and fail in none, dispatched the three companies which he had with him to protect the traders and their merchandise. Of this squadron Capt. Walton had the command, ranking the other two captains, Moss and Rodgers. Capt. Burgwin (having been sent back by Gen. Kearney with about 200 men) being previously apprised of the critical situation of the merchants had already gone to afford them succor. Thus in a short time there were 500 mounted men, besides 300 merchants and teamsters, at Valverde ready to oppose any hostile movement the enemy might choose to make. The merchants had also corraled their wagons in such a manner as to receive troops within and afford them shelter against an enemy, so that the beseiged could fight with as much security as though they were in a fortress.

As to Col. Doniphan, he took his staff (that part of it which happened to be with him) and, attended by three or four other men, proceeded with great haste to Cuvarro, not far from the river Puerco, making great marches and encamping on the ground wherever nightfall chanced to overtake him. This was on the 2d day of November.

At Cuvarro the colonel fell in with a few of Lieut. Col. Jackson's men, most of whom being sick were left behind attended by their friends, that they might recover and not be left without aid in that wild country. Of those who were sick a great number died, their diseases being such that the physicians could not relieve them. These diseases were typhoid fever, rheumatism, blumy, and other complaints produced by intense cold and great exposure. The patients became entirely helpless, and frequently lost the use of their legs. So they died. Others of them surviving for a time were conveyed back to Socorro and Albuquerque, where some of them also died and others recovered.

It was at Cuvarro that Adjt. G. W. Butler, of Col. Doniphan's staff, a brave and gallant man, beloved by all the regiment, was seized with a violent distemper, induced by cold, and died, much lamented, on the 26th of November. He was buried (and also the rest of the dead, for others died near the same time) with as much honor as could be shown to brave and gallant men in that destitute country, for it was not possible to procure coffins for the dead as in the United States, there being no timber there. Their bodies were wrapped in blankets, deposited in the grave, the vault being covered by broad rocks to prevent the wolves disturbing the dead, and then a certain number of rounds being fired over the grave and the last one into it, the earth was heaved in and the "last resting place" completed in the usual manner. Thus were interred those who died in the service of their country.

Col. Doniphan advanced vigorously into the mountains, as we shall presently notice, attended by only a few men.

At the same time Col. Doniphan departed to the Navajo district the detachment under command of Capt. Walton, with the baggage train, began to march toward Valverde on the 2d of November, passing through many ranchos on the river and also the villages Pajaritto and Padillas and the pueblo of Isleta, near which the soldiers encamped that night. The inhabitants of these places did not molest our men nor manifest any hostility toward them, but sold them such things to eat as they could spare and whatever commodities the soldiers desired to purchase. Now, during the night there were a great shouting and yelling and the firing of guns and ringing of bells, and also singing and dancing, among the Pueblos of Isleta. Certain of the soldiers, thinking perhaps an attack was meditated by these people on our camp during the night, volunteered to go and learn what might be the occasion of so much noise and tumult. When they arrived there, they beheld various lights about the streets and squares and groups of men and maidens, fantastically dressed and tattooed, dancing and singing with great merriment. On approaching a little nearer they beheld on the tops of three tall lances or javelins the scalps of three Navajo warriors, the long, straight, black hair sweeping in the wind. The Pueblos were celebrating a war dance. The men, inquiring how these scalps were obtained, received this account from the Pueblos:

About three days ago a party of Navajos, between whom and us there are continual wars, descended from the mountains and seized one of our women, five of our children, and a great number of sheep and cattle, and mules, and having killed eight Mexicans and Pueblos, went off with their booty. These facts being reported to Capt. Burgwin while on his way to Valverde, Lieut. Grier with about 60 men was detached to go in pursuit of this marauding party of Navajos, themselves numbering 70. Lieut. Grier having pursued them about two days (most of his men, however, having given over the pursuit on account of their horses failing) came up with them in a canyon of the mountains, charged upon them killing and scalping three of them, rescuing the captives, and recovering the stock.

Lieut. Grier had one of his men slightly wounded and an arrow lodged in his saddle near his thigh. However, he made good his retreat. It was thus the Pueblos of Isleta obtained the trophies which they were proudly displaying at the war dance. This detachment now moving slowly down the river completed in five days' march about 35 miles, passing through the villages Sineca, Lunaz, Chavez, and Jarrales. Encamping near the latter place, the inhabitants furnished wood for the soldiers and various articles of food, such as chickens, bread, cheese, molasses, melons, meal, and flour at a moderate price. That night some of the men witnessed the nuptial ceremonies of the alcalde's daughter. She was married to a wealthy " ranchero " by the " cura " of the place.

From thence the march was continued through Belen and Sabinaz to the River Puerco, making only about 25 miles in three days. Here the detachment met Capt. Burgwin's command returning to Alburquerque, there being no danger of an attack on the merchant wagons. As it was now cold and disagreeable the soldiers staid in camp three days. The next day they marched 12 miles over deep sand drifts and dry rocky creeks and stopped for the night in a cottonwood grove, a pleasant retreat where they staid three more days. From this place, on the 21st of November, Capt. Rodgers' company returned to La Joya, on the east side of the river, to bury Lieut. Snell, one of their officers who had died the previous day. This officer was much esteemed by his men. Capt. Rodgers was also, at the same place, disabled by the kick of a horse. So the company was now commanded by Lieut. Harrison. From thence in one days' march they passed Soccorro and Huertaz, making about 22 miles. These are the last Mexican settlements on the west bank of the river until you come to El Paso Del Norte. The next day (23d) they marched 12 miles and encamped in a cottonwood forest where there was grass, wood, and water, intending to spend one or two days at that place.

About tattoo the soldiers were suddenly aroused from their repose by the appearance in camp of a friendly Mexican, who had been dispatched thither by the merchants with a letter addressed to the "commandante," requesting him to march with all possible haste to their relief; that they expected very soon to be attacked by a strong Mexican force. Two Americans came into camp next morning and confirmed what the Mexican had said, therefore the volunteers began to clean up their guns, adjust their flints, and see that their cartridge boxes were well supplied, for they now believed that an action would soon take place. A speedy march of 15 miles was completed in less than half the day, which brought them to the Green Valley where the caravans had corralled for defense. They encamped in a large forest of cottonwood trees on the west bank of the river near the ruins of Valverde. The pasturage was excellent in the adjacent mountains. The exigency for succor, however, did not prove as great as was represented.

This being a favorable place from whence to afford protection to the caravan of traders, and also a convenient spot to procure pasturage for the animals, as well as a good position to shelter the men from the wind and violent snow storms, it was thought fit to make it a permanent encampment. It was also convenient to the water. Therefore this place became the headquarters of the commissary and quartermaster departments of the regiment, and the point from which Col. Doniphan, when he should collect his scattered forces together from the Navajo country, was to invade the State of Chihuahua. This was the 24th of November.

Lest it should be supposed that the 300 men who were detailed as a wagon guard to watch over and protect the interest of the merchant caravan were less willing soldiers, or less desirous of serving the country than those who went against the Navajos, let us consider the nature of the service which they are required to perform. There is no one so ignorant that he does not know it is more agreeable to be actively employed in marching than confined in camps and placed on continual guards and watchings, just as the bears which run wild in the mountains enjoy more liberty than those which are kept in chains or in cages. Besides, this section of the Army suffered much from cold, being stationed in an open valley on an exposed spot of earth, poorly supplied with tents, almost destitute of comfortable clothing, and stinted in provisions. These were brave men and good soldiers. They were daily threatened by attacks from the Apaches on the east and west and by the Mexicans on the south. Much vigilance was therefore necessary.

The traders had formed a corral for defense upon the intelligence obtained through two spies whom they had caught on their way from

El Paso to Santa Fe bearing communications to the principal men in the northern settlements. They represented "that 700 Mexicans were on their way from El Paso with the view to attack and rob the merchants, not knowing they were protected by the military." Two other Mexican spies or couriers were soon after caught by them having in their possession a great many letters and other communications from the priests and leading characters of New Mexico, directed to the authorities of Chihuahua and Mexico, excusing themselves for permitting New Mexico to fall under the power of the "Northern Yankees and Texans," and accusing Col. Armijo of the most arrant cowardice.

On the morning of the 27th the old Mexican shepherd who had been employed to take charge of the flock of sheep belonging to the detachment was missing. None knew whither he had gone. After further inquiry it was discovered that 17 Government mules were also missing. It was now plain how matters stood. He had driven them off the previous night and appropriated them to his own "use and benefit." Not long after it was ascertained that 873 head of sheep, the only dependence the detachment had for subsistence, had also been driven off, but in a different direction and by very different authors. Two men, James Stewart and Robert Speares, were detailed to follow the trail of the sheep and discover the direction in which they had been driven. These two young men carelessly went out without their arms or any means of defense, not expecting to go far before returning to camp. Striking the trail, however, they pursued on with the view to drive the sheep back to camp at once. Proceeding about 6 miles toward the mountains westward they came up with the flock. Hereupon they were instantly attacked by a small party of renegade Navajos and cruelly put to death. One of them was pierced by 13 arrows and the other by 9, after which their heads were mashed and their bodies bruised with rocks in a most shocking manner. As these men did not return it was not known by their companions in camp what had become of them. At length they were searched for, when their dead bodies were found, brought into camp, and decently buried. A detail of 38 men commanded by Lieut. Sublette was sent in pursuit of the murderers. The pursuit having been prosecuted vigorously for 60 or 70 miles into the rocky recesses of the Sierra de los Mimbres, the animals beginning to fail and the number of the party thereby decreasing and no water having been found by the way, the men were compelled to return without recovering the stock or chastising the authors of the bloody deed. In the deep valleys of this rugged range of mountains are extensive forests of pine, cedar, and live oak.

When there was nothing important in camp to engage the attention of the soldiers, and the day was pleasant, they spent their time in contests of wrestling, running, and jumping, also in jokes, songs, and speaking, or else in smoking, lounging, sleeping, card playing, or reading, as the humar might prompt them. Strict guards were, however, kept about the camp day and night, and also a detail was daily made to drive the stock out into the mountains for the purpose of grazing them. These stock guards were always well armed to prevent attacks by the Apaches and Navajos, who watch every opportunity of seizing upon whatever booty may chance to be in their power. The traders, who had a great number of mules and oxen, used the same method of subsisting them, sending a part of their own men out each day as a stock guard.

About this time an English officer, or rather ambassador, made his appearance in the camp of the merchants, bringing proposals to them from the governor of Chihuahua to this effect:

That if they would first dismiss from their employ all their American teamsters and employ in their stead Mexicans, and then upon their arrival at El Paso, where the customs for the State of Chihuahua are received, pay a duty of 13 cents per pound on their importations and such an internal or consumption tariff as should be fixed by law, they would be permitted to come into the city of Chihuahua and allowed the advantages of that market, free from molestation.

So impatient to sell were some of the merchants who had embarked largely in the trade, and who were extremely anxious to have the advantage of the first market, that they were disposed to entertain these overtures with some degree of favor. Others, better acquainted with the Mexican character, looked upon it as a ruse or piece of management to get the merchants into their power and then they could seize and confiscate their goods at pleasure. The spoils could easily be divided afterwards. This, indeed, was their design.

Now, while the great majority of the traders were Americans, there were also among them some English and Mexican merchants who could embrace the governor's terms with safety. These were anxious to reap the first fruits of the Chihuahua market. They therefore manifested symptoms of restlessness and evinced a disposition and even a determination to go on in advance of the army which had guarded them thus far from the depredations of the Indians. This movement could not be tolerated. Lieut. Ogden, with 24 men (which number was afterwards increased to 42), was dispatched to Fray Christobal, at the upper end of the Great Jornada del Muerto, with instructions from Capt. Walton, the commanding officer, to permit no portion of the caravan to pass that point until Col. Doniphan should return from the Navajo country. This order was promptly put into execution by the lieutenant, notwithstanding the efforts of the English and Mexican merchants to elude his vigilance.

On the evening of the 5th, two soldiers, inmates of the same tent, their names J. D. Lard and B. W. Marsh, entered into a quarrel as they stood about their camp fires. At length, the parties becoming somewhat excited and mutually dealing upon each other an assortment of abusive epithets, the latter drew out his pistol and shot the former through the breast. Mr. Lard, after several days, was removed to Soccorro, where he survived but a short time.

This detachment, while it remained at the Valverde camp grounds, lost 17 mules, 873 sheep, a great number of horses and cattle, and 6 brave men, 3 of whom died of cold and through distress of their situation and 3 in the manner above related. The various detachments which had been in the country of the Navajos arrived in camp at Valverde about the 12th of December.

CHAPTER IX.

Lieut. Col. Jackson, with a detachment of three companies, under command of Capts. Reid, Parsons, and Hughes,[1] as already stated, left Santa Fe on the 18th of September and proceeded to Cebolleta, on the River Puerco, to keep the Indians in subordination in that part of the State and there to await further orders. Their first march was from Santa Fe to Del Gardo, more than 20 miles, where they remained in camp two days, during which time they repaired their wagons, harness, saddle trappings, tents, clothes, collected their stock together, packed up their baggage, and did whatever else seemed to demand their attention.

From thence, on the next day, all things being made ready and the soldiers having taken their breakfast, they commenced the march, and during this and four other days completed nearly 100 miles. arriving at the Laguna fork of the River Puerco. This march led through Algodones, Bernalillo, Sandia, Albuquerque, where, crossing the river, it was continued through Pajarrito and other villages, thence striking off westerly to the Puerco. On the morning of the 27th about 50 Pueblo Indians, with their arms in their hands, visited the camp and informed Lieut. Col. Jackson that all the Pueblos from San Domingo to Isleta, many hundred in number, were on their way to Cebolleta to make war upon the Navajos in conjunction with him, insisting that Gen. Kearney had granted them permission to retake their stolen animals and recover their people from captivity, great numbers of whom were in the hands of the Navajos. But as Col. Jackson was rather on a mission of peace than war, he accordingly ordered the Pueblos to return peaceably to their homes until their services should be required. To this they reluctantly consented.

On the hills and spurs of the mountains near the camp were large quantities of petrified timber. In some places entire trunks of trees, the remains of an extinct forest, were discovered, intermixed with the débris on the steep declivities and in the recesses of the craggy mountains. While at this camp Don Chavez, a wealthy proprietor of the Laguna Pueblo, well disposed toward the Americans, came and made an offer of all his possessions, such as sheep, goats, cattle, and other stock to the commander, that his men might not be in want of provisions. The commander, however, accepted only so much of this generous tender as was sufficient to relieve his present necessi-

---

[1] Hughes was chosen captain after the detachment arrived at Cebolleta, Lieut. De Courcy being in command for the present.

ties. Being requested, Don Chavez promised to use his endeavors to induce Sandoval, a chief of one branch or canton of the Navajo tribe, to bring his warriors into Cebolleta and there conclude a treaty of friendship with the Americans. In this he partially succeeded.

After a short march on the 28th, this detachment encamped before Laguana, a rich pueblo containing 2,000 inhabitants. Here the men procured such provisions as they were most in need of, the inhabitants supplying a market wherein they might purchase. Pigs, chickens, bread, cheese, molasses, and other things were brought to them. At this place the men witnessed another grand war dance around the scalps of four Navajo warriors, reared upon four lances, as at Isleta. It appeared that a party of Navajos, about the 24th, had made a sudden incursion from the mountains, plundering some of the houses in the suburbs of Laguna and driving off large flocks of sheep from the neighboring plains and valleys. The Pueblos collected together and pursued them, finally overtaking them, killing four of the party and recovering a portion of the stock. This feast and war dance, which continued without intermission for 15 hours, were meant to celebrate the achievement.

The next day the march was continued up the river, near the margin of which the soldiers encamped and spent the night. Here an amiable young man, by name Gwyn, died and was buried. On the 30th the detachment marched over and pitched camp near to Cebolleta. This place became the headquarters of the detachment, whence various smaller parties of men were sent to the hill country and mountains to put an end to the unjust exactions and contributions, such as loss of life and property, which the Navajos were perpetually levying upon the frontier Mexican and Pueblo villages. The difficult nature of this enterprise, to the conduct of which Lieut. Col. Jackson was appointed, will more plainly appear when it is considered that his mission was of a twofold character. He was first instructed by Gen. Kearney to negotiate a triple league of peace between three powers, the Navajos, Mexicans, and Pueblos, who dwell in New Mexico, and the Americans. The novel spectacle is here presented of the Navajo nation being required, first, to treat with the New Mexicans and Pueblos, their perpetual and implacable enemies; to bind themselves by articles of agreement to obtain from war; to bury their mutual hatred toward each other and become friends for the future; and, second, to treat with the Americans, of whom, perhaps, they had never before heard and of whom they knew nothing, save that they were the conquerors of the New Mexicans (for what causes they could not conceive) and might soon be their own conquerors, as they were now on the confines of the Navajo country, proposing terms of treaty with arms in their hands. The Navajos were willing to treat the Americans with friendship, and even to negotiate a permanent peace with them; but they were unable to comprehend the propriety and policy of entering into a league by which they would be compelled to surrender up the captives and property which they had taken from the New Mexicans and Pueblos by valor in various wars, nor could they understand what right the Americans, "armed ministers of peace," had to impose upon them such conditions. Neither were they able to conceive why it was that the New Mexicans, since they were conquered, had been advanced to the condition of American citizens, so that an injury done to those people should now be resented by the Americans as though it were done them.

And secondly, if he could not effect these amicable arrangements with the Navajos, he was instructed to prosecute against them a hostile campaign. Hence, all the arts of diplomacy, as well as those of war, were required to settle these questions involving the interests of three separate powers.

It was from this place that Sandoval, a noted chief of one of the Navajo cantons, who had a friendly intercourse with the New Mexicans on the frontier, was dispatched by Lieut. Col. Jackson to see the principal men of his tribe and ascertain if they were of a disposition to make an amicable arrangement of existing differences. Sandoval, after an absence of about two weeks, returned and reported that he had seen all the head men of his nation, and that they were chiefly disposed for peace, but that they were unwilling to trust themselves among the New Mexicans, unless they should be furnished with an escort of "white men," whose protection would insure their safety. And further, that before coming into the American camp they wished to see some of the white men among them, that they might talk with them and learn what they desired. Sandoval further reported that the principal habitations, or rather haunts, of the Navajos, were 200 miles west from Cebolleta, in the neighborhood of the great Tcheusca Mountain, the grand dividing ridge between the Atlantic and Pacific waters, and upon the borders of the noted Laguna Colorado, or Red Lake. This beautiful, romantic sheet of water is near the western base of the Tcheusca Ridge of the Cordilleras. It is fed by springs at the base of the great mountain. In a lovely recess of this great mountain and in sight of the fairy lake is a spacious semicircular amphitheater, sculptured by the hand of nature in the side of the solid masses of rock. It faces the southwestward. At each corner of this crescent temple of nature, and isolated from the main mountain, stands a mighty, colossal column of sandstone, horizontally striped with violet and blue veins, towering to the height of 300 feet. They are more than 30 feet in circumference, and as regular and smooth as if they had been polished by the chisel of some master sculptor.

Upon the representation of Sandoval, Capt. Reid applied to Lieut. Col. Jackson to permit him, with a small body of troops, to make an excursion into the country and learn more certainly whether the Navajos were disposed for peace or war. In order to allay their suspicions and inspire them with confidence in the good intentions of the Americans, he thought it best to take only a few men. Accordingly, about the 20th of October Capt. Reid, with 30 men, who gallantly volunteered their services (10 from each of the companies present), accompanied and aided by Lieuts. De Courcy and Wells, set out upon this hazardous enterprise, taking with him three mules, packed with provisions, this being all that the scarcity of the camp would allow at that time, expecting to be gone about 15 days. The New Mexicans were amazed at the temerity of Capt. Reid's proceeding. To enter the country of this powerful and warlike nation, which had for a series of years robbed and plundered their country with impunity, with less than an army, was considered by them as certain destruction. Sandoval, whose geographical knowledge of the country was extensive and minute, was taken as a guide, for no other could be procured. Some suspected that he would lead the party into an ambuscade, the more effectually to ingratiate himself into favor with his people. But he proved faithful. Besides, the New Mexicans have but a very limited knowledge of that mountain country, never departing far from their settlements through fear of the Indians. Nor would a Mexican, though his knowledge of the country were ever so accurate, feel himself safe to accompany so small a number of men on so hazardous an enterprise. This party, in its march, surmounted difficulties of the most appalling nature. It passed over craggy mountains of stupendous height, winding its way up the steep and rugged acclivities, each man leading his horse among the slabs and fragments of great rocks which lay in confused masses along the sides of the mountains, having crumbled from some summit still above, obstructing the passway. Precipices and yawning chasms, fearful to behold, often left but a narrow passage, where a blunder either to the right or left would precipitate horse and man hundreds of feet below, among the jagged and pointed rocks. Indeed, this party ascended and descended mountains, where, at first view, every attempt would seem fruitless and vain, and where the giddy heights and towering masses of granite seem to bid defiance to the puny efforts of man. Until success showed what resolution could accomplish, these things were pronounced utterly impossible. But the energy of the Anglo-Saxons knows no bounds.

The ease with which these few hardy and adventurous men appeared to obviate the difficulties and surmount the obstacles which impeded their progress, and which seemed, until essayed, incredible of performance, afforded convincing argument that, in the affairs of men, to resolve is to conquer; and that men, as least Americans, can accomplish whatever is within the scope of possibility. Having traveled five days, with little or no intermission, through the gorges and fissures of the mountains, and over hills intersected by numerous ravines, with steep and almost impassable banks, they pitched camp near a moderate supply of wood, water, and grass, in a narrow vale formed by projecting spurs of dark basalt and pudding stone, terminating in a succession of rocky ridges. Here they determined to remain a short time, that they might obtain a little rest and refreshment. Here also they met a few of Sandoval's people, who, upon being assured that the Americans meant them no harm, returned with confidence to their several homes near camp. From thence, having proceeded a short distance, they met with an advance party of about 40 Navajo warriors, having with them a few women—an infallible sign of friendly intention. At first they were afraid. Hereupon Capt. Reid, leaving his men in the valley and taking with him Sandoval, his interpreter and guide, rode to the top of the hill, upon which they stood, stopped, and saluted them in a kind manner. After a few friendly signs and some conversation, Sandoval being interpreter, gaining confidence, they approached the captain, rode down with him to the place where the men were pitching camp, and passed the night together, the utmost confidence seeming mutually to prevail. Presents were interchanged and conversation was commenced as they sat around their campfires. The night passed off most amicably.

The next morning, at the instance of the Indians, the party moved on again, having obtained from them this information:

That there was to be a grand collection of the young men and women of the Navajo Tribe at a place 30 miles farther into the country, where some event was to be celebrated by much feasting and dancing. They expressed much solicitude that the captain and his men should be their guests on that occasion, adding, "that most of their people had never seen a white man, but having heard much of the power and wisdom of the Americans, and of the progress of the Army in New Mexico, were very anxious to see and entertain them."

This proposal according with the views of the captain and his brave comrades, whose object was to see as many of the tribes as posible, that whatever impression they made might be general, they agreed to attend. They set out.

When they arrived at the place designated, they found no less than 500 men and women already congregated. Whether these Indians meant to deceive, and lead these few men into an ambuscade, and thereby treacherously entrap and put them to death, was uncertain. However, they resolved to proceed and use the utmost vigilance, and if such an attempt should be made, also to use their arms to the best advantage. Seeing which, the Indians received them with the greatest professions of friendship and kindly made them presents of some excellent sheep and other meats, which were very acceptable, as the captain was now destitute. They pitched camp, which was no sooner done that it was surrounded and filled by Indians, eagerly gratifying their curiosity. The "white men" were amongst them. To have kept these "sons of the forest" at a distance by guards would have appeared but safe and prudent, yet it would have thwarted the purpose of the visit, which was to secure their friendship. To have showed anything like suspicion would have been insulting to their pride and wounding to their feelings. It was therefore perhaps safer to risk the chances of treachery than to use caution which would serve but to provoke. The feasting and dancing continued through the night, during which the captain and his men, at intervals, mixing in the crowd, participated in the festivities and amusements of the occasion, to the infinite satisfaction of their rude but hospitable entertainers. The scene was truly romantic. Contemplate 500 dancers in the hollow recesses of the mountains, with the music of shells and timbrels, giving way to the most extravagant joy, and a band of 30 Americans, armed cap-a-pie with martial accouterments, mingling in the throng! This was the 27th day of October.

The next morning the captain proposed a "grand talk," but was told by the Indians "that none of the head chiefs or men of council were present; that there were no Navajos there" (using the Mexican phrase "pocos, pocos," signifying very few); but at the same time intimating that by one day's march farther into the country they would see muchos (very many), and amongst them the old men of the nation, who, they said, had great knowledge and great experience.

Though this party was small, far from succor, scant of provisions, and in a country without supplies, except such as the Indians possessed, it was nevertheless voted to go on and accomplish the original objects of the excursion. The captain suggested the condition of his commissary stores to his red friends, who assured him that there were numerous flocks of goats, sheep, and cattle farther in the mountains, and that if he chose to accompany them he should be abundantly supplied. They started.

A march of 30 miles over the great dividing ridge of the Cordilleras brought them to the waters of the Pacific and into the very heart of the country occupied by the Navajos, the most powerful and civilized tribe in the West. This day's march led them through fissures, chasms, and canyons in the mountains, whose tops were capped with perpetual snow. Capt. Reid, in a letter to the author, thus describes the perils that surrounded him at this time:

This was the most critical situation in which I ever found myself placed—with only 30 men, in the very center of a people the most savage and proverbially treacherous of any on the continent. Many of them were not very friendly. Being completely in their power, we, of course, had to play the game to the best advantage. As there was no pasturage near the camp, we had to send our horses out. Our numbers were too few to divide, or even all together, to think of protecting the horses, if the Indians were disposed to take them. So I even made a virtue of necessity, and putting great confidence in the honesty of their intentions, I gave my horses in charge of one of the chiefs of these notorious horse stealers. He took them out some 5 miles to graze, and we, after taking supper, again joined in the dance, which was kept up until next morning. Our men happened to take the right course to please the Indians, participating in all their sports, and exchanging liveries with them. They seemed to be equally delighted to see themselves clothed in the vesture obtained from us and to see our men adopting their costume. The emboldened confidence and freedom with which we mixed among them seemed to win upon their feelings and make them disposed to grant whatever we asked. They taxed their powers of performance in all their games to amuse us and make the time pass agreeably, notwithstanding our imminently precarious situation.

We had not arrived at the place of our camp before we were met by all the headmen of the nation. The chief of all, Narbona, being very sick, was nevertheless mounted on horseback and brought in. He slept in my camp all night. Narbona, who was probably 70 years old, being held in great reverence by his tribe for the warlike exploits of his youth and manhood, was now a mere skeleton of a man, being completely prostrated by rheumatism, the only disease, though a very common one, in this country. Conformably to a custom of the chief men of his tribe he wore his finger nails very long, probably 1½ inches—formidable weapons! He appeared to be a mild, amiable man, and, though he had been a warrior himself, was very anxious before his death to secure for his people a peace with all their old enemies, as well as with us, the "new men," as he called us.

Upon the evening after our arrival we held a grand talk, in which all the old men participated. Most of them seemed disposed for peace, but some opposed it as being contrary to the honor of the Navajos, as well as their interest, to make peace with the Mexicans, though they were willing to do so with us. The peace party, however, prevailed, and by fair words and promises of protection I succeeded in obtaining a promise from the principal men that they would overtake me at the Agua Fria, a place some 40 miles from Jackson's camp, from whence we would go together to Santa Fe and conclude the final treaty.[1] The night passed off in a variety of diversions, and in the morning, notwithstanding the most urgent desire on the part of our entertainers that we would stay, I thought it prudent to return, as we were running short of provisions. Our horses were forthcoming without a single exception, and as soon as we caught them we turned our faces toward camp.

Although this expedition was one of much hazard, yet it turned out to be one of much pleasurable excitement and attended with no loss or harm. The country through which we traveled is amongst the finest portions of Mexico—decidedly the best for the growth of stock, and presenting more interest and variety in its features than any over which I traveled. It is, however, very destitute of water, so much so as to make it dangerous for those who travel without a guide. On this account, more than by its mountain fastnesses, it is

---

[1] Capt. Reid at this time was not apprised of the fact that Col. Doniphan, who was invested with full powers to conclude a treaty of peace with the Navajos, had taken his departure from Santa Fe.

impregnable to invasion. The people who inhabit it, and who were the object of our visit, are in many respects singular and unlike any other of the aboriginal inhabitants of this continent. Their habits are very similar to those of the Tartars. They are entirely a pastoral people, their flocks constituting their sole wealth, but little addicted to the chase, and never indulging in it except when the game may be taken on horseback. Their weapons of war are the spear or lance, the bow, and the lasso, in the use of all which they are not excelled. They may be said literally to live on horseback. Of these animals they possess immense droves, and of a stock originally the same with the Mexican horse, yet wonderfully improved. They pay great attention to the breeding of their horses, and think scarcely less of them than do the Arabians. They also possess many mules, but these are generally the proceeds of their marauding expeditions against the Mexicans. Indeed, the whole of New Mexico is subject to the devastating incursions of these lords of the mountains. Of this, however, you know as well as I.

The evening after the captain and his party left the grand camp of the Navajos, on their return to Cebolleta, as an evidence of the sincerity of their professions they dispatched a runner to the Americans, to warn them to take care of their horses, for that some of their young men were ill disposed toward them, and might pursue them with the view of capturing their stock. They, however, effected their return to Jackson's encampment without any serious molestation or any considerable difficulty. The chiefs started, according to promise, to overtake the captain at Agua Fria, but were induced to turn back by a miscreant Navajo, who assured them that if they ventured to Santa Fe they would all be killed. Having had so many evidences of the bad faith of the Mexicans they were naturally suspicious, and therefore abandoned their purpose.

Thus terminated this most extraordinary adventure among the Navajos, which in point of excitement, interest, novelty, and hazard was equal, if not superior, to any enterprise connected with the Navajo expedition. Though this excursion was not productive of any immediate beneficial results, yet it was not without its more remote effects upon the people visited, in making up their estimate of the enterprise and good faith of the Americans. Both the captain and the men whom he led were as gallant as ever drew steel. The party arrived safely at Cebolleta after an absence of 20 days.

Whilst Capt. Reid was on this excursion a band of renegade Navajos came into the neighborhood of Cebolleta and succeeded in driving off most of the stock, both mules and horses, belonging to the detachment under Lieut. Col. Jackson, for the recovery of which Capt. Parsons and Lieut. Jackson, with 60 men, were sent out in pursuit of them. After much difficulty they finally succeeded in recovering a portion of them, and returned to camp about the same time with Capt. Reid. The remaining portion was recovered by Maj. Gilpin.

CHAPTER X.

It has been related that on the 18th of September, Maj. Gilpin, in command of two companies under Capts. Waldo and Stephenson, amounting in all to about 180 men, left Santa Fe, in obedience to an order from Gen. Kearney, and proceeded forthwith to the neighborhood of Abiquiu, on the Rio de Chama, to preserve order and quiet among the border tribes. It was not anticipated that this force would be required to penetrate farther into the mountainous regions of the West than its present encampment at Abiquiu, from whence it was expected that various small parties would make short excursions into the surrounding country to clear it of marauders and depredators, the Navajo expedition being subsequently conceived and projected.

Most of the men composing this detachment had not received their commutation of clothing nor had any of them received any portion of the pay which had long been due them; they would therefore soon be in want of means of protecting themselves against the inclemency of the approaching winter. With troops thus poorly provided, a few baggage wagons, and a scanty supply of provisions, Maj. Gilpin arrived at the Chama about the 25th of the same month. Leaving the greater part of his men in this vicinity, he proceeded with a party of 85 men about 100 miles above the valley of Taos, amongst the Yutas, a fierce and numerous tribe of Indians, with the view to conciliate them and dispose them to a friendly intercourse with the Americans. Having in an incredibly short space of time collected together about 60 of their principal men, he returned with them to Santa Fe, where they entered into treaty stipulations with Col. Doniphan on the 13th of October.

After a short stay at the capital, Maj. Gilpin returned to this encampment at Abiquiu, where he remained in faithful discharge of the duties assigned him until he received orders to march against the Navajos. While in this quarter he preserved the utmost tranquillity amongst the Mexicans, Pueblos, and Yutas, supplied his men with provisions from the adjacent country and villages, procured pack mules, sumpter horses for the Navajo campaign, and sent his provision and baggage wagons from Abiquiu to Santa Fe that he might not be embarrassed by these things in his intended expedition across the mountains.

On the 22d of November, Maj. Gilpin, acting under instructions from Col. Doniphan, left his encampment on the Chama and commenced his march against the Navajo Indians, completing in six days more than 100 miles, having followed the Rio de Chama to its source in the snowy regions, transcending the elevated range of mountains which separate the waters of the two great oceans of the world and descending into the San Juan, a branch of the western Colorado. Maj. Gilpin was accompanied by about 65 Mexican and Pueblo Indian allies, under command of a lieutenant.[1] The perils, hardships, and sufferings of this march were almost incredible, yet they were encountered and endured by the men with Roman fortitude. The rugged ways, the precipitous mountains, the dangerous defiles, the narrow passes, the yawning chasms and fissures in vitreous, volcanic remains, and the giant fragments of rocks which obstructed their passage rendered the march arduous beyond the power of language to describe. The passage of the Carthaginian general over the Appenines and his sudden descent upon the plains of Italy attracted the admiration of all Europe. The march of Bonaparte and McDonough over the snow-capped peaks of the Alps astonished the world. Maj. Gilpin's march over the grander and loftier summits of the Cordilleras, eternally crowned with snow, was certainly an achievement not less arduous or perilous.

On the evening of the 7th so much snow fell that it was with the utmost difficulty the men and animals could make their way among the mountain passes. In many places the snow had slid down from the peaks, as an avalanche, until it had accumulated many feet, and even fathoms, deep. This day some Indians were seen upon the eminences at a distance, watching the movements of our men. They were pursued, but without success. On the next day they appeared in like manner, but in greater numbers. They were again pursued hotly, but they were so active and could escape with so much facility into their mountain fastnesses that it was not possible to capture them. On the 9th the Indians appeared in considerable numbers, as before, upon the distant eminences. By the display of friendly signals they were induced to come into camp. They reported that they had seen some of the American forces and formed a treaty with them. These were no doubt the same whom Capt. Reid had previously visited. Upon this information Maj. Gilpin sent one of them to bear an express to Col. Doniphan, then on his way into the Navajo country, assuring them that no hostilities would be commenced until the messenger's return. Meanwhile the rest of the Indians remained quietly about camp or followed the line of march.

The next two days the detachment traveled down the San Juan 40 miles or more, meandering the stream, and encamping on its margin for water and pasturage. This beautiful, fresh, mountain stream, whose limpid waters reveal the very pebbles and brilliant sands upon the bottom and the fishes which sport in its waves, is about 50 yards wide, and was everywhere filled with Indians, watering their numerous herds of horses, sheep, and other animals. From this cause the pasturage was greatly exhausted near the river, but was more abundant further out into the mountains. The three following days the march was continued toward the Tunicha mountains, whose bleak, colossal summits tower magnificently above the

---

[1] This allied force consisted of 20 Taos Mexicans, commanded by Lieut. Virgil; 20 Pueblos under Tomas; and twenty-five peones in charge of the pack mules. Santiago Concklin was Maj. Gilpin's Mexican and Angel Chavez his Navajo interpreter. Ignacio Salezar and Benezate Vilandi were his guides.

clouds, and are plainly visible from the San Juan, a distance of 75 miles. This part of the march was over barren, sandy plains and immense fields of gypsum, covered with pebbles worn smooth by attrition, which rendered the travel extremely laborious, the whole way being entirely destitute of either wood or grass and only supplied with water, which is both bitter to the taste and nauseating to the stomach.

On the 15th the march was commenced over the Tunicha Ridge, the grandest of mountains, consisting of huge masses of granite piled on granite, until their summits penetrate far into the regions of clouds and perennial snows. The ascent was long and arduous. The men, leading their horses and wading in the snow, were compelled to carry their arms and thread their way amongst the huge slabs of granite and basalt which had crumbled from above and lay in confused masses along the rugged ascent. Many animals were left and perished by the way. Some of them, by a misstep, tumbled headlong over the precipices and fell hundreds of feet below. It was useless, of course, to look into the abysses whither they had fallen, for they were either dashed to pieces on the rocks or buried in fathoms of accumulated snow. This day the Indian express bearer returned to Maj. Gilpin, bringing orders from Col. Doniphan for him to be at Bear Spring on the 20th, stating that he would endeavor to meet him there, requesting him to bring into that place all the Navajo chiefs he could find.

The snow was now deep and the weather excessively cold. The fierce winds whistled along the ragged granite hills and peaks. The prospect was horrid. Half of the animals had given out and were abandoned. Thus were these men situated—half of them on foot, carrying their arms, stinted in provisions, destitute of shoes and clothing, and their way barricaded by eternal rocks and snow. Sometimes when they lay down at night, wrapped in their blankets and the skins of wild beasts, before morning they would be completely enveloped in a new crop of snow, and they would rise at day dawn with benumbed limbs and bristling icicles frozen to their hair and long whiskers. They persevered. This night's encampment was on the bare summit of the Tunicha Mountain, where there was neither comfort for the men nor food nor water for the horses. The desolateness of the place was dreadful. The descent on the 16th was even more terrible than the ascent had been the previous day. The men had to walk, as it was impossible to ride down the precipitous crags and spurs of the mountain. The packs would sometimes slide forward on the mules and tumble them down the rugged ways. The crevices between the rocks were filled with driven snow, many fathoms deep, so that man and horse would often plunge into these through mistake, from whence it was difficult, without assistance, to extricate themselves. Having accomplished the descent at sunset, the men built their camp fires (for they had no tents) on a brook issuing from a cleft in the mountain's side, where they found wood, water, and grass. Here they enjoyed the advantage of a little rest.

The next day the march was continued through lovely valleys and handsome upland, the snow falling excessively all day. The snow had now accumulated in such quantities that it was toilsome to advance at all. This night they stayed at a place called Canon de

Trigo, where the Navajos cultivate considerable quantities of wheat and other small grain. The next morning a great many Indians visited the camp and signified their wish to be friendly with the Americans. This day they came to the Challe and passed within a few miles of the celebrated stronghold or presidio of the Navajos, called El Challe.

On the 19th Maj. Gilpin, with about 30 men, starting at dawn, went on in advance so as to reach the Bear Spring on the 20th, leaving Capt. Waldo to bring up the main body of the detachment. He arrived there safely and in anticipation of Col. Doniphan. Capt. Waldo brought up the rear in good order and time to the place appointed, where he effected a junction with Col. Doniphan's forces. Here they rested.

Let us now turn and consider the difficulties which Col. Doniphan and the men with him had to encounter in arriving at the same place. We have hitherto mentioned how Col. Doniphan left Santa Fe on the 26th of October and with a body of 300 men proceeded to Albuquerque, crossed the river, meditated a separate march into the Navajo district, was diverted from his purpose, compelled to send his troops to Valverde to protect the merchants, and how with a part of his staff and four other men he arrived at Cuvarro on the 5th of November, where he found the detachment under Lieut. Col. Jackson, who had just moved his camp to that place from Cebolleta. Capts. Parsons and Reid had just returned from their excursions into the Navajo country. Capt. Reid's company, in consideration of the duties it had performed and that the men were almost destitute of comfortable clothing to defend themselves against the cold, was permitted to return to Albuquerque to receive from the paymaster at that place their commutation for clothing, which had not yet been paid them. The sum was $42 to the private man and noncommissioned officer.

On the 12th of November Col. Doniphan, while at Cuvarro, received an express from Maj. Gilpin, then on the San Juan, which was brought into camp by a Navajo Indian. Maj. Gilpin represented that he had seen large numbers of Navajos, who pretended to have already entered into treaty stipulations with the United States forces, no doubt alluding to the agreement which they had made with Capt. Reid, and failed to carry out. Col. Doniphan replied to Maj. Gilpin by the same Indian, that no such treaty had been made; that Capt. Reid had been sent out for the purpose by Lieut. Col. Jackson, and had visited many of the Navajo chiefs, but that no definite treaty had been ratified; and instructed him to bring all the Navajos he could find to the well-known Ojo Oso, by the 20th of the month. This the major did.

It was now the 15th of November, when Col. Doniphan and Lieut. Col. Jackson took up the line of march for the Bear Spring, with about 150 men under Capt. Parsons and Lieut. De Courcy; Capt. Hughes and the other sick men being left at Cuvarro. This detachment was also scarce of provisions and had neither tents nor baggage wagons, but made use of pack mules to transport provisions and cooking utensils.

For two days the march was conducted up through a rich valley country, in the direction of the sources of the Puerco. The grass was moderately good for grazing purposes, but wood was scarce and the water muddy and filthy. This district of country was occupied by that canton of the Navajos, of whom Sandoval was the chief. On the evening of the latter day they encamped on a rivulet whose waters came leaping down in foaming cascades from the mountain and then disappeared in the sands of the valley. Having no tents the soldiers quartered on the naked earth in the open air, but so much snow fell that night that at dawn it was not possible to distinguish where they lay until they broke the snow which covered them, and came out as though they were rising from their graves; for in less than 12 hours the snow had fallen 13 inches deep in the valleys and 36 in the mountains.

On the 17th they marched northwesterly, leaving the heads of the Puerco to the right and passing directly over the Sierra Madre. The march was difficult in the valleys, but when they came to ascend the steep spurs and bench lands which lead up to the mountains, a horrid, dreary prospect opened above them. The men and their commanders were almost up to their waists toiling in the snow, breaking a way for the horses and mules to ascend. The lowest point in the main mountain rose to a sublime height, and to the right still towering far above this projected stupendous colossal columns of ragged granite and iron-colored basalt. In reaching the only point where the main ridge could be crossed many smaller mountains and intermediate, deep, narrow, rocky vales were to be passed. The snow in the gaps and narrow places among the rocks was frequently a fathom in depth. After much toil they reached the summit. To accomplish the descent into the valleys on the west side was a labor not much less difficult than that which the soldiers had just finished. They rested a moment and then began the descent. After the most serious and arduous labor they reached the base of the great mountain late at night and took up camp at a spring, the water of which flows toward the Pacific. The depth of the snow was less on the west than in the mountains or on the east side. Finding good grass, wood, and water, the soldiers took their supper and recounted, as they sat around their camp fires, the dangers and adventures of the day. At length their toils were forgotten in the slumbers of the night. The faithful sentinel, who after such a day's labor stood wakeful all night in the snow while his weary comrades slept, does he not, reader, deserve your gratitude? He has no other reward.

Having now passed the mountain they traveled on the 18th over a valley country in a westerly direction; gently rolling hills, then rocky bluffs, then bench lands, then crags and bleak knobs, and then barren, naked, giant masses of gray granite and dark basalt rising on the right and a heavy forest of pines and cedars, always verdant, spreading over the lowlands to the left. In many places these colossal granite peaks shoot almost perpendicularly out of the plain more than 6,000 feet high. The surface of the country continued uniform for the next two days' march, except in some places there were gently swelling hills with grassy recesses between on the one side and a heavy, unbroken forest of evergreens on the other. Here the Navajos pasture their immense droves of horses and mules and keep their numerous flocks of sheep and goats. The aspect of the country continued thus until they arrived at the Bear Spring on the morning of the 21st; Maj. Gilpin, as already noticed, having got there on the day previous with a number of the Navajo chiefs who dwell in the country to the west and northwest of that place, commissioned to bind the nation.

There were now present at the Bear Spring, where the treaty was made, about 180 Americans and 500 Navajo Indians, including all the head chiefs of each of the cantons composing that powerful tribe of mountain lords and scourgers of New Mexico. The parties being all present to whom power was delegated to conclude a lasting peace between three nations, the Navajos, Mexicans, and Americans, the treaty was commenced on the 21st, Col. Doniphan first stating explictly through an interpreter, T. Caldwell, the objects of his visit and the designs and intentions of his Government. One of their chiefs, Sarcilla Largo, a young man very bold and intellectual, spoke for them: " He was gratified to learn the views of the Americans. He admired their spirit and enterprise, but detested the Mexicans." Their speeches were delivered alternately during the whole day. At sunset the parties adjourned to meet again the following morning.

Meanwhile they repaired to their respective camps, the Americans posting out sentinels that they might not be surprised and massacred by the Navajos through treachery, and these that they might not come into the power of the Americans without their own consent.

On the 22d, Capt. Waldo having come in with 150 men, swelling the aggregate number of the Americans present to 330, the treaty was recommenced. Col. Doniphan now explained to the chiefs "that the United States had taken military possession of New Mexico; that her laws were now extended over that Territory, that the New Mexicans would be protected against violence and invasion, and that their rights would be amply preserved to them; that the United States was also anxious to enter into a treaty of peace and lasting friendship with her red children, the Navajos; that the same protection would be given them against encroachments and usurpation of their rights as had been guaranteed the New Mexican; that the United States claimed all the country by the right of conquest, and both they and the New Mexicans were now become equally her children; that he had come with ample powers to negotiate a permanent peace between the Navajos, the Americans, and New Mexicans; and that if they refused to treat on terms honorable to both parties he was instructed to prosecute a war against them." He also admonished them " to enter into no treaty stipulations unless they meant to observe them strictly and in good faith; that the United States made no second treaty with the same people; that she first offered the olive branch, and, if that were rejected, then powder, bullet, and the steel."

Then the same young chief, of great sagacity and boldness, stood up and replied to the American commander thus: "Americans, you have a strange cause of war against the Navajos. We have waged war against the New Mexicans for several years. We have plundered their villages and killed many of their people, and made many prisoners. We had just cause for all this. You have lately commenced a war against the same people. You are powerful. You have great guns and many brave soldiers. You have therefore conquered them, the very thing we have been attempting to do for so many years. You now turn upon us for attempting to do what you have done yourselves. We can not see why you have cause of quarrel with us for fighting the New Mexicans on the west, while you do the same thing on the east. Look how matters stand. This is our war. We have more right to complain of you for interfering in our war than you have to quarrel with us for continuing a war we had begun long before you got here. If you will act justly, you will allow us to settle our own differences."

Col. Doniphan then explained "that the New Mexicans had surrendered; that they desired no more fighting; that it was a custom with the Americans when a people gave up to treat them as friends thenceforward; that we now had full possession of New Mexico, and had attached it to our Government; that the whole country and everything in it had become ours by conquest, and that when they now stole property from the New Mexicans they were stealing from us, and when they killed them they were killing our people, for they had now become ours; that this could not be suffered any longer; that it would be greatly to their advantage for the Americans to settle in New Mexico, and that they then could open a valuable trade with us, by which means they could obtain everything they needed to eat and wear in exchange for their furs and peltries."

Col. Doniphan then invited their young men to the United States to learn trades, as he discovered them to be very ingenious, that they might be serviceable to their people. This pleased them, and they desired very much to accompany him to the United States, but they did not wish to go through Chihuahua, for they feared the Mexicans would kill them. This induced them not to go.

Then the same chief said: "If New Mexico be really in your possession, and it be the intention of your Government to hold it, we will cease our depredations and refrain from future wars upon that people, for we have no cause of quarrel with you, and do not desire to have any war with so powerful a nation. Let there be peace between us." This was the end of the speaking. After which the following articles of treaty were signed by both parties.

MEMORANDUM OF A TREATY ENTERED INTO BETWEEN COL. A. W. DONIPHAN, COM-
MANDING THE UNITED STATES FORCES IN THE NAVAJO COUNTRY, AND THE CHIEFS
OF THE NAVAJO NATION OF INDIANS, VIZ, SARCILLA LARGO, CABALLADA DE MUCHO,
ALEXANDRO, SANDOVAL, KIATANITO JOSÉ LARGO, NARBONA, SAGUNDO, PEDRO JOSÉ
MANUELITO, TAPIO, AND ARCHULETTÉ, AT THE OJO OSO, NAVAJO COUNTRY, NOVEM-
BER 22, 1846.

ARTICLE 1. A firm and lasting peace and amity shall henceforth exist between the American people and the Navajo Tribe of Indians.

ART. 2. The people of New Mexico and the Pueblo Tribe of Indians are included in the term "American people."

ART. 3. A mutual trade, as between people of the same nation, shall be carried on between these several parties, the Americans, Mexicans, and Pueblos being free to visit all portions of the Navajo country, and the Navajos all portions of the American country without molestation, and full protection shall be mutually given.

ART. 4. There shall be a mutual restoration of all prisoners, the several parties being pledged to redeem by purchase such as may not be exchanged each for each.

ART. 5. All property taken by either party from the other since the 18th day of August last shall be restored.

The undersigned, fully empowered to represent and pledge to the above articles their respective nations, have accordingly hereunto signed their names and affixed their seals.

ALEXANDER W. DONIPHAN,
Colonel, Commanding First Regiment Missouri Volunteers.
CONGREVE JACKSON,
Lieutenant Colonel, Commanding First Battalion.
WILLIAM GILPIN,
Major, Commanding Second Battalion.

Signature of the Navajo chiefs:

SARCILLA LARGO (his x mark), CABALLADA DE MUCHO (his x mark), ALEXANDRO (his x mark), SANDOVAL (his x mark), KIATANITO (his x mark), JOSÉ LARGO (his x mark), NARBONA (his x mark), SAGUNDO (his x mark), PEDRO JOSÉ (his x mark), MANUELITO (his x mark), TAPIO (his x mark), ARCHULETTE (his x mark), JUANICO (his x mark), SAVOIETTA GARCIA (his x mark).

The colonel then gave them some presents, which he had carried out from Santa Fe for that purpose, explicitly stating that these presents were made, not by way of purchasing their friendship, for this the Americans were not accustomed to do, but were given as a testimony of his personal good will and friendship toward them and as a sign that peace should exist between them.

In return the chief presented Col. Doniphan with several fine Navajo blankets, the manufacture of which discovers great ingenuity, having been spun and woven without the advantage of wheels or looms by a people living in the open air, without houses or tents. Of these the colors are exceedingly brilliant and the designs and figures in good taste. The fabric is not only so thick and compact as to turn rain, but to hold water as a vessel. They are used by the Navajos as a cloak in the daytime and converted into a pallet at night. Col. Doniphan designs sending those which he brought home with him to the War Department at Washington as specimens of Navajo manufacture.

Thus, after almost unparalleled exertion, a treaty of peace was concluded between the Navajos, New Mexicans, and Americans in a manner honorable to all parties. This was a novel, highly important, and interesting proceeding. The Navajos and New Mexicans had been at war from immemorial time. The frontier between them had been the scene of continual bloodshed and rapine. At this crisis the Americans, the enemies of the one and strangers to the other, step in and accommodate their differences by a triple league, which secures peace between all three. This, together with his previous service and subsequent achievements, not only entitles Col. Doniphan to wear the laurel but also the olive, for he has justly earned the distinguished titles of victor and pacificator.

CHAPTER XI.

On the morning of the 23d the Indians peaceably returned to their pastoral employments, and the Americans, in detached parties, for the sake of convenient traveling, returned to the valley of the Del Norte with the utmost expedition. The men were all in want of provisions, having none except what the friendly Navajos generously gave them, and the grizzly bears and black-tailed deer which they hunted in the mountains. This consideration quickened their marches.

Capt. Parsons and Lieut. De Courcy hastily returned to Cuvarro with their respective commands by the same route they had come to Bear Spring. They arrived there without serious misfortune, having lost only a few horses and pack animals by the way. They found that some of their men, who were left sick at Cuvarro, had died, others were past recovery, and all in a destitute condition, having neither comfortable clothing nor a plentiful supply of provisions. All the sick who were able to bear moving, together with their attendants, were now conveyed down the river Puerco to its mouth, and thence to Soccorro, where they were quartered. Amongst these were Capt. Hughes and Lieut. Jackson. A few only, who were very ill, were left at Cuvarro. Of these some died,[1] and the survivors came on and rejoined their companies. This detachment arrived at the camp near Valverde and formed a juncture with the 300 who remained as a guard to the traders about the 12th of December, much worn by distressing marches. Here they rested.

The detachment under Maj. Gilpin, accompanied by Col. Doniphan, Lieut. Col. Jackson, and Lieut. Hinton, and the three Navajo chiefs, leaving the Ojo Oso on the same day (23d of November), completed 60 miles in two days' march, and came to Zuni, a city built after the manner of the ancient Aztecs; during which they passed over a high rolling country, well timbered with stately pines and cedars, presenting a beautiful contrast to the barren, bleak, rocky ridges of the Sierra Madre and Sierra de los Mimbres, which now rose .on the left.

This route lay over a ledge of gently swelling hills and highlands, dividing the headwaters of the Rivers Gila and Colorado. During this entire march there appeared numerous indications of the precious metals abounding. Blossoms of gold, silver, lead, and some specimens of copper were seen. This whole mountain region of

---

[1] Silas Inyard, C. T. Hopper, Wm. Sterne, and several others, died near Cuvarro.

country is unquestionably rich in mineral wealth. On arriving at
Zuni, Maj. Gilpin quartered his men, as usual, in the open air near
town. Col. Doniphan and a few others, including the three Navajo
chiefs, lodged themselves in a spacious adobe building in the city.
Now, there was a continual war between the Navajos and the Zunians. On this account, these three Navajo chiefs durst not leave the
colonel far at any time, because they feared that the Zunians would
kill them. Col. Doniphan therefore appointed a guard for them,
that they might not suffer any hurt. In the evening of the 25th,
upward of 200 Zunians collected about the colonel's quarters. Having intimated that it was his intention on the next day to endeavor
to bring them to a friendly understanding with the Navajos, their
implacable enemies, the leading warriors of the Zunians drew near
(for they were friendly toward the Americans), and entered into
a dispute with the Navajo chiefs. Fiery speeches were made by each
of the parties. The Zunians thought to lay hold on them and de-
tain them as prisoners of war; but they durst not do this through
fear of the Americans, under whose protection the Navajo chiefs
came in. One of the Navajo chiefs spoke for the rest. He said:

The cause of your present dissatisfaction is just this. The war between us
has been waged for plunder. You kill and drive off our flocks and herds, and
subsist your people upon them, and use them for your own advantage. To
resent this we have plundered your villages, taken your women and children
captives and made slaves of them. Lately you have been unsuccessful. We
have outstolen you, and therefore you are mad and dissatisfied about it. But
there is one thing you can not accuse the Navajos of doing, and that is killing
women and children. You know not many years past, when our women and
children went into the mountains to gather piñons, your warriors fell upon and
killed about 40 of them. This cowardly act was perpetrated when there were
no Navajo warriors to afford them succor.

A chief of the Zuni tribe replied, indignantly repelling the charge,
and threatening to hold the Navajo chiefs as hostages until the
Navajos should deliver up those of their people whom they held as
captives. The Navajo rejoined:

The Zunians may rest assured that we did not come over here relying on their
generosity, magnanimity, or good faith; but, being invited by Col. Doniphan,
we have come to see if we can make a peace with you Zunians, which will be
both honorable and advantageous to us. We rely alone on the integrity of the
Americans and their ability to protect us. We have not the slightest fear of
any injury you may attempt to offer us, for we trust ourselves with a more
honorable people.

Col. Doniphan here interposed and advised them to meet the next
morning and endeavor to form a treaty, stipulating entire friendship
between the two nations; that it would be much better for both parties to live in peace; and that war was a great evil. He then appointed the American camp near the town as the place of meeting.
They met accordingly, and, after much debate, consummated a treaty
of peace and amity on the 26th, just and honorable to both parties.
This was the last treaty Col. Doniphan made with any tribe of
Indians. His labors with the Indians were now finished.

Zuni, one of the most extraordinary cities in the world, and perhaps
the only one now known resembling those of the ancient Aztecs, is
situated on the right bank of the River Piscao, a small branch of the
Gila, or Colorado of California, near 200 miles west of the Del Norte,

and contains a singular and interesting population of upward of 6,000, who derive their support almost exclusively from agriculture. They clothe themselves in blankets and other fabrics of their own manufacture. The Zunians being friendly disposed toward the soldiers, these secured of them a supply of provisions, and also of various fruits in which the country abounds. The Zunis, or Zunians, have long been celebrated not only for honesty and hospitality, but also for their intelligence and ingenuity in the manufacture of cotton and woolen fabrics.

The city of Zuni was thus described by Col. Doniphan to Mr. T. B. Thorpe,[1] of New Orleans:

It is divided into four solid squares, having but two streets, crossing its center at right angles. All the buildings are two stories high, composed of sun-dried brick. The first story presents a solid wall to the street, and is so constructed that each house joins, until one-fourth of the city may be said to be one building. The second stories rise from this vast, solid structure, so as to designate each house, leaving room to walk upon the roof of the first story between each building. The inhabitants of Zuni enter the second story of their buildings by ladders, which they draw up at night, as a defense against any enemy that might be prowling about. In this city were seen some 30 Albino Indians, who have, no doubt, given rise to the story that there is living in the Rocky Mountains a tribe of white aborigines. The discovery of this city of the Zunians will afford the most curious speculations among those who have so long searched in vain for a city of Indians who possessed the manners and habits of the Aztecs. No doubt we have here a race living as did that people when Cortez entered Mexico. It is a remarkable fact that the Zunians have, since the Spaniards left the country, refused to have any intercourse with the modern Mexicans, looking upon them as an inferior people. They have also driven from among them [not until recently, however] the priests and other dignitaries, who formerly had power over them, and resumed habits and manners of their own, their great chief, or governor, being the civil and religious head. The country around the city of Zuni is cultivated with a great deal of care, and affords food not only for the inhabitants but for large flocks of cattle and sheep.

The seven villages of the Moquis are situated about 5 leagues farther to the westward on the same small river. The Moquis are an inoffensive, peaceably disposed people, detesting war and rapine; yet they are both numerous and powerful. They manifest considerable skill in their manufactures, and subsist entirely by grazing and agriculture. Of these people Mr. Gregg thus speaks:

They formerly acknowledged the government and religion of the Spaniards, but have long since rejected both, and live in a state of independence and paganism. Their dwellings, however, like those of Zuni, are similar to those of the interior Pueblos, and they are equally industrious and agricultural, and still more ingenious in their manufacturing. The language of the Moquis, or the Moquinos, is said to differ but little from that of the Navajos.

The American Army did not visit them, as they were at peace with all people, and stood aloof from the wars that continually raged around them.

The affairs of the Indians being thus settled, Maj. Gilpin's detachment, on the evening of the 26th, started for the valley of the Del Norte, by way of Laguna, on the Puerco. His first intention was, however, to proceed directly to Soccorro through the elevated range of mountains, called by the Mexicans Sierra de los Mimbres, but was convinced of the impracticability of that route by the Zunians,

---

[1] This account was written out by Mr. Thorpe and first published in the New Orleans National, of which he is the editor.

who informed him of the great dearth of water which prevailed in that region, and induced him to change his purpose. He then marched hastily to Laguna by a more northern pass over the mountains and fell in with Col. Doniphan at that place, 100 miles from Zuni, on the 2d of December.

It will be remembered that Col. Doniphan, Lieut. Col. Jackson, and seven other men, separating from this detachment, left Zuni on the 27th of November, and by a different maneuver in the mountains, reached Cebolleta, and thence proceeded to Laguna, falling in with Maj. Gilpin, as above related. On the headwaters of the Piscao, and high up in the mountains, Col. Doniphan relates that he came to the ruins of an ancient city. This city, according to the best information he could obtain, had been built more than 200 years, entirely of stone, and had been deserted more than 100 years, as is supposed, on account of the earthquakes in the vicinity. Near the ruins are immense beds of vitreous deposit, and blackened scoria, presenting the appearance of an extensive molten lake in the valleys, and other volcanic remains, with chasms and apertures opening down through this stratum of lava, to an unknown depth. The vitreous surface with its sharp asperites, was exceedingly severe on the feet of the mules and horses, wearing them to the quick in a short time. The figure of the city was that of an exact square, set north and south so that its four sides corresponded with the four cardinal points, being encircled by a double wall of stone, 14 feet apart. These walls were three stories high; two entire stories being above ground, and the other partly above and partly below the surface. The space between these walls was divided into rooms of convenient size (about 14 feet square), all opening into the interior. The remainder of the city, though much in ruins, appeared to have been built on streets running parallel to these walls. In the center was a large square, or plaza, which, from its appearance, might have been used for military parade grounds, and for corralling stock in the nighttime. In these rooms large quantities of red cedar which had been cut of convenient length for fire places, was discovered in a state of entire preservation, having been stored up for more than a century. Col. Doniphan and suite cooked their suppers and made their campfires with some of it and then traveled on. This is all that could be learned of that remarkable ruin.

Both of the routes traveled by Col. Doniphan and Maj. Gilpin from Zuni to Cebolleta and Laguna, and thence to the encampment at Valverde, were pronounced impracticable by the Mexicans. There were indeed long stretches over sandy wastes wherein no water could be obtained. These must be traversed. The soldiers and animals were therefore compelled to pass several consecutive days and nights without eating or drinking. They effected their arrival at Valverde rendezvous in parcels between the 8th and 12th of December, Capt. Stephenson's company only being permitted to return to Albuquerque to receive the commutation for one year's clothing, which had long been due them.

The march of the squadron under command of Maj. Gilpin, ranks among the brightest achievements of the war. This passage over the Cordilleras and Tunicha Mountains, accomplished, as it was, in the depth of winter, when the elements and obstacles were ten times more dreadful than the foe, with men destitute of everything but arms and resolution, meets not with a parallel in the annals of history. From the time of his leaving Santa Fe, including the diversion he made into the country of Yutas, north of Taos, his column marched at least 750 miles, before reaching Valverde, over the loftiest mountains, and most inaccessible regions, on the continent. By distress of marching he lost two brave men, Bryant and Foster, and 150 head of stock. The success of the celebrated Navajo treaty was not less owing to the gallantry and energy of this column in hunting up and bringing in the chiefs of that nation to the appointed place, than to the skill and diplomacy of Col. Doniphan, who brought the negotiations to so happy an issue. The marches of the other two columns, under Col. Doniphan and Lieut. Col. Jackson, and Capt. Reid, were scarcely less arduous or astonishing; nor was the country over which these passed less impracticable; for by reason of hardship and suffering these lost a great number of animals and seven or eight brave soldiers.

Thus terminated this most arduous and difficult campaign against the Navajo Indians, of whom it may not be amiss to give a brief account as touching their manners and habits of life.

The Navajos occupy a district of country scarcely less in extent than the State of Missouri. In their predatory excursions they roam from 30° to 38° of north latitude, and for the period of 250 years have with impunity, except in one to two instances, ravaged the whole Mexican frontier from Socorro to the valley of Taos, plundering and destroying according as their caprices prompted them. Their strong places of retreat are in the Cordilleras, and that entire range of high lands which divides the waters of the Gila and Colorado of the west from those of the Del Norte. They stretch from the borders of New Mexico on the east to the settlements of California on the west. They are supreme lords of this mountain country; and, like the Asiatic Tartars, have no fixed abodes, but follow their flocks. Upon these and the plunder they secure in their frequent incursions upon the New Mexican villages they subsist themselves entirely. They are not addicted to the chase, except where the game may be taken on horseback. The bold and fearless character of the Navajos, together with the magnificent mountain scenery of the country which they inhabit awakens in the mind reflections not unlike those which any-one is apt to entertain of the Highlanders and Highlands of Scotland, from reading the Scottish bards.

Mr. Thorpe, upon the authority of Col. Doniphan, thus alludes to the tribe of American Tartars:

The Navajo Indians are a warlike people; have no towns, houses, or lodges; they live in the open air, or on horseback, and are remarkably wealthy, having immense herds of horses, cattle, and sheep. They are celebrated for their intelligence and good order. They treat their women with great attention, consider them equals, and relieve them from the drudgery of menial work. They are handsome, well made, and in every respect a highly civilized people, being as a nation, of a higher order of beings than the mass of their neighbors, the Mexicans. About the time Col. Doniphan made his treaty a division of his command was entirely out of provisions—the Navajos supplied its wants with liberality.

The art and skill which they possess in manufacturing woolen fabrics (the texture of which is so dense and fine as to be impervious to water), and apparently with such limited means, is really matter of astonishment. The Navajos can easily muster 1,500 warriors for battle; and their aggregate numbers can not be less than 12,000. They are certainly the noblest of the American aborigines.

BLACK-TAILED DEER.

CHAPTER XII.

The manner in which Gen. Kearney settled the affairs, both civil
and military, in New Mexico, and how the forces were disposed in
different parts of that country for the preserving of good order,
tranquility, and subordination among the malcontents, has been
related in the previous chapters. It now remains to speak of Gen.
Kearney's stupendous march over the southern spurs of the Cordilleras to the settlements of California.

On the 25th of September, Gen. Kearney left Santa Fe and commenced his great march for the distant shores of the Pacific, taking
with him his staff officers, 300 of the First Dragoons, baggage and
provision wagons, and about 65 days' provision.

The dragoons were commanded by Capts. (now Maj.) Sumner,[1]
Cooke, Moore, and Burgwin, and Lieut. Noble, in place of Capt. Allen.
Their horses were now sent back to Fort Leavenworth, and mules sub-
stituted in their stead, as it was believed this animal possessed more
endurance and was better adapted to the travel through a dry, mountainous country, mostly destitute of water and grass, than the horse.
The general left orders at Santa Fe for Capt. Hudson's California
Rangers and the battalion of Mormons under Lieut. Col. Allen to
succeed him on the march as soon as the latter corps should arrive at
that place.

The general proceeded this day no farther than Maj. Sumner's
grazing encampment on Santa Fe Creek. Grass and good spring
water were obtained in sufficient quantities for the night's use. The
next morning the ox teams and then the mule teams, as was the usual
practice of the Army, started on the way by daylight; for these
necessarily travel slower than mounted men. The country during
this day's march was thinly covered with grama grass and occasional
cedar shrubs, betokening the greatest sterility. Several mules being
missing and two wagons broken down they encamped on the bank
of the Del Norte, near San Filipe, where they spent the night, during
which some of their mules broke loose and depredated upon the
neighboring cornfields. The complaints of the Pueblos were silenced
by the payment of damages.

This column now moved slowly down the valley of the Del Norte,
passing through Algodones, Bernalillo, Sandia, Albuquerque, where

---

[1] Maj. Sumner subsequently rendered important service at the battles of Churubusco
and Chapultepec.

crossing the river and proceeding about 8 miles farther the general pitched his camp on the 29th near the village Pajarrito. Here, owing to the scarcity of timber, the soldiers were compelled to buy fuel with which to cook their suppers. "A few days previous to this, and shortly after three companies of volunteers crossed the river on their way to Cebolleta," observes Capt. Johnston, "a party of Navajos crossed at this point and killed eight Mexicans on the east bank of the Del Norte. Here," observes the same author, "the sand drifts in various places had accumulated into hills. Drifting sand seems to adhere to its own kindred material. It is fortunate that it is so. This country would otherwise be impassable as well as uninhabitable. The inhabitable portion of New Mexico is confined to the immediate borders of the streams. The bottoms of the Del Norte are about one mile and a half wide on an average so far down, and are elevated but a few feet above the level of the running water. The Del Norte is rapid and regular, and its waters can be tapped at any point without a dam, so that irrigation is carried on successfully. It remains for greater improvements in this respect to develop the resources of the country. A large canal along the base of the hills might carry all the waters of the Del Norte and be a means of transportation, while its surplus water could be employed in the winter for filling reservoirs, and during the summer to convey water directly upon the fields. In this way the country could be made to support ten times its present population. The rains of this country all fall upon the mountain tops, and the valleys are thus dependent upon irrigation, as the water only reaches them in the big drains of nature. From our camp, during the night, we could see upon the distant hills the camp fires of the shepherds who lead their flocks afar from their habitations."

From thence this column marched in three days about 36 miles, passing through Paparrito, Padillas, Isleta, Sineca, Lunas, Belen, Sabinaz, and encamped opposite La Joya, during which some portions of the country were under a high state of cultivation, while in other places the earth was entirely bare or covered by white efflorescences of soda. The river was occasionally skirted by clusters and groves of alamas. Here the soldiers took some fine turtle and catfish out of the Del Norte upon which they feasted sumptuously during the night.

The next day, which was the 3d of October, the general lay in camp awaiting the arrival of the Mexican caretas and the ox teams which had fallen one day in the rear. "During the day an express came in from Polvadera, 12 miles down the river, informing the general that the Navajos had attacked the village, and he had been sent by the alcalde to bring the Artillery, where they were still fighting when he left. Capt. Moore was sent with Company C in defense of the Mexicans, and orders were sent to-day to Col. Doniphan (at Santa Fe) to make a campaign into the Navajo country."

The following day the general came to Polvadera, where he learned from Capt. Moore that about 100 Navajos had visited the place and driven off into the mountains a great quantity of stock, but that no battle had taken place, as they appeared mutually to dread each other. "The general here gave permission to the people of New Mexico, living on the Rio Abarjo, to march against the

Navajos in retaliation for the many outrages they had received at their hands." Thus it will appear that the Pueblos, who offered their serives to Lieut. Col. Jackson before arriving at Cebolleta, and which were rejected, were not acting without instructions from the head of the Government.

Thence, on the 5th, the march was continued through Limitar, Soccorro, and Huertus. It was at Soccorro the general took possession of certain mules, of which the alcade had deprived the legal owners in consequence of their carrying on contraband trade with the Apaches, and which he claimed as the rightful perquisites of his office. They now became the property of the American Government, and were appropriated accordingly. The American Army had not hitherto visited any of the settlements thus far south in the great Del Norte Valley. The inhabitants, therefore, gazed with astonishment and admiration upon an army passing orderly and silently through the country, abstaining from acts of violence and outrage, as though it were in the country of an ally.

Mexican cart.

Thence, having progressed, on the 6th, about 3 miles, this column was met by Lieut. Kit Carson with a party of 15 men (among them 6 Delaware Indians) direct, on express, from Monterey with sealed dispatches for Washington. He represented California as being in quiet possession of the Americans. The general then said: " Lieutenant, you have just passed over the country we intend to traverse, and you are well acquainted with it; we want you to go back with us as our guide and pilot us through the mountains and deserts." Carson replied: " I have pledged myself to go to Washington and I can not think of neglecting to fulfill that promise." The general then said: " I will relieve you of all responsibility and intrust the mail in the hands of a safe person, who will carry it on speedily." Carson finally consenting, " turned his face to the westward again, just as he was on the eve of entering the settlements after his arduous trip and when he had set his hopes on seeing his family. It requires a brave man to give up his private feelings thus for the public good; Carson is one such."

Carson's party were not till then apprised of the conquest of New Mexico by the American troops, and, therefore, although they had lost most of their animals, intended, if the New Mexicans should prove hostile, to make as speedy a transit across that country as possible, during which they counted on procuring such an outfit and supply of provisions as would enable them to pass the plains and reach the States. The column now moved on 10 miles, encamping in a beautiful cottonwood grove, where the general issued orders reducing his command to 100 men. California being in quiet possession of the Americans, there appeared to be no advantage in carrying a strong force to that distant country. The rest of the command was now put under requisition to supply these with the best possible outfit for the long and arduous campaign. The new organization for the expedition stood thus: Gen. Kearney, with his aids-de-camp, Capts. Turner and Johnston; Maj. Swords, quartermaster; Griflin, assistant surgeon; Lieuts. Warner and Emory, topographical engineers; and two companies of the First Dragoons (50 men each) commanded by Capt. Moore and Lieut. Hammond, including the section of mountain howitzers under Lieut. Davidson, each company being furnished with three wagons, drawn by eight stout mules.

This evening the Apaches brought unto the general four young men as guides. Their geographical knowledge was extensive and accurate, yet they could not tell what route was practicable for wagons. Fitzpatrick was dispatched to Santa Fe and thence to Fort Leavenworth with the mail from California. The other three companies of the First Dragoons and the principal part of the baggage train were sent back under Maj. Sumner to winter at Albuquerque.

From thence in three days' march they made 50 miles, crossed the river, and encamped southwest of the Jornada Mountain, which is a heap of volcanic cinders and igneous rocks; during which they passed much rough road, where the rocks, asperities, and thickets of mesquite rendered it necessary to send in advance a pioneer party with axes and picks to clear the way. The wagons progressed slowly, some of them were already broken, and many of the mules began to fail. The general determined to send from this place to Maj. Sumner for mules to haul the six wagons back to the valley of the Del Norte, and resolved to resort at once to pack mules and sumpter horses as a means of transporting his baggage and provisions, for he now foresaw the route would be impracticable to either light carriages or heavy wagons.

Accordingly, Corpl. Clapin and one Mexican, his name Zones, were dispatched for the purpose about midnight, with orders to ride to Maj. Sumner's camp, 60 miles, without stopping. This they did. Meanwhile Capt. Cooke was employed in opening a road for the howitzers and pack animals. The next four days they remained in camp, awaiting the arrival of the mules and pack saddles.

At this point on the Del Norte were discovered signs of the otter, the catamount, the wildcat, the raccoon, the deer, and the bear; also of the crane, the duck, the goose, the plover, and the California quail. This latter differs from the quail of the United States, the male having a dark bluish and the female a reddish plumage. On the 13th Lieut. Ingalls came up, bringing the pack saddles and the United States mail, containing general orders for Gen. Kearney, and other letters and papers. These were answered and all future communication with the States closed, for they had now passed beyond the reach of mail facilities.

On the 15th this little army struck off from the Rio Del Norte in a southwesterly direction, ascending at once 200 feet to an elevated plain intersected by numerous deep ravines and dashing mountain streams running through great chasms and filled with the finest fish. Having completed a progress of 24 miles over a country where the hills were capped with iron-colored basaltic rocks, and the valleys and margins of the streams beautified with a new caste of tropical walnut, oak, hackberry, birch, and mesquite, the men encamped on a mountain rivulet, cooked their suppers, and stayed for the night.

Marching the next two days, they passed over a beautiful country, watered by fresh, leaping mountain streams issuing from the southern spurs of the Sierra de los Mimbres, bordered and shaded by a small growth of live oak, walnut, acacia, grapevines, canissa, and Spanish bayonet, and also fringed by the richest growth of grama grass, and came to the river Minifres, about 3 miles beyond which they encamped on a small creek in a cedar grove near heaps of volcanic glass and igneous rocks, where they obtained a plentiful supply of fine grama grass for their stock. Here they rested for the night.

The next day the march was continued. Smoking fires were made on the tops of the hills near the way, as friendly signals to invite the Apaches into camp. At sunset they arrived at the celebrated copper mine in the northern part of the State of Chihuahua, which Capt. Johnston thus describes:

The veins of sulphuret of copper run through a whitish, silicious rock, like the blue veins running through white marble; they vary in their knees, but traverse the whole substance. The rock breaks easily, and the pick appears to be the only tool used formerly. Occasional veins of pure copper, very yellow from the quantity of gold it contains, traverse the whole mass. I saw in the rollers lying over the mine masses of the blue limestone, supposed to be cretaceous; the water had filled many of the abandoned chambers of the mine; in others, the flies had perched themselves in great numbers, to pass the winter. The fort, which was erected to defend the mines, was built in shape of an equilateral triangle, with round towers at the corners; it was built of adobe, with walls 4 feet thick. The fort was in tolerable preservation; some remains of the furnaces were left, and piles of cinders; but no idea could be formed of the manner of smelting the ore, except that charcoal in quantities was used. Several hundred dollars' worth of ore had been got ready for smelting, when the place was abandoned. McKnight, who was nine years a prisoner in Chihuahua, made a fortune here, and abandoned the mines in consequence of the Apache Indians cutting off his supplies. At one time they took 80 pack mules from him. The mine is very extensive, and doubtless immensely valuable. Water is abundant, and pasture fine, and many lands which will furnish breadstuffs by cultivation. Wood is very abundant, and particularly in the vicinity.

From thence in one day's march they completed 30 miles, passing the San Vicentia Spring and the high rocky ridges that separate the waters of the Gulf of Mexico from the Gulf of California. Several mules failed on this march, and were abandoned amongst the rocks and crags.

The next morning Red Sleeve, an Apache chief, with 20 of his warriors and some squaws, visited the camp, and gave assurances of their friendly intentions and wishes. They were habited after the manner of the Mexicans, with wide drawers, moccasins turned up in front, and leggins to the knees, with a keen dagger knife inserted in the folds of the leggin on the outside for convenient use in cases of sudden assault. Their hair was long and flowed loosely in the wind; they mostly had no headdress. To turn the scorching rays of an almost vertical sun from their faces and preserve their eyes some of them used a fantastic kind of shield made of rawhide and dressed buckskin, while others of them employed a fan of twigs or a buzzard's wing for the same purpose. They were armed in part with Mexican fusils, partly with lances, and bows and arrows. The general gave Red Sleeve and two other chiefs papers, showing that he had held a talk with them, and that they had promised perpetual friendship with the Americans.

Also another Apache chief came into camp and harangued the general thus: "You have taken Santa Fe; let us go on and take Chihuahua and Sonora; we will go with you. You fight for the soul; we fight for plunder; so we will agree perfectly; their people are bad Christians; let us chastise them as they deserve." The general, of course, rejected his proposal, and so they all went away. This day the march was down a deep valley of rich grama grass, watered by a cool rivulet, with high hills and piles of volcanic rock on either hand; and having completed 5 miles they came to the famous river Gila, "a beautiful mountain stream about 30 feet wide and a foot deep on the shallows, and hemmed in by mountains, the bottom being not more than a mile wide. The signs of beaver, bear, deer, and turkey, besides the tracks of herds of Indian horses, were plain to be seen on the sand." Now, turning south, they advanced about 2½ miles farther, and encamped at the base of a ledge of hills, with summits of dark, ragged, iron-colored rocks, where the river passes through a deep fissure or canyon, impassable by cavalry. Here the soldiers took some fish from the river, which were of delicate and excellent flavor. Therefore they feasted that night.

Thence after 11 days they came to the river San Francisco, emptying into the Gila by the left bank—during which they passed over rough mountains of dingy rock, and encountered the most serious opposition from the deep ravines and chasms and precipitous bluffs, which everywhere obstructed the way and prevented the march.

From the summit of these mountains, near Sierra del Buso, a magnificent scene opens to view. The Gila, winding its tortuous way through innumerable valleys and deep canyons; the dark, iron-colored peaks of the mountains limiting the horizon toward the southwestward; and the broad plain south of Del Buso, extending from the Del Norte to the Gila, richly carpeted with the grama, all exhibit a picture of a grand and sublime nature. The whole country appears to be a succession of valleys, hills, highlands, rocky ridges, mountains, and lofty peaks of granite, and black, igneous rocks, reaching far above the clouds. It was during their passage through one of these mountain ranges that one of the howitzers and the draft mules tumbled down a steep declivity in the nighttime and entirely disappeared in a deep chasm or ravine, whence they were extricated by Lieut. Davidson after much labor uninjured.

During this march they were necessitated, in consequence of the rocky and precipitous ranges of mountains which frequently traverse the river and through which the water has forced its way in deep canyons and rocky passes, to cross and recross the Gila several times. On one occasion they were compelled to make a detour on the south side of 14 miles to avoid one of those deep, rocky defiles, through which the river flows in dashing falls and foaming cascades, utterly

impassable by man or horse. Also in the valleys near the spurs and
projecting points of the smaller class of mountain ranges the diluvion
is cut into immensely deep gutters and channels, which render the
passage of an army almost impossible.

While encamped on the San Francisco small groups of Gilan
made their appearance on the tops of the distant hills and spurs o
the mountains. They made friendly signals. Hereupon the Ameri
cans called them, and sent Capt. Moore and Lieut. Carson as mes
sengers to them, bearing a white flag. The messengers shook them by
the hand, and spoke to them kindly; but they could not be induced
to come into camp. The reason of their extreme timidity toward
the Americans is said to be this:

They have been harshly dealt with by Americans in the employment of
Chihuahua, who have hunted them at $50 a scalp as we would hunt wolves
and one American decoyed a large number of their brethren in the rear of a
wagon to trade and fired a field piece among them.

This produced great havoc among them and lasting dread of the
Americans.

From thence they passed the Gila again, and having traveled 8
miles, halted to refresh themselves at the head of a canyon preparatory
to commencing the march over the Jornada or sand plain, 60 miles
in extent, without water. Here evidences of a former settlement
were discovered, such as a profusion of red pottery scattered over
the ground. They now, after a few hours rest, began their passage
over a tall, rugged chain of mountains, leaving the river where it
dashed, foaming through the gorge, skirted by clustering alamos
They ascended the mountains by an Indian trail, and, after traveling
10 miles, halted near a spring high up among the masses of rock
This day's march was arduous. Three mules used in drawing the
artillery failed and one of the howitzers got broken. So rough and
inaccessible were the ways that Lieut. Davidson and party were
obliged to abandon the howitzers and come into camp for a guard to
protect them from injury until the next morning. Accordingly a
detail of six men was dispatched long after dark to watch over them
until daydawn, when they were conveyed into camp. This was near
the mouth of the San Francisco.

A novel species of the cactus, which had made its appearance on
the hillsides and among the maguey and Spanish bayonet, deserves to
be noticed. This species, called by the Mexicans pateja, is sometimes
30 feet high, 2½ feet in diameter, bears a fine fruit, and is notched
with 15 flutes, with an interior structure of wood, corresponding to
each of the flutes.

The next morning the Apaches, in considerable numbers, perched
on the distant hilltops and knobs, evinced by friendly signals a desire to hold council with the Americans. After some effort one of
them was induced to trust himself in camp and given some presents:
then came another and another, each in turn gaining confidence that
the Americans did not intend to capture or injure them. They promised to conduct the general to water, 6 miles farther on the route, and
expressed a desire to trade mules to the men. They then went away.
Water was accordingly found.

"The wigwams of the Apaches," observes Capt. Johnston, " scarce
peep above the brushwood of the country, being not more than 4

feet high, slightly dug out in the center, and the dirt thrown around the twigs, which are rudely woven into an oven shape, as a canopy to the house. A tenement of a few hours' work is the home of a family for years or a day."

After a march of four days, wandering and bewildered among the hills and rocks and on the desert, they again reached the river below the canyon, where they rested and awaited the arrival of the howitzers one day. The next day they marched about 18 miles, frequently crossing the Gila and finally encamping on the right bank. Dark, rocky, projecting spurs of the mountains approach near the river, covered with thickets of the mezquite and the creosote plant. The valley was covered in places by the fragments of broken pottery. Some Apaches came to the tops of the mountain peaks and hailed the column, displaying friendly signals. At length they were prevailed on by Capt. Moore to come into camp. They desired to conciliate the Americans. They stayed one night and, having begged tobacco, went away.

The following day they marched down the Gila, crossing from one side to the other not less than a dozen times in 14 miles in consequence of the rough rocky points, which extend to the stream, rendering it impossible to pass altogether on either side* This river, during a greater part of its course, runs through immensely deep valleys, with lofty bluffs on either hand, or through great chasms where the mountains close into the water's edge. In these deep canyons where the bluffs stand perpendicularly and rise to a frightful height the water dashes along, foaming and roaring over the points of rocks, sometimes winding tortuously and sometimes gliding volubly and rectilineally down the vent between the mountains. Pottery was still discovered and the ruins of several ancient buildings.

After a march of 6 miles on the 10th of November, passing over plains which had once sustained a dense population, they came to an extensive ruin, one building of which, called the Hall of Montezuma, is still in a tolerable state of preservation. This building was 50 feet long, 40 wide, and had been four stories high, but the floors and the roof had been burned out. The joists were made of round beams 4 feet in diameter. It had four entrances—north, east, south, and west. The walls were built of sun-dried brick, cemented with natural lime, which abounds in the adjacent country, and were 4 feet thick, having a curved inclination inward toward the top, being smoothed outside and plastered inside. About 150 yards from this building to the northward is a terrace 100 yards long and 70 wide, elevated about 5 feet. Upon this is a pyramid 8 feet high and 25 yards square at the top. From the top of this, which had no doubt been used as a watchtower, the vast plains to the west and northeast for more than 15 miles, lie in plain view. These lands had once been in cultivation, and the remains of a large ascequia or irrigating canal could be distinctly traced along the range of dilapidated houses.

About the same day they came to the Pimo villages on the south side of the Gila. Capt. Johnston observes:

Their answer to Carson when he went up and asked for provisions was, "Bread is to eat; not to sell; take what you want." The general asked a Pimo who made the house I had seen. "It is the Casa de Montezuma," said he. "it was built by the son of a most beautiful woman who once dwelt in yon mountain. She was fair and all the handsome men came to court her: but in vain. When they came they paid tribute, and out of this small store she fed all people in times of famine, and it did not diminish. At last as she lay asleep a drop of rain fell upon her navel and she became pregnant and brought forth a son, who was the builder of all these houses."

He appeared unwilling to discourse further about them, as though some melancholy fate had befallen the people who formerly inhabited them. These were his ancestors. At length, observing that there were a great many similar buildings in the north, south, and west, he was silent. Some other Pimos Cocomiracopas visited the camp. Messengers were now sent into their villages to purchase melons, fruits, and provisions. These soon came, although the distance was several miles. They wanted white beads for what they had to sell and knew the value of money. Seeing us eating the interpreter told the general that he had tasted the liquor of Sonora and New Mexico and would like to taste a sample of that of the United States. The dog had a liquorish tooth, and when given a drink of French brandy pronounced it better than any he had ever tasted. The Mirocopa messenger came to ask the general what his business was and where he was going. He said his people were at peace with all the world, except some of their neighbors, the Apaches, and they did not desire any more enemies. He was, of course, told to say to his chief that our object was merely to pass peaceably through their country; that we had heard a great deal of the Pimos and knew them to be a good people.

These Pimos approached the Americans with the greatest confidence and suavity of manners, possessing a natural grace of carriage, great good humor, and unbounded loquacity. They are a virtuous, honest, and industrious race and subsist entirely by agriculture and grazing and clothe themselves with woolen and cotton fabrics of their own manufacture. The Pimos and Cocomiracopas at present live neighbors to each other, the latter having recently migrated from the mouth of the Gila and the Colorado. They are distinct races and speak different tongues. These, together with the Miracopas, number more than 4,000 souls.

CHAPTER XIII.

" On the morning of the 12th," says Capt. Johnston, " we awoke to hear the crowing of the cock and the baying of the watchdog, reminding us of civilization afar off in the green valleys of our country." Leaving some mules with the chief barrebutt, they marched down through the settlements of the Pimos and Cocomiracopas, all of which are on the south side of the Gila, and having completed a distance of 15 miles encamped near the base of a mountain lying west of their villages. Both the houses and costumes of these Indians are similar. Their winter lodges consist of a ribwork of poles, about 15 feet in diameter, of convenient height, thatched with twigs and straw and covered over with a layer of dirt, in the center of which they build their fires. Their summer shelters are of a much more temporary nature, being constructed after the manner of a common arbor, covered with willow rods, to obstruct the rays of the vertical sun. " The fable of the Pimos is," says our author, " that their first parents were caught up to heaven, and from that time God lost sight of them, and they wandered to the west; that they came from the rising sun." The chief of the Pimos said to the general " that God had placed him over his people, and he endeavored to do the best for them. He gave them good advice, and they had fathers and grandfathers who gave them good advice also. They were told to take nothing but what belonged to them and to ever speak the truth. They desired to be at peace with everyone; therefore they would not join us or the Mexicans in our difficulties." He shook hands with us and bade us welcome, and hoped we might have good luck on our journey. He said we would find the chief of the Maricopas, a man like himself, and one who gave similar counsel to his people.

The entire plains adjacent are susceptible of irrigation and have once sustained a numerous population, as is evidently shown by the ruins, and the remains of pottery scattered over the earth. These indications of the existence of a former race are still more numerous on the Salt and San Francisco Rivers.

The next morning, while they lay in camp, preparatory to commencing the march over the tesotal jornada, or journey of 40 miles without water, the chiefs of the Comomiracopas visited the general, and through an interpreter said: " You have seen our people. They do not steal. They are perhaps better than others you have seen. All of our people have sold you provisions. It is good to do so when people have commodities to exchange. If you had come here hungry and poor, it would have afforded us pleasure to give you all you wanted without compensation. Our people desire to be friendly with the Americans."

From thence in 10 days' march, following the course of the Gila, they came to the confluence of that stream with the Colorado, near

which they encamped. Just before their arrival at this place signs
of a body of horsemen were discovered along the river, which excited some apprehension. It was at first conjectured that it might
be Gen. Castro, on his way from Sonora, with a body of cavalry, to
regain California. Lieut. Emory, with 20 men, was sent out to reconnoiter, when presently he discovered it to be some Californians,
with 500 horses, on their way to Sonora. He brought a few of them
to the general, one of whom said: "There is a party of 800 armed
Californians in the Pueblo de los Angeles opposed to the Americans,
and also a party of 200 at San Diego, friendly to the United States."
Another said: "The Mexicans at the Pueblo de los Angeles are quiet,
and the Americans have quiet possession of the whole country."
They both agreed that there were three ships of the line at San
Diego. The next morning a few of them were again brought into
camp, one of whom was discovered by Lieut. Emory to have in his
possession a package of letters. Some of these letters were directed
to Gen. Castro. The seals were broken and the letters read by Gen.
Kearney. One of the letters gave an account of an insurrection in
California and the placing of Don Flores at the head of the insurrectionists at Pueblo de los Angeles. This was addressed to Gen. Castro.
In another letter to a different person it was asserted that a body of
80 Mexican cavalry had vanquished 400 Americans at the ravines
between the Pueblo and San Pedro and captured a cannon called
Teazer. These leters were resealed by Capt. Turner and returned
to the Mexican, who was then dismissed with them. The general now
supplied his men with fresh animals, as many of theirs by this time
had failed in crossing the deserts and mountains. They now rested
two days before starting upon the desert, or jornada, of 90 miles
without water, which lay on the route.

They passed the great Colorado of the west, below the mouth of
the Gila, which was deep and rapid; yet all got over safely and began
the march upon the desert, which was continued with little intermission three days and nights, when they came to the Camisa, where
they found a supply of water in a canyon of the mountains. Here
they enjoyed the advantage of a little repose. Thence they marched
over a rugged, rocky road, among hills and mountains, and after four
days came to Warner's rancho, during which they lost many animals
and suffered much from hunger and fatigue, being compelled to subsist a part of the time on horseflesh. Here again they rested.

This rancho is 60 miles from San Diego and 80 from the Pueblo
de los Angeles. Learning that there was a herd of mules 15 miles
from this place belonging to Don Flores, the leader of the insurgents
at the pueblo, Lieut. Davidson, with 27 men, was dispatched by Gen.
Kearney at dark, with instructions to procure a sufficient number of
horses and mules to remount the men. About this time Mr. Stokes
an Englishman, came to Gen. Kearney and informed him "that
Commodore Stockton, with the greater part of his naval force, was
at San Diego." The general immediately dispatched a letter to the
commodore, informing him of his arrival in the country and expressing his intention to march directly to San Diego. The next day
Lieut. Davidson and Carson returned, having in possession a large
mulada. In a short time a party of French and Englishmen and a
Chilean came to claim their stock, averring their intention to leave
the country. The general restored them a portion of the animals and
put the remainder into service.

From thence on the 4th of December they advanced 15 miles and came to the old mission of Santa Isabella, en route to San Diego, where it was Gen. Kearney's intention to communicate with the naval force under Commodore Stockton; and " on the 5th " observes Mr. Stanley, who accompanied Gen. Kearney on this expedition, " we met Capt. Gillespie and Lieut. Beall, of the United States Navy, with an escort of 35 men. After making a late camp, Gen.. Kearney heard that an armed body of Californians was encamped about 9 miles from us. Lieut. Hammond, with a small party, was sent out to reconnoiter. He returned about 12 o'clock with intelligence that the camp was in the valley of San Pascual, but learned nothing of the extent of the force, although it was thought to be about 160. At 2 o'clock on the morning of the 6th the reveille sounded, and at 3 our force was formed in the order of battle and the march resumed. We arrived about daylight at the valley. The enemy were encamped about a mile from the declivity of the mountain over which we came, and as Lieut. Hammond had been discovered on the night previous, the Californians were waiting in their saddles for our approach.

" From a misapprehension of an order, the charge was not made by our whole force or with as much precision as was desirable, but the Californians retreated on firing a single volley to an open plain about half a mile distant. Capt. Johnston and one private were killed in this charge. The retreat of the enemy was followed with spirit by our troops, skirmishing the distance of half a mile. When they reached the plains our force was somewhat scattered by the pursuit. The Californians, taking advantage of this disorganization, fought with desperation, making great havoc with their lances. It was a real hand-to-hand fight, and lasted half an hour. They were, however, driven from the field, with what loss we could not learn. Our loss was severe, 17 being killed and 14 wounded. Among the killed were Capt. Johnston, who led the charge of the advance guard; Capt. Benj. Moore, and Lieut. Hammond. Gen. Kearney, Capt. Gillespie, and Lieut. William H. Warner were slightly wounded. Several noncommissioned officers were killed.

" We encamped on the field and collected the dead. At first, Gen. Kearney thought to move on the same day. The dead were lashed on mules, and remained two hours, or more, in that posture. It was a sad and melancholy picture. We soon found, however, that our wounded were unable to travel. The mules were released of their packs, and the men engaged in fortifying the place for the night. During the day the enemy were in sight, curveting their horses, keeping our camp in constant excitement. Three of Capt. Gillespie's volunteers started with dispatches to Commodore Stockton. The dead were buried at night, and ambulances made for the wounded; and the next morning we started in face of the enemy's spies, being then about 38 miles from San Diego. In our march we were constantly expecting an attack—spies could be seen on the top of every hill, but with a force of 100 men, many of whom were occupied with the care of the wounded, we did not leave our trail.

" We had traveled about 7 miles, when, just before sunset, we were again attacked. The enemy came charging down a valley—about 100 men, well mounted. They were about dividing their force, probably with a view of attacking us in front and rear, when Gen. Kearney ordered his men to take possession of a hill on our left. The enemy, seeing the movement, struck for the same point, reaching it before us, and as we ascended they were pouring a very spirited fire upon us from behind the rocks. They were soon driven from the hill, only one or two being wounded on our side. Here, therefore, we were compelled to encamp, and also to destroy the most cumbersome of our camp equipage. A white flag was sent to Señor Pico, the Californian commandant, and an exchange of prisoners effected—our bearers of dispatches having been intercepted by the enemy. We were more fortunate in getting an express through to San Diego for a reinforcement, and at the expiration of four days, during which we lived on the meat of mules, horses, and colts, without bread or other condiment, we were joined by a reenforcement of 200 men, and on the 11th of December resumed our march. Not a Californian was to be seen as we proceeded, and on the 12th we reached San Diego and received from the officers a hearty welcome," having completed a march of 1,090 miles from Santa Fe.

Another account makes the American loss 20 killed and 15 wounded; among the former were Capts. Moore and Johnston and Lieut. Hammond, of the First Dragoons; Sergts. Moore, Whitehurst, and Cox, and Corpls. Clapin and West, and 10 privates of the First Dragoons, 1 private of the topographical engineers, and 1 volunteer. The wounded were Gen. Kearney; Lieut. Warner, of the topographical engineers; Capts. Gillespie and Gibson, of the Volunteers, and Mr. Robidou, interpreter, and 10 privates of the First Dragoons. Gen. Kearney's official account of this hard-fought action is as follows:

As the day dawned on the 6th of December we approached the enemy (160) at San Pascual, who was already in the saddle, when Capt. Johnston made a furious charge upon them with his advance guard, and was in a short time after supported by the dragoons, soon after which the enemy gave way, having kept up from the beginning a continual fire upon us. Upon the retreat of the enemy Capt. Moore led off rapidly in pursuit, accompanied by the dragoons, mounted on horses, and was followed, though slowly, by the others on their tired mules. The enemy were mounted, and among the best horsemen in the world. After retreating about half a mile and seeing an interval between Capt. Moore, with his advance, and the dragoons coming to his support, rallied their whole force, charged with their lances, and, on account of their greatly superior numbers, but few of us in front remained untouched. For five minutes they held the ground from us, when, our men coming up, we again drove them, and they fled from the field, not to return to it, which we occupied and encamped upon.

A most melancholy duty now remains for me; it is to report the death of my aid-de-camp, Capt. Johnston, who was shot dead at the commencement of the action; of Capt. Moore, who was lanced just previous to the final retreat of the enemy; and of Lieut. Hammond, also lanced, and who survived but a few hours. We had also killed 2 sergeants, 2 corporals, and 10 privates of the First Dragoons, 1 private of the Volunteers, and one man, an engage in the topographical department. Our howitzers were not brought into action. The enemy proved to be a party of about 160 Californians, under command of Andres Pico, brother of the late governor; the number of their dead and wounded must have been considerable, though I had no means of ascertaining how many, as just previous to their final retreat they carried off all except six.

After the strife of the battle was over the surgeon came to Gen. Kearney, who sat bleeding at three wounds, and offered to afford him all the relief that was in his power. " First go and dress the wounds of the soldiers," said he, " who require attention more than I do, and when you have done, then come to me." The surgeon proceeded to execute the order; but while busily employed he looked around and saw the general fall backward, exhausted by loss of blood. The surgeon immediately ran to his support, raised him from the ground, restored him, and dressed his wounds.

CHAPTER XIV.

Col. Stevenson—Commodore Sloat and Lieut. Col. Fremont—Gen. Castro—Commodore Stockton—The revolution in California—Mr. Talbot—The insurgents under Flores and Pico—Gen. Kearney marches upon Angeles—Battles of San Gabriel and the Mesa—Capital recovered—The capitulation.

It is not proposed in this chapter to give a historical account of the movements of the Pacific squadron, commanded by Commodores Sloat and Stockton in taking possession of the coast of California, nor, indeed, of the land forces under Lieut. Col. Fremont, except so far as may serve to illustrate the operations of Gen. Kearney while in that country.

In the instructions furnished Gen. Kearney by the War Department on the 12th of September, 1846, he was assured that a regiment of volunteers had been raised in the State of New York, commanded by Col. J. D. Stevenson, whose term of service would not expire until the close of the War with Mexico, which would immediately sail for California, and would, when arrived there, constitute a portion of his command, to act as land forces. The Secretary of War, writing to Gen. Kearney under date of June 3, 1846, further adds:

It is expected that the naval forces of the United States, which are now, or soon will be, in the Pacific, will be in possession of all the towns on the seacoast, and will cooperate with you in the conquest of California. Arms, ordnance, munitions of war, and provisions to be used in that country will be sent by sea to our squadron in the Pacific for the use of the land forces.

A company of United States Artillery, commanded by Capt. Tompkins, aided by Lieut. Halleck, engineer, was also dispatched to the bay of Monterey to cooperate with Gen. Kearney and the marine forces in holding possession of California.

In the month of July, 1846, Commodore John D. Sloat, commanding the United States naval forces in the Pacific Ocean, acting in anticipation of instructions from the Navy Department and on his own responsibility and clear conception of duty as a naval officer (having on the 7th heard of the existence of war between the United States and Mexico), anchored in the Bay of Monterey with the Pacific Squadron, and in less than 24 hours raised the American flag in the old capital of the country. The gallant marines, led on by the commodore, proceeded on land, invested the city, and, without bloodshed or strenuous opposition, took formal possession in the name of the Government of the United States.

About the same period a corps of volunteers, consisting of American emigrants to California, commanded by Gen. Ide and Capt. Grigsby, raised the independent flag of the "Bear and the Star" in the settlements on the Sacramento and held that part of the Province in quiet possession. Their intention was to establish an independent government of their own in the event the United States

117

forces did not cooperate with them in wresting the country from the hands of the haughty Mexicans. These were styled the "Bear men." Lieut. Col. Fremont was at this period on the Bay of San Francisco, near the settlements of Sonoma, in command of the topographical corps, which had gone out from Missouri early in 1846, and a few California volunteers. Hearing of the capture of Monterey, he ventured to raise the standard of his country, that he might cooperate with the naval forces in the peaceable conquest of California. Thus was California bloodlessly and peaceably commenced to be revolutionized and placed under the American flag and American protection. The cities and settlements were soon occupied by the American arms, and the inhabitants, at first, treated with a clemency and consideration which very much conciliated and disposed them to desire a peace and connection with the United States. They were accordingly protected in their persons and property in the amplest manner.

This brilliant and highly important service having been rendered the country in a manner that met the cordial approval of the Executive, Commodore Sloat, whose modesty is only equaled by his gallantry, returned to the United States, leaving Commodore R. F. Stockton commander in chief of the coast and of the bays and harbors. Commodore Stockton, in his instructions from the Navy Department, was permitted to establish in California a temporary civil government until the same should be abrogated or modified by competent authority. It may not be amiss in this connection to observe that Commodore Sloat had been instructed by Mr. Bancroft, Secretary of the Navy, to blockade and hold possession of the bays and ports of San Francisco, Monterey, and San Diego, and, if he deemed it advisable, also to hold the ports of Guymas, Mazatlan, and Acapulco in a state of vigorous blockade. These instructions descended to Commodore Stockton, his successor in the command of the Pacific naval forces.

Commodore R. F. Stockton and Lieut. Col. J. C. Fremont completed the conquest which the gallant and modest Commodore John D. Sloat and his marines had so gloriously and auspiciously begun. In a short time the whole of California was in the hands of the Americans, and the American flag waved from every important place in the country. The civil functions of the government were at an end, and the governor and his forces dispersed amongst the mountains and deserts. Gen. Castro, commander in chief, with a small body of men, escaped to Sonora, having addressed the subjoined proclamation to the Californians:

Fellow citizens: I carry away my heart full of the heaviest weight in taking leave of you. I go out of the country in which I was born, but in the hope of returning to destroy the slavery in which I leave you. I will come the day in which our unfortunate country can chastise exemplarily an usurpation so rapacious and so unjust and in the face of the world exact satisfactions for its wrongs. My friends, I confide in your loyalty and patriotism, and in proof of the confidence which you merit from me I leave to you my wife and innocent children. They have no fortune, and are even without means of subsisting. I leave them to your favor and guidance, considering that I lose all to save national honor.

I acknowldge the faithfulness that you have constantly manifested toward me. I believe it is right for me to exhort you again not to abandon the sentiments of fidelity for the mother country; preserve in your bosoms the holy fire of liberty, and the day of vengeance will come. Never deny the Mexican name. Fellow citizens, adieu. In taking leave of you I feel my soul inundated with bitterness, considering I leave you as slaves; but the glorious day will come when you will break your chains and again be free and independent. God and liberty.

Commodore Stockton next proceeded with a part of his force to San Pedro, where, disembarking them, he formed a junction with Lieut. Col. Fremont, in command of a small body of California volunteers who had been recently enrolled for the service. With their united forces they now marched to the Pueblo de los Angeles, the new capital of the country. Upon their approach Gen. Castro and his troops fled without offering the slightest resistance. The Americans entered the city and raised the flag of the Stars and Stripes. Commodore Stockton, having issued a proclamation to the people of California setting forth certain obnoxious ordinances and regulations, which subsequently proved the ground of the attempted revolution of Flores and Pico, and leaving Capt. Gillespie with 19 volunteers to garrison the capital, returned to San Pedro. Not long afterwards the revolution breaking out, the insurgents compelled Capt. Gillespie to capitulate and retire with his slender force to San Pedro. It is due to Capt. Gillespie, however, to state that the capitulation, under the circumstances, was highly honorable to him and his men. The forces of the enemy were overwhelming. The capital was now repossessed by the Californians.

Meanwhile Mr. Talbot, of the topographical corps, under Lieut. Col. Fremont, who had been stationed with 16 men at Santa Barbara, was hotly beseiged by an insurrectionary force for a considerable time. Finally, however, he and his men, with much peril and difficulty, effected their escape to the mountains. After wandering among the rocks and fastnesses for several days, and suffering incredibly from fatigue, hunger, and other privations, they arrived at Monterey in the greatest destitution.

Not far from this period Commodore Stockton, leaving a sufficient garrison in Monterey and a part of the fleet in the bay, sailed with three ships of war for the harbor of San Diego with the view of marching thence against the insurgents, who were posted in considerable numbers at the Pueblo de los Angeles. At San Diego, on the 12th of December, he formed a junction of his marine and volunteer forces with the overland detachment of the First Dragoons of the United States Army, under immediate command of Gen. Kearney. The malcontents had concentrated at Angeles and armed themselves with the design of recovering the country from the hands of the Americans. They were 600 strong and were headed by Don Mariana Flores and Don Andres Pico, the latter of whom commanded the Californians on the 6th of December in the action at San Pascual. Having compelled the garrison, which was stationed at Angeles upon the conquest of the country to capitulate; driven all the Americans from the interior to the seaboard; and come near defeating the marine expedition of Capt. Marvine, the insurgents confidently hoped to reestablish the former power and government of California.

On the 29th of December Gen. Kearney and Commodore Stockton, in joint command of 500 men, consisting of marines, California volunteers, a detachment of the First Dragoons of the United States Army, and a battery of artillery, left San Diego upon the march against the insurgent forces at the Pueblo de los Angeles, a distance of 145 miles. The entire force was on foot, with the exception of about 60 volunteer mounted riflemen, commanded by Capt. Gillespie.

On the 8th of January the insurgents showed themselves, 600 strong, with four pieces of artillery, occupying the heights, prepared to dispute the passage of the river San Gabriel. Gen. Kearney now drew up his forces in order of battle, passed the river under a heavy fire from the enemy, charged the heights, drove him from his strong position, and gained a most signal victory. This action lasted one hour and a half. The next day (the 9th), continuing the march toward the capital, on the plains of the mesa, the insurgents, having concealed their forces and cannon under the cover of a ravine until the Americans were within gunshot, opened a galling fire upon their right flank and at the same instant charged them in front and rear. In a short time, however, the insurgents were repulsed with considerable loss and driven from the field. The loss of the Americans on both days was 2 killed and 15 wounded; that of the enemy was estimated in killed and wounded at no less than 85. On the 10th the Americans repossessed the city without further opposition, while the bayonets and lances of the retreating insurgents glittered on the adjacent hills and mountains.

Lieut. Col. Fremont, with his battalion of 400 mounted California volunteers, whom he had recently enrolled for the service in the settlements of New Helvetia, Sonoma, and the northern districts, had performed a march of 120 miles, from Santa Barbara to San Fernando, while Gen. Kearney was marching from San Diego, in the hope that the former would be able to effect a junction with him in time to cooperate against the malcontents. In this expectation, however, the general was disappointed.

After the battle of the 9th Andres Pico, the second in command of the insurgent forces, having, as some say, more than once forfeited his parole of honor, and expecting little clemency from Gen. Kearney, escaped with a few of his adherents, and on the 12th, meeting Lieut. Col. Fremont on his way to Angeles, effected with that officer (who as yet was not fully apprised of what had transpired) a stipulation securing immunity for his crimes. This treaty was afterwards approved by the commander in chief from motives of policy. The following is Commodore Stockton's account of the affair:

HEADQUARTERS, CIUDAD DE LOS ANGELES,
January 11, 1847.

SIR: I have the honor to inform you that it has pleased God to crown our poor efforts to put down the rebellion and to retrieve the credit of our arms with the most complete success. The insurgents determined, with their whole force, to meet us on our march from San Diego to this place, and to decide the fate of the territory by a general battle.

Having made the best preparation I could in the face of a boasting and vigilant enemy, we left San Diego on the 20th day of December (that portion of the insurgent army who had been watching and annoying us having left to join the main body) with about 600 fighting men, composed of the detachment from the ships, aided by Gen. Kearney with a detachment of 60 men on foot, from the first regiment of United States dragoons, and by Capt. Gillespie, with 60 mounted riflemen.

We marched nearly 140 miles in 10 days, and found the rebels on the 8th day of January in a strong position on the high bank of the River San Gabriel, with 600 mounted men and four pieces of artillery, prepared to dispute our passage across the river.

We waded through the water, dragging our guns after us, against the galling fire of the enemy, without exchanging a shot until we reached the opposite shore, when the fight became general, and our troops having repelled a charge of the enemy charged up the bank in a most gallant manner and gained a complete victory over the insurgent army.

The next day on our march across the plains of the mesa to this place, the insurgents made another depserate effort to save the capital and their own necks. They were concealed with their artillery in a ravine until we came within gunshot, when they opened a brisk fire from their fieldpieces on our right flank and at the same time charged on our front and rear. We soon silenced their guns and repelled the charge, when they fled and permitted us the next morning to march into town without any further opposition.

We have rescued the country from the hands of the insurgents, but I fear the absence of Col. Fremont's battalion of mounted riflemen will enable most of the Mexican officers who have broken their parole to escape to Sonora.

I am happy to say that our loss in killed and wounded does not exceed 20, whilst we are informed that the enemy has lost between 70 and 80.

This dispatch must go immediately, and I will await another opportunity to furnish you with the details of these two battles and the gallant conduct of the officers and men under my command, with their names.

Faithfully, your obedient servant,

R. F. STOCKTON,
Commodore, etc.

To the Hon. GEORGE BANCROFT,
Secretary of the Navy, Washington, D. C.

HEADQUARTERS, CIUDAD DE LOS ANGELES, .
January 15, 1847.

SIR: I have the honor to inform you of the arrival of Lieut. Col. Fremont at this place, with 400 men; that some of the insurgents have made their escape to Sonora, and that the rest have surrendered to our arms.

Immediately after the battles on the 8th and 9th they began to disperse, and I am sorry to say that their leader, Jose Ma. Flores, made his escape and that the others have been pardoned by a capitulation agreed upon by Lieut. Col. Fremont.

Jose Ma. Flores, the commander of the insurgent forces, two or three days previous to the 8th, sent two commissioners with a flag of truce to my camp to make a "treaty of peace." I informed the commissioners that I could not recognize Jose Ma. Flores, who had broken his parole, as an honorable man or as one having any rightful authority or worthy to be treated with; that he was a rebel in arms; and that if I caught him, I would have him shot. It seems that, not being able to negotiate with me and having lost the battles of the 8th and 9th, they met Col. Fremont on the 12th instant on his way here, who, not knowing what had occurred, entered into a capitulation with them, which I now send you; and, although I refused to do it myself, still I have thought it best to approve it.

The Territory of California is again tranquil, and the civil government formed by me is again in operation in the places where it was interrupted by the insurgents.

Col. Fremont has 400 men in his battalion, which will be quite sufficient to preserve the peace of the Territory, and I will immediately withdraw my sailors and marines and sail as soon as possible for the coast of Mexico, where I hope they will give a good account of themselves.

Faithfully, your obedient servant,

R. F. STOCKTON,
Commodore, etc.

To the Hon. GEORGE BANCROFT,
Secretary of the Navy, Washington, D. C.

To all to whom these presents shall come, greeting:

Know ye that in consequence of propositions of peace or cessation of hostilities being submitted to me, as a commandant of the California battalion of United States forces, which has so far been acceded to by me as to cause me to appoint a board of commissioners to confer with a similar board to be appointed by the Californians, and it requiring a little time to close the negotiations, it is agreed upon and ordered by me that an entire cessation of hostilities shall take place until to-morrow afternoon (Jan. 13), and that the said Californians be permitted to bring in their wounded to the mission of San Fernandez, where also, if they choose, they can remove their camp to facilitate said negotiations.

Given under my hand and seal this 12th day of January, 1847.

J. C. FREMONT,
Lieutenant Colonel, United States Army,
and Military Commander of California.

The commissioners appointed on the part of Lieut. Col. Fremont to settle the terms of the capitulation were Maj. P. B. Reading, L. McLane, and W. H. Russell, formerly of Missouri. Those selected by Andres Pico were J. A. Carrilo and A. Olvera. The first article of this capitulation required the insurgents to deliver up to Lieut. Col. Fremont their artillery and public arms and peaceably return to their homes, yield obedience to the laws of the United States, and not again take up arms during the continuance of the war. They were also required to aid in preserving tranquillity throughout California. In the second article the American commissioners guaranteed to the insurgents protection of life and property, whether on parole or otherwise, immediately upon their complying with the conditions of the first article. The remaining articles were unimportant.

The revolution of Flores was now crushed; the insurgents had taken refuge in the deserts and mountains or dispersed to their several homes; the American flag was again hoisted in every part of the province; and general peace and quietude once more prevailed.

CHAPTER XV.

Having settled the affairs of the Government at Angeles and
restored the supremacy of the laws, wherein they had been interrupted by the insurrectionists, Gen. Kearney and Commodore Stockton hastily returned to San Diego, where they arrived about the 23d
of the same month, the former marching his dismounted dragoons by
land and the latter conducting his marine forces to San Pedro and
sailing thence for the port of San Diego.

It was on this return march that Gen. Kearney, dismounting,
walked 145 miles with the common soldiers, covered with dust and
sweat, having placed on his horse one of the sick men, whose feet
were worn and blistered and who, from exhaustion, was unable to
proceed farther.

About this time the gallant Willard P. Hall, of the Missouri Volunteers, Col. Doniphan's regiment, and Member elect to Congress, came
up, met Gen. Kearney in the road, and reported to him the near approach to California of the Mormon battalion, under command of
Lieut. Col. Cooke. Hereupon Mr. Hall, seeing the general toiling in
the dust with the common soldiers, generously offered him his charger,
observing, " General, take my horse and ride; I am younger than you
and will walk." The general refused, saying, " No, thank you; I am
a soldier and can walk better than you, as I am accustomed to it."

On the 15th of November, 1846, a small detachment of 45 volunteers, commanded by Captains Burrows and Thompson, met and
totally defeated 200 Californians on the plain of Salinas, near Monterey, with considerable slaughter. The loss on the side of the Americans was 4 killed and 2 wounded. Among the former were Capt.
Burrows and Pvt. Ames, of St. Louis, Mo. About the 25th of January, 1847, and shortly after the return of the troops from Angeles
to San Diego, Capt. Emory, of the topographical corps, assistant
acting adjutant general to the overland expedition after the death of
Capt. Johnston, sailed as bearer of dispatches from Gen. Kearney to
Washington City, passing by the Isthmus of Panama.

It will be remembered that the Mormons had not arrived at Santa
Fe when Gen. Kearney took his departure thence for California.
Arriving shortly afterwards, however, Capt. Cooke was dispatched
from the Del Norte, below Socorro, by Gen. Kearney, to conduct them,
as their lieutenant colonel, to their destination, on the Pacific coast,
in the place of Capt. Allen, who died at Fort Leavenworth. Their

outfit being in readiness, they left Santa Fe and commenced their march on Sunday, the 18th day of October, 1846, following the route of Gen. Kearney down the Rio del Norte to a point 25 miles below the Jornada Mountain, where they struck off westerly over the southern spurs of the Sierra de los Mimbres. Lieut. Col. Cooke, perceiving that these spurs terminated abruptly and that a broad plain spread out to the southward of them, very rightly conjectured that there might be found a pass from the Del Norte to the Gila without encountering a single mountain. He therefore directed his course about 60 miles farther south than that of Gen. Kearney, thence striking out across the high plain, bordered by the precipitous points of the Sierras, out of which flowed cool streams of delicious water. These streams, issuing from the mountains, run down upon and fertilize the plain and lose themselves in the sand not far distant.

Before leaving the Del Norte Valley, Lieut. Col. Cooke sent a part of his baggage train, and all the sick Mormons back to Fort Pueblo, on the Arkansas, above Fort Bent, at which place a large number of Mormon families were collecting, with the view of emigrating to California early in the spring of 1847. Accordingly, an emigration of not less than 900 Mormon families started from this and other points, including the Council Bluffs, and are now on their way thither.

Also Lieut. Abert, of the Topographical Corps, with a small party returned to the United States about the same time, passing the plains in the inclement season of winter. Being caught in a snowstorm about the 20th of February, which continued without intermission for 36 hours, some of his men froze to death, and the Pawnees robbed him of all his mules and other animals.

Lieut. Col. Cooke, with his troops, now prosecuted his march over the high plain, through an aperture in the great Cordilleras, finding generally water and pasture, and meeting with no opposition on his way. He passed the deserted village, San Bernadino, which had once been very rich in cattle and other herds, but was now entirely abandoned on account of the frequent and desolating incursions of the Apaches. Thence he passed over to the San Pedro River, down which he continued his march for 60 miles. Thence striking off, he passed through Teuson, and arrived at the Gila, intersecting Gen. Kearney's route at the Pimo settlement.

On a certain occasion, the guides desired Lieut. Col. Cooke to march from the Ojo Vacca to Yanos in Chihuahua. This at first he assented to, but finding that the route urged by his guides led him too far south, he struck directly west, and found water after a march of 12 miles. The next day he marched southwesterly, and encamped at night without water. At daybreak on the morning following, his command was again in motion, and after marching about 25 miles arrived at a plain destitute of grass or other vegetation, and as smooth and hard as polished marble; upon which neither the nails of the shod animals nor the iron tires of the loaded wagons produced the slightest impression, extending 40 or 50 miles from north to south and 2 or 3 miles wide. Immediately after crossing this hard plain (resembling the dry bed of a lake) in its narrowest direction, the party came upon springs furnishing an abundance of cool and delightful water. Here they all rejoiced and took rest.

On another occasion, when Lieut. Col. Cooke and his party were encamped within about 6 miles of the little town of Teuson, in the State of Sonora, where 150 dragoons and two pieces of artillery had been stationed, the commandante having express orders from the governor not to permit their passage, three commissioners were sent into camp to inquire into Col. Cooke's business and intentions, and to ask what terms he would exact of them in passing through the place. The commissioners also entreated him not to pass through the town, but to turn aside and march in some other direction, assuring him that he could do this with impunity and without molestation. He, however, told them that he would require of the commandante one piece of artillery and certain small arms, and the submission of the place; the arms and cannon to be restored to them upon his departure. The commissioners then retired.

The next morning the lieutenant colonel, with his troops drawn up in order of battle, marched directly toward the town. Upon approaching it, he was met by a messenger, who said: "Sir, your terms are hard and such as the commandante never can and never will accede to." Whereupon the messenger returned. Col. Cooke now passed the order down the lines to "load." However, the men did not load their pieces, for very soon a great dust was seen to rise beyond the town, and a body of horsemen at a distance scampering off across the plain with the utmost expedition, leaving behind only such as were too old and helpless to effect their escape by flight. The men now entered the place, where they found an abundance of wheat for their animals and some fruit and provisions to satisfy their keen appetites. Therefore all now fared well. Then they resumed the march.

Upon arriving at the Pimo villages or settlements, the chief of this honest and simple race of people delivered to Lieut. Col. Cooke a letter and a bale of Indian goods, which Gen. Kearney had left in his charge for that purpose. He also delivered to him 22 mules, which, having failed, Gen. Kearney had abandoned at different places. The Pimo Indians had collected these together, knowing that Cooke's forces were to pass that way. This is a remarkable instance of the honesty and good faith of the Pimos, a very peculiar and interesting race of people. "The Sonorans," said the honest chief, "have endeavored several times to prevail on me, both by promises and threats, to deliver this property up to them, but I would let nobody have it except my friend, Gen. Kearney, or some of his people." Lieut. Col. Cooke commended him for his strict honesty and integrity, and told him that in acting thus he would always enjoy the friendship and good opinion of the Americans. They then separated.

Now falling into Gen. Kearney's trail they marched down the Gila, crossed the Colorado below the confluence of the two rivers, proceeded through the Jornada of 90 miles in extent, and arrived at San Diego about the close of January, 1847, as already related. Meanwhile Commodore Shubrick arrived at Monterey on the 15th of January, on board the *Independence*, and superseded Commodore Stockton in command of the Pacific Squadron and the coast of California.

Gen. Kearney,[1] with Capt. Turner and Lieut. Warner, of the Topographical Corps, on the 2d of February went aboard the war vessel *Cyane* and proceeded directly to Monterey, leaving the Mormons at San Diego, and Lieut. Col. Fremont, in command of the California battalion at the Pueblo de los Angeles, as temporary governor of the country, acting under appointment from Commodore Stockton; Angeles now being considered the capital and seat of the new government.

Upon his arrival at Monterey Gen. Kearney waited upon Commodore Shubrick, then in command of the fleet in the bay, and let him know his instructions from the War Department, and the extent of his authority. Commodore Shubrick, and subsequently Commodore Biddle, most heartily and cordially cooperated with Gen. Kearney in carrying out his instructions. Thus harmony existed between the land and naval forces. Gen. Kearney, for certain reasons,[2] however, refused to organize for the people of California a civil government similar to that which he had previously provided for the inhabitants of New Mexico, as his instructions permitted him.

On the 1st day of March, 1847, Gen. Kearney assumed the reins of the civil government (Commodore Shubrick being in command of the naval forces), and on the same day issued the following proclamation to the inhabitants of California:

The President of the United States having devolved on the undersigned the civil government of California, he enters upon the discharge of his duties with an ardent desire to promote, as far as possible, the interests of the country and well being of its inhabitants.

The undersigned is instructed by the President to respect and protect the religious institutions of California, to take care that the religious rights of its inhabitants are secured in the most ample manner, since the Constitution of the United States allows to every individual the privilege of worshiping his Creator in whatever manner his conscience may dictate.

The undersigned is also instructed to protect the persons and property of the quiet and peaceable inhabitants of the country, against each and every enemy, whether foreign or domestic; and now assuring the Californians that his inclinations no less than his duty demand the fulfillment of these instructions, he invites them to use their best efforts to preserve order and tranquillity, to promote harmony and concord, and to maintain the authority and efficacy of the laws.

It is the desire and intention of the United States to procure for California as speedily as possible a free government like that of their own Territories, and they will very soon invite the inhabitants to exercise the rights of free citizens in the choice of their own representatives, who may enact such laws as they deem best adapted to their interests and well being. But until this takes place, the laws actually in existence, which are not repugnant to the Constitution of the United States, will continue in force until they are revoked by competent authority, and persons in the exercise of public employments will for the present remain in them, provided they swear to maintain the said Constitution and faithfully to discharge their duties.

The undersigned, by these presents, absolves all the inhabitants of California of any further allegiance to the Republic of Mexico, and regards them as citizens of the United States. Those who remain quiet and peaceable will be protected in their rights, but should any take up arms against the government of this Territory, or join such as do so, or instigate others to do so—all these he will regard as enemies, and they will be treated as such.

---

[1] About this time Maj. Swords, quartermaster, was dispatched on board a vessel to the Sandwich Islands to purchase a supply of provisions for the Army, there being no supplies in California.

[2] These reasons were, perhaps, the dissatisfaction that existed among the Americans who had emigrated to California, the acts of Commodore Stockton being partially in force, and the personal responsibility the work would involve.

When Mexico involved the United States in war, the latter had not time to invite the Californians to join their standard as friends, but found themselves compelled to take possession of the country to prevent its falling into the hands of some European power. In doing this there is no doubt that some excesses, some unauthorized acts, were committed by persons in the service of the United States, and that, in consequence, some of the inhabitants have sustained losses in their property. These losses shall be duly investigated, and those entitled to indemnification shall receive it.

For many years California has suffered great domestic convulsions; from civil wars, like poisoned fountains, have flowed calamity and pestilence over this beautiful region. These fountains are now dried up; the Stars and Stripes now float over California, and as long as the sun shall shed its light they will continue to wave over her and over the natives of the country and over those who shall seek a domicile in her bosom, and under the protection of this flag agriculture must advance, and the arts and sciences will flourish like seed in a rich and fertile soil.

Americans and Californians from henceforth one people! Let us, then, indulge one desire, one hope; let that be for the peace and tranquillity of our country. Let us unite like brothers and mutually strive for the improvement and advancement of this our beautiful country, which within a short period can not fail to be not only beautiful but also prosperous and happy.

Given at Monterey, capital of California, this 1st day of March, in the year of our Lord 1847 and of the independence of the United States the seventy-first.

S. W. KEARNEY,
Brigadier General, United States Army, and Governor of California.

Gen. Kearney now sent orders to Lieut. Col. Fremont, at Angeles, requiring him to muster his men into the United States service regularly and agreeably to law and repair with them to Monterey, where they could be mustered for discharge and payment, and also to bring with him the archives of the State and other documents and papers. At the same time he also sent an order to Lieut. Col. Cooke to march with a part of his Mormon force from San Luis Rey to Angeles and relieve Lieut. Col. Fremont. The California volunteers refused to be mustered into service as required, and therefore Lieut. Col. Fremont could not obey the orders of Gen. Kearney. Toward the close of March Lieut. Col. Fremont, unattended, left Angeles and repaired to Monterey. Here he had an interview with Gen. Kearney, who in a short time ordered him back to Angeles to transact certain business important to be accomplished before their returning to the United States. Fremont being delayed in the execution of this work, Gen. Kearney, accompanied by Mr. Hall, of Doniphan's regiment, started for the pueblo, where they arrived on the 12th of May. The general, Mr. Hall, Lieut. Col. Fremont, and others now returned to Monterey, arriving there near the close of the month.

Gen. Kearney, the lawgiver and land traveler, having completed the work assigned him by his Government, and being now on the eve of returning to the United States, disposed his forces in a manner to preserve entire submission and tranquillity in the country. The Mormons, whose term of service would expire on the 16th of July, were stationed at San Diego, San Luis Rey, and Angeles. Col. Stevenson, with two companies of his regiment and one company of the First Dragoons, under Capt. Smith, were also posted at Angeles. One company of Col. Stevenson's regiment and one of light artillery, under Capt. Tompkins, were retained as a garrison in Monterey.

Four companies of the New York regiment, under Lieut. Col. Burton, were garrisoning Santa Barbara, of which force, however, a squadron of two companies, under command of Lieut. Col. Burton, were ordered to proceed by sea to Lower California, where they would disembark at La Paz, hoist the American flag, and take possession of the country. Of this regiment, also, one company, under Capt. Nagle, would remain in the San Joaquin Valley, a detachment of 30 men would stay at Sutter's settlement, and the remainder, under Maj. Hardy, would garrison the town of San Francisco.

Commodore Biddle having returned from China on the 2d of March assumed the chief command of the naval forces on board the *Columbus*. Commodore Shubrick, with the *Independence* and *Cyane*, had been ordered to sail down the coast and blockade the ports of Guymas and Mazatlan. Col. R. B. Mason, of the First Dragoons, who was sent out by the Government for the purpose, was left commander in chief of all the land forces and ex officio governor of California. Therefore, on the 31st of May, Gen. Kearney took his departure from Monterey and in company with Lieut. Col. Cooke, Maj. Swords, Capt. Turner, and Lieut. Radford of the Navy, also Lieut. Col. Fremont, the Hon. Willard P. Hall, Asst. Surg. Sanderson, and 13 of the Mormon battalion and 19 of Lieut. Col. Fremont's topographical party, making an aggregate of 40 men, returned to the United States by way of the Southern Pass and arrived at Fort Leavenworth on the 22d [1] of August following, having twice crossed the continent. On the 21st of June this party passed the main ridge of the Sierra Nevada, riding 35 miles chiefly over snow from 5 to 25 feet deep, under which water was running, and in many places in great torrents. Near the Great Salt Lake Gen. Kearney and escort humanely gathered up and buried the bones of the emigrant party who so miserably and wretchedly perished of cold and hunger during the winter of 1846. Gen. Kearney immediately repaired to Washington, whence he will proceed to Southern Mexico and join Gen. Scott's division of the Army. Thus terminated the overland expedition to California, which scarcely meets with a parallel in the annals of history.

---

[1] Gen. K. arrested Col. Fremont on their arrival at Fort Leavenworth August 22. The trial is now in progress at Washington. Commodore Stockton and suite left the settlements of California on the 19th of July and, by the overland route, arrived at St. Joseph in October.

CHAPTER XVI.

Concentration of the forces at Valverde—Mitchell's escort—Passage of the great "Jornada del Muerto"—Arrival at Don Anna—Frank Smith and the Mexicans—Battle of Brazito—The piratical flag—Doniphan's order—Burial of the dead—False alarm—Surrender of El Paso—Release of American prisoners.

Col. Doniphan, upon his return from the Navajo country, dispatched Lieut. Hinton from Soccorro to Santa Fe with orders to Col. Price, commanding the forces at the capital, to send him 10 pieces of cannon and 125 artillerymen. Col. Doniphan especially requested that he would send Capt. Weightman's company of light artillery, leaving it discretionary with Maj. Clark whether he would remain at Santa Fe or accompany the expedition against Chihuahua. He chose the latter.

The camp at Valverde [2] was made the place of rendezvous at which all the detachments and parcels of the regiment were to reunite. In fact, the regiment was to be reorganized. Lieut. De Courcy was appointed adjutant in the place of G. M. Butler, who died at Cuvarro; Sergt. Maj. Hinton resigned and was elected lieutenant in De Courcy's stead; Palmer, a private, was appointed sergeant major; also Surg. Penn and Asst. Surg. Vaughan, having previously resigned and returned to Missouri, T. M. Morton now became principal surgeon and J. F. Morton and Dr. Moore assistant surgeons.

With indefatigable labor and exertion Lieuts. James Lea and Pope Gordon, assistant quartermaster and commissary, had procured an outfit and a supply of provisions for the expedition. These they had already at Valverde or on the way thither when the detachments returned from the campaign against the Navajos. The merchant trains had received permission to advance slowly down the country until the Army should take up the line of march, when they were to fall in rear with the baggage and provision trains, that they might be the more conveniently guarded.

About the 1st of November Dr. Connelly, Doane, McManus, Valdez, and James McGoffin proceeded to El Paso in advance of the Army and contrary to order to ascertain upon what conditions their merchandise could be introduced through the customhouse into the Chihuahua market. They were, immediately upon their arrival at El Paso, seized and conducted under an escort of 26 soldiers to the city of Chihuahua, where they remained in surveillance until liberated by the American Army.

While Col. Doniphan was yet in the mountains Lieut. Col. Mitchell, of the Second Regiment, and Capt. Thompson, of the regular

---

[2] On the 17th day of December, at Valverde, Pvt. W. P. Johnson, of Capt. Waldo's company, was honorably discharged from the service of the United States and permitted to return home to attend to the interests of his constituents, having been chosen a member of the Missouri Legislature.

service, conceived the bold project of opening a communication between Santa Fe and Gen. Wool's army, at that time supposed to be advancing upon Chihuahua. For this purpose a volunteer company consisting of 103 men raised from the different corps at Santa Fe was organized under the name of the " Chihuahua Rangers," commanded by Capt. Hudson and Lieuts. Todd, Sproule, and Gibson. This force having advanced down the valley of the Del Norte some distance below Valverde, and hearing of a strong Mexican force near El Paso, dared not venture farther, but returned and joined Col. Doniphan's column, which was then about being put in motion. All things were now ready for the march.

Accordingly, for the sake of convenience in marching over the " Jornado del Muerto," or Great Desert, which extends from Fray Christobal to Robledo, a distance of 90-miles, the colonel dispatched Maj. Gilpin in the direction of El Paso on the 14th of December, in command of a division of 300 men; on the 16th he started Lieut. Col. Jackson, with an additional force of 200; on the 19th he marched in person with the remainder of his command, including the provision and a part of the baggage trains.

In passing this dreadful desert, which is emphatically the " Journey of the dead," the men suffered much, for the weather was now become extremely cold and there was neither water to drink nor wood for fire. Hence, it was not possible to prepare anything to eat. The soldiers, fatigued with marching, faint with hunger, and benumbed by the piercing winds, straggled along the road at night—for there was not much halting for repose—setting fire to the dry bunches of grass and the stalks of the soap plant, or palmilla, which would blaze up like a flash of powder and as quickly extinguish, leaving the men shivering in the cold. For miles the road was most brilliantly illuminated by sudden flashes of light, which lasted but for a moment, and then again all was dark. At length toward midnight the front of the column would halt for a little repose. The straggling parties would continue to arrive at all hours of the night. The guards were posted out. The men without their suppers laid down upon the earth and rested. The teamsters were laboring incessantly night and day with their trains to keep pace with the march of the Army. By daydawn the reveille roused the tired soldier from his comfortless bed of gravel and called him to resume the march without taking breakfast, for this could not be provided on the desert. Such was the march for more than three days over the Jornado del Muerto.

On the 22d Col. Doniphan overtook the detachments under Lieut. Col. Jackson and Maj. Gilpin near the little Mexican town Dona Ana. Here the soldiers found plenty of grain and other forage for their animals, running streams of water, and abundance of dried fruit, corn meal, and sheep and cattle. These they purchased; therefore they soon forgot their sufferings and privations which they had experienced on the desert. Here they feasted and reposed.

The Army now encamped within the boundaries of the State of Chihuahua. The advanced detachments under Lieut. Col. Jackson and Maj. Gilpin, apprehending an attack from the Mexicans, about the 20th had sent an express to Col. Doniphan, then on the desert, requesting him to quicken his march. Capt. Reid, with his company, had proceeded about 12 miles below Dona Ana for the purpose of making a reconnoissance and of acting as a scout or advanced guard. While encamped in the outskirts of a forest, on a point of hills which commanded the Chihuahua road, on the night of the 23d one of the sentinels hailed the Mexican spies in the Spanish language. The spies, mistaking the sentinel for a friend, advanced very near. At length, discovering their mistake, they wheeled to effect their escape by flight. The sentinel leveled his rifle-yager and discharged the ball through the bodies of two of them. One of them tumbled from his horse, dead, after running a few hundred yards and the other at a greater distance. Their dead bodies were afterwards discovered. This sentinel was Frank Smith, of Saline.

On the morning of the 24th the whole command, including Lieut. Col. Mitchell's escort and the entire merchant, provision, and baggage trains, moved off in the direction of El Paso, and, after a progress of 15 miles, encamped on the river for water. The forage was only moderately good, therefore the animals, which were not tethered, rambled and straggled far off into the adjacent boskets and thickets during the night. The weather was pleasant.

On the morning of the 25th of December a brilliant sun, rising above the Organ Mountains to the eastward, burst forth upon the world in all his effulgence. The little army, at this time not exceeding 800 strong, was comfortably encamped on the east bank of the Del Norte. The men felt frolicksome indeed. They sang the cheering songs of Yankee Doodle and Hail Columbia. Many guns were fired in honor of Christmas Day. But there was no need of all this, had they known the sequel.

At an early hour the colonel took up the line of march with a strong front and rear guard. The rear guard, under Capt. Moss, was delayed for a considerable part of the day in bringing up the trains and the loose animals which had rambled off during the night. A great number of men were also straggling about in search of their lost stock. These were also delayed.

While on the march the men most earnestly desired that, if they had to encounter the enemy at all, they might meet him this day. They were gratified, for having proceded about 18 miles, the colonel pitched his camp at a place called Brazito, or the Little Arm, on the east bank of the river, in an open, level, bottom prairie, bordered next the mountains and river on the east and southeast by a mezquite and willow chaparral. Here the front guard had called a halt.

While the men were scattered everywhere in quest of wood and water for cooking purposes and fresh grass for their animals, and while the trains and straggling men were scattered along the road for miles in the rear, a cloud of dust, greater than usual, was observed in the direction of El Paso, and in less than 15 minutes some one of the advance guard, coming at full speed, announced to the colonel " that the enemy was advancing upon him." [1] The bugler was summoned. Assembly call was blown. The men, dashing down their loads of wood and buckets of water, came running from all quarters, seized their arms, and fell into line under whatever flag

---

[1] It is said that Col Doniphan and several of his officers and men were at this moment engaged in playing a game of three-trick loo. At first he observed that the cloud of dust was perhaps produced by a gust of wind and that they had as well play their hands out. In another moment the plumes and banners of the enemy were plainly in view. The colonel quickly sprang to his feet, threw down his cards, grasped his saber, and observed, ' Boys, I held an invincible hand, but I'll be d—d if I don't have to play it out in steel now." Every man flew to his post.

was most convenient. As fast as those in the rear came up they also fell into line under the nearest standards. The officers dashed from post to post, and in an incredibly short space of time the Missourians were marshaled on the field of fight.

By this time the Mexican general had drawn up his forces in front and on the right and left flanks of Col. Doniphan's lines. Their strength was about 1,300 men, consisting of 514 regular dragoons, an old and well-known corps from Vera Cruz and Zacatecas, and 800 volunteers, cavalry and infantry, from El Paso and Chihuahua, and 4 pieces of artillery. They exhibited a most gallant and imposing appearance, for the dragoons were dressed in a uniform of blue pantaloons, green coats trimmed with scarlet, and tall caps plated in front with brass, on the tops of which fantastically waved a plume of horse hair or buffalo's tail. Their bright lances and swords glittered in the sheen of the sun. Thus marshaled, they paused for a moment.

Meanwhile Col. Doniphan and his field and company officers appeared as calm and collected as when on drill and in the most spirited manner encouraged their men by the memory of their forefathers, by the past history of their country, by the recollection of the Battle of Okeechobee, which was fought on the same day in 1837, and by every consideration which renders life, liberty, and country valuable, to cherish no other thought than that of victory.

Before the battle commenced and while the two armies stood marshaled front to front the Mexican commander, Gen. Poncé de Leon, dispatched a lieutenant to Col. Doniphan bearing a black flag. This messenger, coming with the speed of lightning, halted when within 60 yards of the American lines and waved his ensign gracefully in salutation. Hereupon Col. Doniphan, advancing toward him a little way, sent his interpreter, T. Caldwell, to know his demands. The ambassador said, "The Mexican general summons your commander to appear before him." The interpreter replied, "If your general desires peace, let him come here." The other rejoined, "Then we will break your ranks and take him there." "Come, then, and take him," retorted the interpreter. "Curses be upon you; prepare, then for a charge; we neither ask nor give quarters," said the messenger, and waving his black flag over his head galloped back to the Mexican lines.

At the sound of the trumpet the Vera Cruz dragoons, who occupied the right of the enemy's line of battle, first made a bold charge upon the American left. When within a few rods the yagermen opened a most deadly fire upon them, producing great execution. At the same crisis Capt. Reid with a party of 16 mounted men (for the rest were all on foot) charged upon them, broke through their ranks, hewed them to pieces with their sabers, and thereby contributed materially in throwing the enemy's right wing into confusion. A squad or section of dragoons, having flanked our left, now charged upon the commissary and baggage trains, but the gallant wagoners opened upon them a well-directed fire, which threw them into disorder and caused three of their number to pay the forfeit of their lives.

The Chihuahua infantry and cavalry were posted on their left and consequently operated against our right wing. They advanced within gunshot and took shelter in the chaparral, discharging three rounds upon our lines before we returned the fire. At this crisis Col. Doniphan ordered the men to "lie down on their faces and reserve their fire until the Mexicans came within 60 paces." This was done. The Mexicans, supposing they had wrought fearful execution in our ranks, as some were falling down while others stood up, began

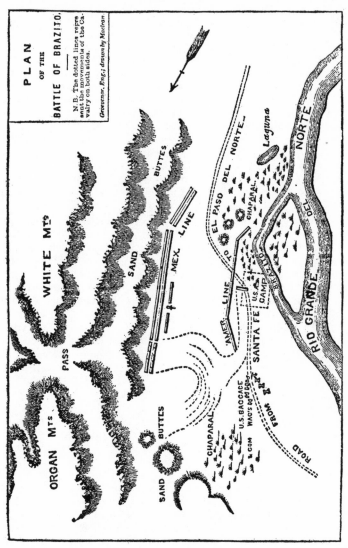

PLAN
OF THE
BATTLE OF BRAZITO.

N. B. The dotted lines represent the movements of the Cavalry on both sides.

Grosvenor, Eng.; drawn by Maclean

WHITE M^{ts}

ORGAN M^{ts}

PASS

SAND BUTTES

CHAPARAL

SAND

BUTTES

MEX. LINE

EL PASO DEL NORTE

Laguna

NORTE

CHAPARAL

AMER. LINE

U.S. CAMP

SANTA FE

RIO GRANDE

DEL

FROM

U.S. BACCAGE

MAC'S Rd 500

1 COM

ROAD

now to advance, and exultingly cry out "Bueno, bueno"; whereupon our whole right wing, suddenly rising up, let fly such a galling volley of yager-balls into their ranks that they wheeled about and fled in the utmost confusion.

By this time the Howard company and others occupying the center had repulsed the enemy with considerable loss, and taken possession of one piece of his artillery and the corresponding ammunition.

This was a brass 6-pound howitzer. Sergt. Calaway and a few others of that company first gained possession of this piece of can non, cut the dead animals loose from it, and were preparing to turn it upon the enemy when Lieut. Kribben, with a file of artillerymen was ordered to man it.[1]

The consternation now became general among the ranks of the Mexicans, and they commenced a precipitate retreat along the base of the mountains. Many of them took refuge in the craggy fast nesses. They were pursued by the Americans about 1 mile; Capt Reid and Capt. Walton, who by this time had mounted a few of hi men, followed them still further. All now returned to camp and congratulated one another on the achievement. The Mexican los was 71 killed, 5 prisoners, and not less than 150 wounded, among whom was their commanding officer, Gen. Poncé de Leon. Also considerable quantity of ammunition, baggage, wine, provisions blankets, guns, and several stands of colors were among the spoils A number of horses were killed and several were captured. The Americans had 8 men wounded, none killed.

In this engagement Col. Doniphan, his officers, and men displayed the utmost courage and determined resolution to conquer or perish in the conflict. Defeat would have been ruinous. Therefore all the companies vied with each other in endeavoring to render the country the most important service. The victory was complete on the part of the Americans. The battle continued about 30 minutes and was fought about 3 o'clock p. m., on Christmas Day, at Brazito 25 miles from El Paso.

Not more than 500 of Col. Doniphan's men were present when the battle commenced. The rest fell into line as they were enabled to reach the scene of action. Those who had been far in the rear dur ing the day when they heard the firing came running in great haste with their arms in their hands, to bring aid to their comrades, who were then engaged with the enemy. This created such a dust that the enemy supposed a strong reinforcement was marching to our sup port. This circumstance, also, contributed to strike terror into the Mexican ranks.

By this defeat the Mexican Army was completely disorganized and dispersed. The volunteer troops returned with the utmost expedi tion to their respective homes, while the regular troops continued their flight to Chihuahua, scarcely halting for refreshment in E Paso. On the retreat many of the wounded died. Several were found dead by the roadside and the chaparral near the battle field was stained with the blood of the retreating foe. The field was all trophied over with the spoils of the slain and the van quished. Martial accouterments, sacks and wallets of provi sions, and gourds of the delicious wines of El Paso were pro fusely scattered over miles of surface. These supplied our soldiers with a Christmas banquet. The whole affair resembled a Christ mas frolic. This night the men encamped on the same spot where they were when attacked by the Mexicans. Having eaten the bread and drunk the wine which were taken in the engagement, they re posed on their arms, protected by a strong guard.

On the following morning the dead were buried and the wounded Mexican prisoners comfortably provided with means of conveyance to

---

[1] The other three pieces of artillery were not brought into the action.

El Paso. Every needful attention was also given our own wounded by the surgeons. The column now, in perfect order, with the baggage, provision, hospital, ammunition, and merchant trains in the rear, and a strong rear and front guard and a party of flankers on the right and left, moved cautiously in the direction of El Paso, apprehending another attack. After an advance of 15 miles camp was selected near a small salt lake, where there was a moderate supply of natural forage, such as grass and rushes. From this point Col. Doniphan sent back an express for the artillery to hasten forward, for he anticipated strenuous opposition at El Paso.

While encamped here one of the picket guard, discovering a party of Mexicans passing along the base of the mountains toward the east, in which they had taken shelter during the day, endeavoring to make good their retreat to El Paso under cover of the night, fired upon them. This produced an alarm in camp. The men were cooking their suppers; some of them had spread their beds for repose. Col. Doniphan ordered the fires to be extinguished. Whatever was in the vessels on the fire cooking was now turned topsy-turvy in the effort to put out the light. For a moment all was confusion. Quickly, however, Col. Doniphan drew up his men in line of battle and awaited the approach of the enemy. Lieut. Col. Jackson in the hurry to parade his men mounted his mule bareback, with his sword and shotgun. Many of the men were in ranks barefoot and only half clad, for they had been roused from slumber. Finally, no enemy appearing, the soldiers were ordered to repair to their tents and sleep on their arms. They ran, leaping and hallooing and cursing the false alarm. Before day another false alarm called them out in a similar manner. Therefore this night the soldiers were much vexed.

The same order of march which had been adopted on the previous day was continued on the 27th, until the column reached El Paso. On arriving at the Great Pass, or gorge in the mountains, through which the river appears to have forced its way, debouching into the valley below, over a system of rocky falls, in dashing cataracts, the colonel was met by a deputation of citizens from El Paso, bearing a white flag, proposing terms of peace and offering to surrender the place into his hands, beseeching at the same time that he would use his clemency toward them in sparing their lives and protecting their property. This the colonel was inclined to do. It was now about 3 miles to the city. All moved on, rejoicing in the prospect of rest and something to appease the appetite.

Thus, on the 27th, the city of El Paso [1] was possessed by the American troops without further opposition or greater effusion of blood. It was now night. Therefore the soldiers encamped and enjoyed the advantage of a little repose.

The men at first were encamped on a bare spot of earth south of the Plaza, where the wind drove the sand furiously through the camp, dreadfully annoying both man and beast. In this comfortless situation the soldiers remained for several days. At length, after great suffering from the driven sands, which filled the eyes, nostrils,

---

[1] " When you learn," observes an intelligent volunteer, " that this place is the key by which you enter New Mexico you will see at once the importance of the place. All communications passing from Lower Mexico in the direction of Santa Fe must necessarily pass through this place or within a few miles of it. Is it not, therefore, most surprising that with 2,240 fighting men in the town besides the regular soldiers, 514, who were stationed there, they should have surrendered the place so easily?"

and mouth to suffocation, the men were quartered in houses near the square.

One of the first acts of Col. Doniphan after taking possession of El Paso was the liberating of three American citizens who, without crime, had been immured in a dungeon for five months and one day. Thus have Americans been deprived of their liberty in Mexico. Col. Doniphan was their deliverer.

These three American citizens—Hudson, Pollard, and Hutchinson—had started from Van Buren, in Arkansas, with the view of proceeding to Upper California, where they intended settling; and, arriving safely at Santa Fe, they agreed to hire Graham, a Scotchman, to pilot them through the mountains to San Diego. Having purchased an outfit at Santa Fe, they were conducted by Graham down the Del Norte to El Paso, who told them the best route led from that place to Guadeloupe Calvo, and thence by San Bernadino to the mouth of the Gila, whence they could easily arrive at San Diego. They followed their pilot. On reaching El Paso, however, Graham became intoxicated and informed against them, representing to the prefecto of the place that they were Texan spies, whereupon they were apprehended and lodged in prison, where they lay until delivered by the American Army.

CHAPTER XVII.

On the morning of the 28th three commissioners, deputed by the citizens of El Paso, came into the American camp to negotiate more fully the terms of capitulation and the nature of the peace which had been partially agreed upon the previous day. Col. Doniphan instructed them to say to the inhabitants of the settlement of El Paso " that he did not come to plunder and ravage, but to offer them liberty; that the lives and property of such as remained peaceable and neutral during the existence of the war would be fully and amply protected; but that such as neglected their industrial pursuits and instigated other peaceable citizens to take up arms against the Americans would be punished as their crimes deserved." He also encouraged them to industry and the prosecution of their daily labor, advising them to prepare a market wherein his soldiers might purchase such things as they needed, excepting spiritous liquors, the sale of which he interdicted. He further assured them " that his commissary and quartermaster would purchase of them such supplies of provisions and forage as his men and animals might require, and that the beautiful settlement of El Paso should not be laid waste and destroyed by his soldiers." These things were done as Col. Doniphan promised.

On the same day an assessment was made of all the corn, wheat, and provender which could be found in the city, that the quartermaster might know whence to draw supplies in case the proprietors refused to sell to the American Army. When the estimate had been completed it appeared that there were several hundred thousand fanegas of corn and wheat and a vast quantity of fodder and other forage for horses and mules.[1] Also a search for public arms, ammunition, and stores was instituted, that if such things were found to abound the army might not be in want of the means of defense; and also that the Mexicans, in case they attempted an insurrection, might not have in their power the means of prosecuting their designs with success or of inflicting permanent injury upon our men. Therefore the field officers and captains and lieutenants, with files of men, went into all the houses, treating the families with respect, taking nothing save arms and other munitions of war; neither did they abuse any person.

---

[1] Col. Doniphan issued an order to the soldiers, forbidding them to take any property from the Mexicans without paying its just equivalent to the owner. A waggish volunteer who was standing by observed, " Colonel, you don't care if we take mice (maize), do you? " The colonel, not suspecting his motive, replied in the negative. The volunteer went away and in a short time returned to camp with great quantities of corn for his horse and those of his companions, for the Mexicans call corn mice, i. e., maize. The colonel enjoyed the joke.

When this search was completed it was discovered that the colone
had come in possession of more than 20,000 pounds of powder, lead
musket cartridge, cannon cartridge, and grape and cannister shot
500 stands of small arms, 400 lances, 4 pieces of cannon, severa
swivels and culverins, and several stands of colors.

On the 30th a body of cavalry under Maj. Gilpin and Capt. Rei
was sent to the Presidio del Eclezario, 22 miles farther down th
river, for the purpose of making a reconnoissance. Here a stron
body of Mexicans had been recently stationed, but abandoned th
post when Col. Doniphan entered El Paso. Several wagonloads o
ammunition and one piece of cannon were discovered cached, o
buried, in the sand.[1] These also were afterwards sent for by the com
mander. This body of cavalry, having returned, reported a stron
Mexican force on its march from Chihuahua to recover El Paso fro
the hands of the Americans. So the Army was not yet free fro
apprehension.

The Americans now having complete possession of El Paso, an
treating the inhabitants with great humanity, even those who fough
against them under a black, piratical flag at Brazito (for many o
them were walking about town with bandages around their head
and their arms in slings, and their other wounds bound up, which the
had received in that action), they in turn generously and gratuitousl
supplied many of the soldiers with such things as they required t
eat and drink, as though unwilling to be excelled in kindness. Thi
is the character of the El Paseños. The soldiers spent much of thei
time pleasantly in feasting upon a variety of the best viands an
finest fruits, such as fresh pears, quinces, apples, oranges, and drie
pears, apples, peaches, and grapes which far excel the raisin fo
deliciousness of flavor. Besides these there was a great variety o
sweetmeats in the market, and also mezcal and pulque and beer an
the richest wines. The soldiers enjoyed all these luxuries after s
much privation.

Shortly after Col. Doniphan's arrival at El Paso the proclamatio
of Angel Trias, governor of Chihuahua, to the Mexican troops befor
the Battle of Brazito fell into his hands, a copy of which, translate
by Capt. David Waldo, here follows:

Soldiers: The sacrilegious invaders of Mexico are approaching the city o
El Paso, an important part of the State, where the enemy intend establishin
their winter quarters, and even pretend that they will advance farther into ou
territory. It is entirely necessary that you go—you defenders of the hono
and glory of the Republic—that you may give a lesson to these pirates.

The State calculated much upon the aid that would be given by the valian
and war-worn citizens of the Pass, but treason has sown there distrust, and th
patriotic people, by a disgraceful mutiny, retreated at 30 leagues distance fro
the small force under the command of Gen. Kearney when they might hav
taken him and his force prisoners at discretion. Subordination and disciplin
were wanting.

You go to reestablish the character of those Mexicans and to chastise th
enemy if he should dare to touch the soil of the State, the.State ennobled by th
blood of the fathers of our independence. I confide in your courage, and alon
I recommend to you obedience to your commanders and the most perfect dis
cipline.

All Chihuahua burn with the desire to go with you, because they are a
Mexicans, possessed of the warmest enthusiasm and the purest patriotism

---

[1] At this fort was also discovered a great number of bloody bandages, for the Mexican
who were wounded at Brazito had been conveyed thither to receive surgical attention.

They will march to join you—at the first.signal the circumstances of the war demand reinforcements; they shall be forwarded, let it cost the State what it may. To the people of Chihuahua no sacrifice is reckoned when the honor of the Republic is at stake.

The enthusiasm with which you march and the sanctity of your noble cause are sure evidences of victory. Yes; you are led by the god of battles and your brows shall be crowned with laurels. Thus trusts your friend and companion.

ANGEL TRIAS.

CHIHUAHUA, *November 9, 1846.*

On the morning of the 1st of January, 1847, a great cloud of dust was seen rising in the direction of Chihuahua similar to that usually produced by the march of an army of cavalry. The picket guard came dashing in at full speed. Assembly was blown by the bugler. All apprehended an attack. The soldiers ran to their arms in great haste. The officers paraded their respective commands. The standards were displayed. The men were drawn up in order of battle. The Mexican pieces of artillery recently taken and the howitzer captured at Brazito were put into an attitude of defense by a file of men under Lieut. Kribben. The men who had straggled from camp into town came running for their arms with the utmost expedition. Col. Doniphan, who now had his quarters in the town, also came running on foot with his holster pistols swung across his left arm, having his drawn sword in his right hand. Lieut. Col. Mitchell, with a small body of cavalry, galloped off in the direction of the rising dust, and, having made a reconnoissance, reported that the dust proceeded from an atajo of pack mules and a train of Mexican caretas coming into town. This was another false alarm. The soldiers were now moved and quartered in houses near the square for better defense, both against the enemy and the high winds, which rage continually during the winter season in that mountainous country.

The merchants and sutlers upon arriving at El Paso hired rooms and storehouses, where they exhibited their goods and commodities for sale. Many of them sold largely to the inhabitants, whereby they considerably lightened their burdens. Certain of the merchants advanced Col. Doniphan sums of money for the use of the Commissary and Quartermaster Departments of the Army, taking for these accommodations checks on the United States Treasury. To a limited extent also they furnished some of the soldiers with clothing and other necessaries.

About the 5th [1] a lieutenant and a number of mechanics were sent up to the falls to repair the gristmills at that place. Large quantities of wheat were now ground and the flour, unbolted, put up in sacks for the use of the army. For the present, therefore, the soldiers were bountifully supplied.

Near the mills the Mexican Army, a short time previous to the battle at Brazito, had constructed a cordon or system of field works extending from the mountains and connecting with the river on the west side at the falls. Here, at first, it was proposed to give the "northern invaders" battle, than which it is difficult to conceive a stronger position for defense; but Gen. Cuilta, chief in command at

---

[1] Capts. Waldo, Kirker, Maclean, and a Mexican went on a hunting excursion up the Del Norte River. They were absent 8 or 10 days, during which they had much sport. They chased several small parties of Mexicans, and visited the house of the friendly Mexican whose son had volunteered to serve under Gen. Poncé at Brazito and was unfortunately shot while endeavoring to come over to the American lines in that action.

that time, being seized with an indisposition, Gen. Poncé led the troops to Brazito, where he suffered a total defeat. The next day Capt. Stephenson and about 100 men, including some who had been left sick at Socorro and Albuquerque and had recovered, came up, escorting a large train of commissary wagons. This train had been ordered down from Santa Fe when the troops came out of the Navajo country.

The soldiers (such of them as were not on duty at any time) now engaged in various pastimes and amusements with the Paseños, sometimes visiting and conversing with the fair señoritas of the place, whose charms and unpurchased kindness almost induced some of the men to wish not to return home, and at other times gleefully dancing at the fandango. When the weather was pleasant the streets about the plaza were crowded with Mexicans and American soldiers engaged in betting at monte, chuck-a-luck, twenty-one, faro, or some other game at cards. This vice was carried to such an excess at one time that Col. Doniphan was compelled to forbid gambling on the streets in order to clear them of obstruction.

Capt. James Kirker, who had gained so much celebrity as an Indian fighter, and who for many years past has been successfully employed by the State of Chihuahua against the Apaches, hearing that the American forces were advancing upon El Paso, left his family at Coralitus and hastened to join his countrymen that he might show his fidelity and patriotism. This conduct of Capt. Kirker was no less unexpected than it was terrifying to the Chihuahuans, for he, who had so long been the terror of the Apaches, had now joined with his countrymen, to be henceforward equally the terror of the Chihuahuans. Capt. Kirker, on account of his great knowledge of the country and acquaintance with the language and customs of the Mexican people, became subsquently of the most essential service to Col. Doniphan as an interpreter and forage master. He returned with the army to the United States.

The universal kind treatment which the El Paseños received from the Americans not only induced them to think well of the conduct of the Army, but disposed them favorably toward the American Government, for they began to consider how much more liberty and happiness they might enjoy having connection with this Republic than in their present state. They saw also that the Americans were not disposed to plunder; for, being conquerors, they notwithstanding purchased of the conquered those things they wished to use and forcibly took nothing. Nor would they permit the Apaches to kill and plunder the Mexican people. This pleased them, for they dread the Apaches. Besides, when a subaltern officer took provisions for his men or forage for the animals, he gave the owner of the property an order on the quartermaster. Such order was always accepted and promptly redeemed. This, too, gave the Mexicans great confidence in the solvency and fairness of the American Government.

Now, there are a great many wolves which come down from the neighboring mountains into the suburbs of El Paso and kill the flocks when not penned in their folds, and also feed upon the offal about the shambles and slaughter pens. They kept up a dolorous serenade during the nights, and in many instances were so bold as almost to drive the sentinels from their posts. Oftentimes the sentinels were compelled to shoot them in self-defense, as they would a prowling enemy. This would usually create a false alarm.

On one occasion several beeves had been slaughtered in a fold, or corral, for the use of the army. During the night the scent of the offal attracted the wolves. A considerable number of them coming down from their lairs among the rocks leaped into the corral and feasted sumptuously. The walls of the corral were many feet higher on the inside than on the outside, so, at daydawn, when the wolves wished to retire, they could not repass the walls. The soldiers, therefore, in the morning, taking their sabers, went in amongst them, and, after much sport, killed them all. In such amusements did the soldiers delight.

On a certain occasion while the army remained here two sentinels, Tungitt and Clarkin, were found sleeping on their posts, and their guns taken from them by the officer of the guard. This is a capital offense. They were brought before Col. Doniphan under arrest, who thus addressed them: " Gentlemen! You have committed a very high offense against the laws of the country and propriety. By your neglect you have exposed the lives of all; you have laid the whole camp liable to be surprised by the enemy. Are you not sensible of the enormity of these offenses?" To which they replied in the affirmative, "but we were tired and exhausted and could not preserve our wakefulness; we will endeavor not to commit a similar offense in future." "Then go," says Col. Doniphan, "and hereafter be good soldiers and faithful sentinels. I will excuse you for the present." They departed, and were never known to be in default again.

About the 10th of January [1] we learned of the insurrection which had been set on foot in New Mexico by Gen. Anchulette, Chavez, Ortiz, and others, and captured certain of their emissaries, endeavoring to instigate the inhabitants of El Paso to attempt the same there. This matter, being timely detected and exposed at El Paso by the vigilance of both officers and men, was crushed before the plan was matured. Also certain other Mexicans were detected in secretly carrying on a correspondence with the troops at Chihuahua, whereby they were endeavoring to plot and work our destruction. Among these was Ramond Ortiz, the curate of El Paso, a very shrewd and intelligent man, and the same whom Kendall's graphic pen has immortalized. All of these were now held in custody under a strict guard.

The time was now occupied in procuring a supply of provisions and a suitable outfit for the contemplated march upon Chihuahua. Preparatory to this, also, and for the more perfect organization and better discipline of the troops, the intermediate time was consumed in regimental and company drills, in cavalry charges, and sword exercises. These wholesome military exercises gave greater efficiency to the corps, and it is due to the high-minded, honorable men who composed this column to bear testimony to the prompt and cheerful manner in which they performed every duty and submitted to every burden upon which they foresaw their safety as an army depended.

---

[1] About this time an American, his name Rodgers, escaped from Chihuahua and reported to Col. Doniphan that Gen. Wool had abandoned his march upon that city and that a formidable force was preparing to defend the place.

Such was the spirit of the soldiers under the command of Col. Doniphan.[1]

On the 18th Capt. Hughes and Lieut. Jackson, with 10 men, who had been left sick at Socorro, and a few days afterwards Lieuts. Lea, Gordon, and Hinton, who had been sent back to Santa Fe for provisions and the artillery, arrived at El Paso and rejoined their companies. About this time also five intelligent young men, who fought bravely at Brazito, died of typhoid fever, and were buried with the honors of war in the El Paso cemetery.[2]

> Peace to the shades of the virtuous brave,
> Who gallantly bore the perils of war,
> Who found an humble, yet honored grave,
> From kindred, home, and country far.

On the 25th the author made the subjoined statements of the resources of the rich valley of El Paso to the War Department after several weeks' careful observation, which was ordered to be printed:

FOR THE CONSIDERATION OF THE WAR DEPARTMENT, AT WASHINGTON CITY.

The United States forces under command of Col. Alexander W. Doniphan took possession of the city of El Paso, in the Department of Chihuahua, on Sunday, the 27th of December, 1846, two days after the Battle of Brazito, the strength of his command being about 900 men.

My object in this communication is to give the War Department and the country at large some idea of the resources of the fruitful valley of El Paso and of its importance to the United States. The settlement of the El Paso extends from the falls of the Rio Grande on the north to the Presidio on the south, a distance of 22 miles, and is one continuous orchard and vineyard, embracing in its ample area an industrious and peaceable population of at least 8,000. This spacious valley is about midway between Santa Fe and Chihuahua and is isolated from all other Mexican settlements by the mountains that rise on the east and west and close into the river on the north and south. The breadth of the valley is about 10 miles. The falls of the river are 2 miles north of the "plaza publica," or public square, and affords sufficient water power for grist and saw mills enough to supply the entire settlement with flour and lumber.

The most important production of the valley is the grape, from which are annually manufactured not less than 200,000 gallons of perhaps the richest and best wine in the world. This wine is worth $2 per gallon and constitutes the principal revenue of the city. Thus the wines of El Paso alone yield $400,000 per annum. The El Paso wines are superior in richness of flavor and pleasantness of taste to anything of the kind I ever met with in the United States, and I doubt not that they are far superior to the best wines ever produced in the valley of the Rhine or on the sunny hills of France. There is little or no rain in this elevated country and hence the extraordinary sweetness and richness of the grape. Also, quantities of the grape of this valley are dried in clusters and preserved for use during the winter months. In this state I regard them as far superior to the best raisins that are imported into the United States from the West Indies and other tropical climates.

If this valley were cultivated by an energetic American population it would yield, perhaps, ten times the quantity of wine and fruits at present produced. Were the wholesome influences and protection of our republican institutions extended to the Rio del Norte, an American population possessing American feelings and speaking the American language would soon spring up here. To facilitate the peopling of this valley by the Anglo-American race, nothing would contribute so much as the opening of a communication between this rich valley and the Western States of our Union by a turnpike, railroad, or some other thoroughfare which would afford a market for the fruits and wines of this river country. Perhaps the most feasible and economical, though not the most direct, plan of opening an outlet to the grape valley of the Rio Grande would be the construction of a grand canal from this place, following the meanderings of the river to its highest navigable point. If a communication by either of

---

[1] On Jan. 11 J. T. Crenshaw was appointed sergeant major, vice Palmer, resigned.
[2] These were James M. Finley, J. D. Leland, G. J. Hackley, J. Clark, and a Mr. Dyer.

these routes were opened this valley would soon become the seat of wealth, influence, and refinement. It would become one of the richest and most fashionable parts of the continent. A communication between the valley of the Mississippi and that of the Rio del Norte affording an easy method of exchanging the products of the one for those of the other will do more than any other cause to facilitate the westward march of civilization and republican government. It would be an act of charity to rid these people of their present governors and throw around them the shield of American protection.

That the idea of a canal following the course of the Del Norte may not appear impracticable it may not be amiss to state that no country in the world is better adapted for the construction of canals than this valley. As the earth is sandy, canals are easily constructed; but there is a kind of cement intermixed with the sand that renders the banks of canals as firm as a wall. There is already a grand canal, or "acequia," leading out from the river above the falls, extending through the entire length of the valley of El Paso, irrigating every farm and vineyard, thence to the Presidio, where it rejoins the river.

Pears, peaches, apples, quinces, and figs are produced here in the greatest profusion. The climate of this country is most salubrious and healthful—the scenery is grand and picturesque beyond description. The inhabitants here suffer more from the depredations of the Apaches than from any other cause. They are frequently robbed of all they possess in one night by the incursions of these lawless plunderers. A few companies of American dragoons would, however, soon drive them from their hiding places in the mountains and put an end to their depredations.

Add to the fruits and wines of this rich valley a vast quantity of corn, wheat, and other small grain, and the surplus productions of the place will, under its present state of agriculture, amount to near $1,000,000 per annum. What then would be the amount of the surplus under the advantages of American agriculture? The entire valley of the Del Norte, from Albuquerque to Chihuahua, a distance of 500 miles in length, is as well adapted to the cultivation of the grape as the particular valley adjacent to El Paso.

I have thought proper to make these suggestions to the War Department, as there is no corps of field and topographical engineers with this branch of the western army, whose duty it would have been to make such a report.

Very respectfully,

JOHN T. HUGHES.

His Excellency W. L. MARCY,
    Secretary of War.

EL PASO, *January 25, 1847.*

The Apache Indians were continually making incursions from the mountains upon the settlements of El Paso, plundering and robbing whomsoever chanced to fall in their way, whether Mexican or American, and driving off large herds of mules and flocks of sheep. On one occasion they drove off 280 mules belonging to Algea and Porus, Mexican merchants, traveling under the protection of the American Army. They had previously driven off 20 yoke of oxen belonging to the commissary trains near the little town Dona Ana. And subsequently, when the army was encamped about 35 miles below El Paso, they stole a parcel of work oxen from Mr. Houke, an American trader, and made their escape to the mountains. The next morning information of the fact was given, when Mr. Houke, Lieut. Hinton, and three other men pursued them, and after a toilsome march of about 60 miles overtook the villains, killed one of their number, recovered the oxen, and returned to the army.

CHAPTER XVIII.

Departure from El Paso—Doniphan's position—Ramond Ortiz—Two deserters—Battalion of merchants—Passage of the desert—The Ojo Caliente—Marksmanship—Lake of Encenillas—Dreadful conflagration—Capt. Reid's adventure—The reconnoissance—Plan of the march—Battle of Sacramento—Surrender of Chihuahua.

Col. Doniphan delayed at El Paso 42 days awaiting the arrival of the artillery under Maj. Clark and Capt. Weightman, which he had ordered Col. Price to forward immediately upon his return from the Indian campaign. Col. Price, having his mind turned on quelling the conspiracy which had been plotted by Gen. Archulette, and fearing, if he should send the artillery away, that it would too much weaken his force and embolden the conspirators, hesitated several weeks before he would comply with the order. At length, however, he dispatched Maj. Clark with 117 men and six pieces of cannon, four 6-pounders, and two 12-pound howitzers, which, after indefatigable exertion and incessant toiling through the heavy snows, arrived at El Paso on the 1st of February.

On the 8th the whole army, the merchant, baggage, commissary, hospital, sutler, and ammunition trains, and all the stragglers, amateurs, and gentlemen of leisure, under flying colors, presenting the most martial aspect, set out with buoyant hopes for the city of Chihuahua. There the soldiers expected to reap undying fame—to gain a glorious victory—or perish on the field of honor. Nothing certain could be learned of the movements of Gen. Wool's column, which at first was destined to operate against Chihuahua. Col. Doniphan's orders were merely to report to Gen. Wool at that place, not to invade the State. Vague and uncertain information had been obtained through the Mexicans that Gen. Wool's advance had, at one time, reached Parras, but that the whole column had suddenly deflected to the left for some cause to them and us equally unknown. Thus was Col. Doniphan circumstanced. With an army less than 1,000 strong he was on his march leading through inhospitable, sandy wastes against a powerful city, which had been deemed of so much importance by the Government that Gen. Wool, with 3,500 men and a heavy park of artillery, had been directed thither to effect its subjugation. What, then, must have been the feelings of Col. Doniphan and his men when they saw the States of Chihuahua and Durango in arms to receive them, not the remotest prospect of succor from Gen. Wool, and rocks and unpeopled deserts intervening, precluding the possibility of successful retreat? "Victory or death" were the two alternatives. Yet there was no faltering, no pale faces, no dismayed hearts. At this crisis had Col. Doniphan inquired of his men what was to be done the response would have been unanimously given, Lead us on. But he needed not to make the inquiry, for he saw de-

144

picted in every countenance the fixed resolve "To do or die." Col. Doniphan's responsibility was therefore very great. The undertaking was stupendous. His success was brilliant and unparalleled. Who, then, will deny him the just meed of applause? A deep gloom enshrouded the State of Missouri. Being apprised of Gen. Wool's movements, the people of the State were enabled to appreciate the full extent of the danger which threatened to overwhelm us. They saw our imminently perilous situation. They felt for the unsuccored army. The executive himself was moved with sympathy and fearful apprehension for its safety. But neither he nor the people could avert the coming storm or convey timely warning to the commander of this forlorn hope. He had therefore to rely upon steel and the courage of his men. The event is known.

The colonel took with him Ramond Otiz, Pino, and three other influential men of the malcontents as hostages for the future good behavior of the inhabitants of El Paso. " By this means the safety of traders and of all other persons passing up or down the country was guaranteed, for they were forewarned that if any depredations were committed upon citizens of the United States at El Paso they would be put to death."

Since that time no outrages have been perpetrated at El Paso upon any American citizen. It was at El Paso that two American soldiers conceived for two fair young Mexican girls an affection so strong and ardent that they did not choose to march any further with the army. Having marched with their companies one or two days' they deserted camp at night and returned to those they loved and in a short time married them.

On the evening of the 12th the column reached a point on the Del Norte, about 50 miles below El Paso, where the road, turning to the right, strikes off at right angles with the river across the Jornada, of 65 miles in extent, running through deep sand drifts nearly the whole way. On this desert tract there is not one drop of water. Here, therefore, the command came to a halt and tarried one day that the men might prepare victuals and such a supply of water, as they had means of conveying along with them, for the desert journey.

Col. Doniphan now called upon the merchant caravan to meet and organize themselves into companies and elect officers to command them. This he did that he might avail himself of their services in the event that the troops, which he already had, should not prove sufficiently strong to cope with the enemy at Chihuahua. The merchants and the teamsters in their employ were quickly organized into two efficient companies under Capts. Skillman and Glasgow, forming a battalion commanded by Samuel C. Owens, of Independence, who they elected major.

This was a very effective corps, for both the merchants and the teamsters were well armed and were very brave men. Besides having a large capital invested in merchandise, they had the double incentive to fight bravely, first, for their property, and, then, for their lives. These numbered about 150 well-armed men. Here all the Mexican powder and other munitions of war, which the colonel had taken at El Paso and for which he had not the means of transportation, were destroyed. The powder was burnt and the cannister shot and arms thrown into the river.

A few days previous to this Cufford & Gentry, a strong firm, the former an Englishman and the latter an American, both traveling with British passports, secretly and dishonorably abandoned the merchant caravan, and, contrary to their promise to Col. Doniphan, slipped off at night with 45 wagons and hastened on to Chihuahua, and from thence to Zacatecas.

Now, Harmony, a Spaniard, and Porus, a Mexican, fearing lest Doniphan might be defeated at Chihuahua, were loath to proceed with their wagons any farther, and desired to turn back to El Paso and there make sale of their merchandise. This could not be permitted without endangering the safety of all; for the only safety was in union. Therefore, Lieut. Col. Mitchell, Capt. Reid, and Lieut. Choteau, with 16 men, went back several miles to compel these men to bring up their trains. At first they pretended that the Apaches had stolen all their mules, wherefore they could not move their wagons. But being threatened they soon brought their animals from a place where they had purposely concealed them that they might be permitted to remain. In a short time they were brought up and forbidden to leave the army again.

While at this place the author held a conversation with Ortiz, the curate, in regard to the project of M. Guizot " to preserve the balance of power" by placing the son of Louis Philippe or some other monarch on the "throne of Mexico." The curate observed: "Such an idea is too preposterous to deserve a serious consideration. The Mexicans, and especially those in the northern States, would treat the proposition, if made to them seriously, with the indignation and contempt which it so richly merits. Mexicans, not less than Americans, love liberty. Mexico would rather be conquered by a sister Republic—rather lose her national existence—than submit to be governed by a foreign prince."

Having buried two brave men, Maxwell and Willis, on the 14th the army bade adieu to the Great River of the North and commenced its march upon the dreadful desert. Some of the men having no canteens or other means of carrying water filled the sheaths of their sabers and swung the naked blades jingling at their sides. C. F. Hughes, quartermaster sergeant, had terrible work to force the trains along through the heavy sand drifts. Oftentimes he was compelled to double his teams and have a dozen or more men rolling at the wheels to induce the wagons to move at all.

The mules were weak and sunk up to their knees in the sand; the wagons stood buried almost to the hubs. Thus were they embarrassed. The teams could not move them. The soldiers and teamsters would often leap down from their horses and mules and roll the wagons along with their hands until they got where the sand was lighter. Thus it was all through the desert. After an arduous march of 20 miles the army encamped upon the plain without wood or water. On the next day, toward sunset, the army passed through a gap or canyon in a range of mountains which traverses the desert from north to south. This mountain shoots up abruptly from the plain into an innumerable set of knobs and rocky peaks, consisting of dark, iron-colored masses of basalt and puddingstone and in some places of volcanic cinders. At this point Lieut. Gordon, and Collins, interpreter, with 12 other men, fell in company with Kirker's scouting party, which had been in advance several days. Kirker's party consisted of 8 men. The whole, now (being 23 in number) under Lieut. Gordon, proceeded far in advance of the army, by direction from the colonel, for the purpose of making reconnoissance at Carrizal, where they had understood a body of Mexicans were posted. This place is on the other side of the desert. Before their arrival there, however, the Mexican soldiery abandoned the place. Therefore they entered it and took military possession in the name of the United States Government, the alcalde, without offering the slightest resistance, giving a written certificate of submission, in which he claimed the colonel's clemency and threw himself on the generosity of the American Army. He was not disappointed in receiving the amplest protection. By this time there was not a drop of water in the canteens and all were suffering extremely with thirst. At this hour one of the artillerymen came up from Santa Fe, having in possession the United States mail, the only one of consequence which had been received for six months. Though at this crisis nothing could have been so refreshing to the body as cool water, yet newspapers and letters from home had a wonderfully cheering and talismanic influence on the mind. Not a word, however, could be learned of the movements of the army of Gen. Wool. After a toilsome march of 24 miles, about midnight the column halted to allow the men and animals a little rest. But they had no refreshment, for the men were again obliged to spend the night without their suppers and without water. The animals also were nearly perishing of thirst. It was now still 21 miles to water, over a heavy, sandy road, and the teams had already become feeble and broken down. Ortiz, the benevolent curate, although a prisoner and under a strict guard, generously gave many of the soldiers a draft of water, which he had provided to be brought from the Del Norte in a water vessel. For this and other instances of kindness toward the author, he now makes his grateful acknowledgments.

The next morning by daydawn the army was on the march. The mules and horses were neighing and crying piteously for water. Some of them were to weak to proceed farther. They were abandoned. Notwithstanding the eagerness of the men to get to water, a strong front and rear guard were detailed, as usual, to prevent surprise by the enemy. Toward night, when the column had arrived within 5 miles of the Laguna de los Patos, the men could no longer be restrained in the lines, but in the greatest impatience hurried on in groups to quench their burning thirst. The commander seeing this, and knowing how his men suffered—for he, too, suffered equally with them—did not attempt to prevent it, but, taking his whole force, hastened on to the lake as quick as possible, that all might be satisfied, having left an order for Capt. Parsons, who commanded the rear guard that day, to leave the trains, that his men might have water and rest. It was near sunset. Meanwhile, the quartermaster sergeant and the resolute and hardy teamsters had the task of a Hercules before them in bringing up the trains through the deep, heavy, sand drifts. Having arrived within about 10 miles of the Laguna, they found it impossible to advance farther. The rear guard had left them, with the view of getting water and then returning. They were sometimes compelled to quadruple the teams to move a wagon through the deep sand. The animals were dying of

thirst and fatigue. Thirty-six yoke of oxen had been turned loose.
Two wagons were abandoned amidst the sand hills. Eight thousand
pounds of flour and several barrels of salt had been thrown out upon
the ground. Also some of the sutlers threw away their heavy
commodities which they could not transport. The trains never
could have proceeded 10 miles farther. But the God who made the
fountain leap from the rock to quench the thirst of the Israelitish
army in the desert now sent a cloud, which hung upon the summits
of the mountains to the right, and such a copious shower of rain descended that the mountain torrents came rushing and foaming down
from the rocks, and spread out upon the plains in such quantities
that both the men and the animals were filled. Therefore they
stayed all night at this place where the godsend had blessed them,
and being much refreshed, next morning passed out of the desert.
All were now at Laguna de los Patos, where they stayed one day to
recruit and gain strength. This is a beautiful lake of fresh water.
It was here that W. Tolley, a volunteer, who, as it is said, left a
charming young bride at home, drank so excessively of the cool,
refreshing element, after so many days of toil on the desert, that he
soon died. He was buried near the margin of the lake. Thus the
army passed the desert, 65 miles in extent.

On the morning of the 18th the column and trains were again in
motion. C. F. Hughes, in consideration of the service he had rendered in passing the desert, was now relieved from further duty by
Mr. Harrison. To the right, at the distance of several miles from
the Laguna, rises a stupendous, pyramidal rock, many thousand feet
high. The existence of such abrupt, detached, masses of mountains
shows that the earth, by some wonderful agency, had been convulsed
and upheaved. Who will say that the flood which inundated the
Old World may not have been produced by the sudden unheavement
and emergement of the Western Continent from the ocean by some
all-powerful agency? A march of 18 miles brought the army to
Carrizal, where there was much cool and delightful water and where
forage was obtained in abundance.

At meridian on Sunday, the 21st, the command reached the celebrated "Ojo Caliente," or Warm Spring, where the men were again
permitted to rest a few hours and make preparations for crossing
another desert, 45 miles wide, without water. From this place Capt.
Skillman, with 12 volunteers, was dispatched to the Laguna de
Encenillas to keep up a close espionage on the movements of the
enemy, for it was now anticipated that he would give battle at that
place. The Ojo Caliente is at the base of a ledge of rocky hills
and furnishes a vast volume of water, about blood warm, which runs
off in the direction of the Patos. The basin of the spring is about
120 feet long and 75 wide, with an average depth of 4 feet. The
bottom consists of sparkling, white sand and the water is perfectly
transparent. No effort by disturbing the sand was sufficient to
becloud or muddy the crystal water.[1]   Col. Doniphan and many of
his officers and men now enjoyed the most luxurious and rejuve-
nescent bathing. Thus refreshed, the march was commenced upon
the desert. Having advanced 12 miles, the men were encamped on

[1] This Ojo Caliente was formerly the seat of a princely hacienda belonging to Porus, a
Spanish nabob, who at one time had grazing on his pastures more than 36,000 head of
cattle and sheep.

the plain, without wood or water, indispensable requisites for comfort in a military camp after a hard day's march.

Continuing the march the next day, a canyon was passed in a high and craggy range of mountains traversing the desert. These huge masses of basalt, which rise in many places 2,000 feet almost perpendicularly, were capped with snow. Having completed 22 miles, the men halted for the night on a rocky, flinty spot of earth, where there was neither wood, water, nor grass. Nor was it possible for the men to have the least comfort, as it was extremely cold. They tethered their animals and, wrapping themselves up in their blankets, lay down on the earth without taking supper.

The next day we marched 12 miles, and came to the Guyagas Springs. These issue in leaping, gushing, cool streamlets out from the western base of a system of rocky bluffs, and refresh the neighboring plain. Here the men and animals slaked their burning thirst. Under the jutting rocks and archways of this mountain range were seen dependent spar, crystal of quartz, and the most brilliant stalactites. Here a drove of 12 or 13 antelopes, which had been feeding on the sides of the cliffs, seeing the men marching and the banners and guidons fluttering, were affrighted at the unusual sight, and came bounding down from the rocks as though they would break through the ranks, but as they neared the lines the men fired upon and killed them all while bounding along. They were used for food. This evidence of marksmanship struck the Mexican prisoners with astonishment and caused them more than ever to dread the American rifles. Here in a narrow valley, with lofty, rocky ridges on either hand, the men were dismounted and allowed to rest for the night, during which M. Robards, a good soldier, died and was buried.

From thence they marched the next day 15 miles, and again encamped on the plain without wood or water. Here part of the spies returned and reported that there were 700 Mexicans at Encenillas with artillery. Early the following morning (which was the 25th) Col. Doniphan drew up his forces in order of battle and marched over to the north margin of the lake. Here he allowed his men a short respite and some refreshment. This lake is about 20 miles long and about 3 miles wide, and at the point where the army first encamped there were near the margin white efflorescences of soda on the surface of the ground. Either this efflorescent soda or the water of the lake when put in flour will quickly cause it to rise or leaven. It was used instead of saleratus.

While nooning, the fire from one of the tents caught into the tall, dry grass and, by a high wind, was furiously driven over the plain, threatening destruction to everything before it. In a short time the fire, which had broken out in a similar manner from the camp near the Guyagas Springs, having almost kept pace with the army, came bursting and sweeping terribly over the summits of the mountains and, descending into the valley, united with the fire on the margin of the lake. The conflagration, now roaring and crackling, irresistibly swept along. The flame rose in dashing and bursting waves 20 feet high, and threatened to devour the whole train. The army was now put upon the march, and the trains endeavored to advance before the flames, but in vain. The wind blew steadily and powerfuly in the direction the army was marching. The conflagration, gaining new strength from every puff of wind, came raging and sweeping like a wave. The column of flame, displaying a front of many miles, steadily advanced along the margin of the lake. This was a more terrible foe than an "army with banners." The fire now gained upon the trains. The ammunition wagons narrowly escaped. The artillery was run into the lake. Some of the wagons still passed onward.

The road runs parallel to the lake, and about 200 yards from it. Col. Doniphan and his men endeavored to trample down the grass from the road to the lake, in a narrow list, by frequently riding over the same ground. They also rode their horses into the water, and then quickly turned them upon the place where the grass was trodden down, that they might moisten it, and thereby stop the progress of the fire between the road and the lake. But still the flames passed over and heedlessly swept along. Capt. Reid, with the Horse Guards, adopting a different plan, upon the suggestion of a private, ordered his men to dismount about 2 miles in advance of the trains, and with their sabers hew and chop down the grass from the road to the lake, on a space 30 feet broad, and throw the cut grass out leeward. This was done. Fire was now set to the grass standing next to the wind, which burned slowly until it met the advancing conflagration. Thus the fire was checked on one side of the road.

On the other side the volume of flame, increasing as the gale rose, rolled along the plain and over the mountains, roaring and crackling and careering in its resistless course until the fuel which fed it was exhausted. The men spent the night on the bare and blackened earth, and the animals stood to their tethers without forage.

On the southwestern side of this lake, and near its margin, stands the princely hacienda of Don Angel Trias, governor of Chihuahua. On this estate immense herds of cattle and flocks of sheep are produced. But the Mexican soldiers, 700 of whom on the morning of the 25th had been seen at the hacienda, had driven them all off, to prevent the Americans from subsisting on them. On the night of the 25th, and before it was known that the soldiery had evacuated the post, Capt. Reid, with 25 of the Horse Guards, volunteered to make a reconnoissance of the enemy and report his position and strength. As, in the event the enemy was still occupying his position at the hacienda, strong guards would most probably be posted near the roads leading into the place from above and below the lake, the scouts, to prevent falling upon the guards and to take the enemy by surprise, if it should be deemed advisable to attack him, crossed the lake, which was near 3 miles wide and both deep and boggy and hitherto considered impassable. Reaching the opposite shore, they saw no sentinel. Therefore they approached nearer. Still they saw no sentry. Cautiously and with light footsteps and in almost breathless silence, without a whisper or the jingling of a saber, and under cover of the dark, they advanced a little. They heard the sound of music and at intervals the tramping of horses. Perhaps it was the military patrol. None knew.

They now rode around the hacienda; but the high walls precluded the possibility of seeing within. No satisfactory reconnoissance could therefore be made. Not wishing to return to camp without effecting their object, the captain and his men, like McDonald and his madcaps at Georgetown, made a sweeping dash, with drawn saber and clattering arms, into the hacienda, to the infinite alarm of the inhabitants. They now had possession. The 700 soldiers had started, about an hour previous, to Sacramento. This was a bold and hazardous exploit. Then they quartered in the place, which contains several hundred inhabitants, and were sumptuously entertained by the administrador del hacienda.[1] The next morning they rejoined the army, then on the march, having with them several wild Mexican cattle. The whole force now moved on to a fort called Sanz, on a creek discharging into the Laguna de Encenillas. Here they encamped.

The next day the army and trains, including the merchant wagons, were drawn up in order of battle, ready to maneuver expeditiously in the event of a sudden attack. The enemy was known to be at no great distance.[2] Thus the march was continued until night over a level, beautiful valley, with a high range of mountains running along on the left and, at a greater distance, also on the right. A short time before sunset Lieut. Col. Mitchell, Lieuts. Winston and Sproule, Corpl. Goodfellow, the author, and one other volunteer, having proceeded about 9 miles in advance of the column, and within 5 miles. of the enemy's fortified position at Sacramento, ascended a high, rocky peak of the mountain and, with good telescopes, enjoyed a fair view of the whole Mexican encampment. The enemy's whole line of fieldworks was distinctly viewed, the position of his batteries ascertained, and his probable numbers estimated. The result of this reconnoissance was duly reported to Col. Doniphan, whereupon he immediately called a council of officers and matured a plan for the conduct of the march on the following day. This night, also, the army encamped on a tributary of the lake of Encenillas.

On Sunday, the 28th of February, a bright and auspicious day, the American army, under Col. Doniphan, arrived in sight of the Mexican encampment at Sacramento, which could be distinctly seen at a distance of 4 miles. His command consisted of the following corps and detachments of troops:

The First Regiment, Col. Doniphan, numbering about 800 men; Lieut. Col. Mitchell's escort, 97 men; artillery battalion, Maj. Clark and Capt. Weightman, 117 men, with a light field battery of six pieces of cannon; and two companies of teamsters, under Capts. Skillman and Glasgow, forming an extra battalion of about 150 men, commanded by Maj. Owens, of Independence, making an aggregate force of 1,164 men, all Missouri volunteers. The march of the day was conducted in the following order: The wagons, near 400 in all, were thrown into four parallel files, with spaces of 30 feet between each. In the center space marched the artillery battalion; in the space to the right, the first battalion; and in the space to the left, the second battalion. Masking these in front marched the three companies intended to act as cavalry, the Missouri Horse Guards, under Capt. Reid, on the right, the Missouri Dragoons, under Capt. Parsons, on the left, and the Chihuahua Rangers, under Capt. Hud-

---

[1] These fearless men were Capt. Reid, C. Human, F. C. Hughes, W. Russell, J. Cooper, T. Bradford, Todd, I. Walker, L. A. Maclean, C. Clarkin, Long, T. Forsythe, Tungitt, Brown, W. McDaniel, J. P. Campbell, T. Waugh, J. Vaughan, Boyce, Stewart, Antwine, and A. Henderson and I. Kirker, interpreters, and one or two others.
[2] Capt. Skillman this day pursued one of the enemy's spies into the mountains so closely that he captured his horse, but the Mexican, leaping off, escaped on foot among the rocks.

son, in the center. Thus arranged, they approached the scene of action.[1]

The enemy had occupied the brow of a rocky eminence rising upon a plateau between the River Sacramento and the Arroya Seca and near the Sacramento Fort, 18 miles from Chihuahua, and fortified its approaches by a line of fieldworks, consisting of 28 strong redoubts and intrenchments. Here, in this apparently secure position, the Mexicans had determined to make a bold stand, for this pass was the key to the capital. So certain of victory were the Mexicans that they had prepared strings and handcuffs in which they meant to drive us prisoners to the City of Mexico, as they did the Texans in 1841. Thus fortified and intrenched, the Mexican Army, consisting, according to a consolidated report of the adjutant general which came into Col. Doniphan's possession after the battle, of 4,220 men, commanded by Maj. Gen. José A. Heredia, aided by Gen. Garcia Condé, former minister of war in Mexico, as commander of cavalry; Gen. Mauricia Ugarté, commander of infantry; Gen. Justiniani, commander of artillery; and Gov. Angel Trias, brigadier general, commanding the Chihuahua Volunteers, awaited the approach of the Americans.

When Col. Doniphan arrived within 1½ miles of the enemy's fortifications (a reconnoissance of his position having been made by Maj. Clark), leaving the main road which passed within the range of his batteries, he suddenly deflected to the right, crossed the rocky arroya, expeditiously gained the plateau beyond, successfully deployed his men into line upon the highland, causing the enemy to change his first position, and made the assault from the west. This was the best point of attack that could possibly have been selected. The event of the day proves how well it was chosen.

In passing the arroya the caravan and baggage trains followed close upon the rear of the army. Nothing could exceed in point of solemnity and grandeur the rumbling of the artillery, the firm moving of the caravan, the dashing to and fro of horsemen, and the waving of banners and gay fluttering guidons as both armies advanced to the attack on the rocky plain, for at this crisis Gen. Condé, with a select body of 1,200 cavalry, dashed down from the fortified heights to commence the engagement. When within 950 yards of our alignment, Maj. Clark's battery of 6-pounders and Weightman's section of howitzers opened upon them a well-directed and most destructive fire, producing fearful execution in their ranks. In some disorder they fell back a short distance, unmasking a battery of cannon, which immediately commenced its fire upon us. A brisk cannonading was now kept up on both sides for the space of 50 minutes, during which time the enemy suffered great loss, our battery discharging 24 rounds to the minute. The balls from the enemy's cannon whistled through our ranks in rapid succession. Many horses and other animals were killed and the wagons much shattered. Sergt. A. Hughes, of the Missouri Dragoons, had both his legs broken by a cannon ball. In this action the enemy, who were drawn up in columns four deep, close order, lost about 25 killed, besides a great number of horses. The Americans, who stood dismounted in two ranks open order, suffered but slight injury.

---

[1]An eagle, sometimes scaring aloft and sometimes swooping down amongst the fluttering banners, followed along the lines all day and seemed to herald the news of victory. The men regarded the omen as good.

Gen. Condé, with considerable disorder, now fell back and rallied his men behind the intrenchments and redoubts. Col. Doniphan immediately ordered the buglers to sound the advance. Thereupon the American Army moved forward in the following manner to storm the enemy's breastworks:

The artillery battalion, Maj. Clark, in the center, firing occasionally on the advance; the First Battalion, commanded by Lieut. Cols. Jackson and Mitchell, composing the right wing; the two select companies of cavalry under Capts. Reid and Parsons, and Capt. Hudson's mounted company, immediately on the left of the artillery; and the Second Battalion on the extreme left, commanded by Maj. Gilpin. The caravan and baggage trains, under command of Maj. Owens, followed close in the rear. Col. Doniphan and his aids, Capt. Thompson, United States Army, Adjt. De Courcy, and Sergt. Maj. Crenshaw acted between the battalions.

At this crisis a body of 300 lancers and lazadors were discovered advancing upon our rear. These were exclusive of Heredia's main force and were said to be criminals turned loose from the Chihuahua prisons, that by some gallant exploit they might expurgate themselves of crime. To this end they were posted in the rear to cut off stragglers, prevent retreat, and capture and plunder the merchant wagons. The battalion of teamsters kept these at bay. Besides this force there were 1,000 spectators—women, citizens, and rancheros—perched on the summits of the adjacent mountains and hills, watching the event of the day.

As we neared the enemy's redoubts, still inclining to the right, a heavy fire was opened upon us from his different batteries, consisting in all of 16 pieces of cannon. But owing to the facility with which our movements were performed and to the fact that the Mexicans were compelled to fire plungingly upon our lines (their position being considerably elevated above the plateau, and particularly the battery placed on the brow of the Sacramento Mountain with the design of enfilading our column), we sustained but little damage.

When our column had approached within about 400 yards of the enemy's line of fieldworks the three cavalry companies, under Capts. Reid, Parsons, and Hudson, and Weightman's section of howitzers were ordered to carry the main central battery, which had considerably annoyed our lines and which was protected by a strong bastion. The charge was not made simultaneously, as intended by the colonel, for this troop, having spurred forward a little way, was halted for a moment under a heavy cross fire from the enemy by the adjutant's misapprehending the order. However, Capt. Reid, either not hearing or disregarding the adjutant's order to halt, leading the way, waved his sword, and, rising in his stirrups, exclaimed, "Will my men follow me?" Hereupon Lieuts. Barnett, Hinton, and Moss, with about 25 men, bravely sprang forward, rose the hill with the captain, carried the battery, and for a moment silenced the guns. But we were too weak to hold possession of it. By the overwhelming force of the enemy we were beaten back and many of us wounded. Here Maj. Samuel C. Owens, who had voluntarily charged upon the redoubt, received a cannon or musket shot which instantly killed both him and his horse. Capt. Reid's horse was shot under him, and a gallant young man of the same name immediately dismounted and generously offered the captain his.

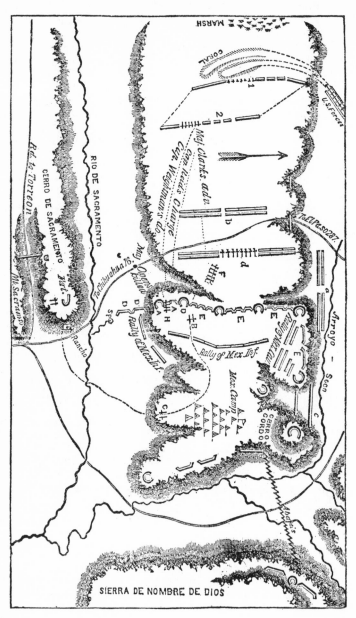

PLAN OF THE BATTLE OF SACRAMENTO.

Explanation.

◖ ⊔ ⊔ Redoubts and intrenchments, filled with Mexican infantry.
1. First position U. S. forces. 2. Second do. a, First position Mexican cavalry. b, Second position Mexican do. c, First position Mexican infantry. d, Second position Mexican cavalry and infantry.
A A—Red. and intrench. stormed by Capt. Reid's Horse Guards.
B—First position of the howitzers on hill.
C—Sec'd " " " "
D D D—Redoubts and intrenchments taken by 1st batt.
E E E E—Red. and Intrench. taken by 2d bat. and Mo. Drag.
F—Major Clark's batt. dispersing the rally of Mexican cav.
H—Fourth position Major Clark's batt., from which he silenced the fort on Sacramento hill.

List of Officers.

Col. A. W. Doniphan, Comm. U. S. Forces.—Staff—Capt. Thompson, U. S., D. A. A. de C.—Lieut. De Courcy, Adjt.
Surg., Morton ; Asst. S., Moore & Morton.
Artillery ; Maj. Clark, Adjt. Walker, Capt. Weightman.—Sect'n Howitz. ; Lieuts. Chouteau and Evans.
Six lb'rs ; Lts. Dorn, Kribben, Labeaume.
Cavalry ; Missouri Horse Guards, Capt. Reid.—Lts., Hinton, Barnett, Moss and Hicklin.
Miss. Drag. ; Capt. Parson.—Lts., Winston & Harrison.
Chihuahua Rang. ; Capt. Hudson.—Lts. Sproule & Todd.
Infantry : Lt. Cols., Mitchell and Jackson—Maj. Gilpin.—Capts., Waldo, Walton, Moss, Stevensons, Hughes, and Rogers.—Lts., Reed, Clayton, Childs, Lea. Graves, Sublette, Ogden, Miller, Bush, M'Danald, Campbell, Gordon, Jackson, Wright, Duncan and Murray.

NOTE.—Strength of the U. S. Forces : Total, 924—6 pieces artillery.—Loss, 1 killed and 11 wounded (3 mortally).—Mexican : 4224—10 pieces artillery and 9 culvs.—Killed 320, wounded, 560, 72 prisoners.

CHARGE OF CAPT. REID, AT SACRAMENTO.

NOTE.—As Lieut. Col. Jackson, at the head of the first battalion, charged over the enemy's breastworks, with his long shotgun in one hand and his drawn saber in the other, almost the only order he gave, just at that time, was : " Now, boys, every man for his turkey ! " And, it is said, almost every man singled out his " yallow fellow," as the colonel called the Mexicans, and brought the bead to bear upon him with as much certainty as if he were shooting at wild game in the forests of Missouri.

The next morning after the battle, Col. Doniphan called on his battalion officers for a report of their respective commands. Majs. Clark and Gilpin each furnished a detailed account of the conduct of the troops under his immediate control. When he called on Lieut. Col. Jackson for his report he observed : " Colonel ! I am not a writing man—all I have to say is, that my men fought like h—ll, and whipped everything before them ! "

The next day after the battle, Dr. Reese, who had been carried to Parral, as a prisoner, effected his escape. On his return to Chihuahua, he met many of the Mexicans, on the retreat towards Durango. The retreating host permitted him to pass on uninterrupted. At length he met a Mexican in full gallop, and almost frantic with despair. The Doctor hailed him, and asked him whither he was going, in such haste. " Corrajo ! I am running from those d—n—d hairy Americans ! They fight like devils incarnate ! "

One of the lieutenants of the Mexican artillery stood to his guns, until he was wounded and captured. Col. Doniphan asked him if he did not know, before the action came on, that the Mexicans would be defeated. The lieutenant replied. " I did not ; and if they had stood to their posts, as I encouraged them to do, you never could have driven us from our strong position. I am now your prisoner ; but I do not regret fighting for the liberty and honor of my country. I will still encourage my people to resist foreign invasion." Col. Doniphan was so well pleased with the patriotic devotion of the young officer, that he immediately gave him his liberty.

By this time the remainder of Capt. Reid's company, under Lieut. Hicklin, and the section of howitzers under Capt. Weightman and Lieuts. Choteau and Evans, rose the hill and supported Capt. Reid. A deadly volley of grape and canister shot mingled with yager balls quickly cleared the intrenchments and the redoubt. The battery was retaken and held. Almost at the same instant Capts. Parsons and Hudson, with the two remaining companies of cavalry, crossed the intrenchments to Reid's left and successfully engaged with the enemy. They resolutely drove him back and held the ground.

All the companies were now pressing forward and pouring over the intrenchments and into the redoubts, eagerly vieing with each other in the noble struggle for victory. Each company, as well as each soldier, was ambitious to excel. Companies A, B, C, and a part of Company D, composing the right wing, all dismounted, respectively under command of Capts. Waldo, Walton, Moss, and Lieut. Miller, led on by Lieut. Cols. Jackson and Mitchell, stormed a formidable line of redoubts on the enemy's left, defended by several pieces of cannon and a great number of resolute and well-armed men. A part of this wing took possession of the strong battery on Sacramento Hill, which had kept up a continued cross-firing upon our right during the whole engagement. Cols. Jackson and Mitchell, and their captains, lieutenants, noncommissioned officers, and men generally behaved with commendable gallantry. Many instances of individual prowess were exhibited. But it is invidious to distinguish between men where all performed their duty so nobly.

Meanwhile the left wing also dismounted, commanded by Maj. Gilpin, a gallant and skillful officer, boldly scaled the heights, passed the intrenchments, cleared the redoubts, and, with considerable slaughter, forced the enemy to retreat from his position on the right. Company G, under Capt. Hughes, and a part of Company F, under Lieut. Gordon, stormed a battery of three brass 4-pounders strongly defended by embankments and ditches filled by resolute and well-armed Mexican infantry. Some of the artillerists were made prisoners while endeavoring to touch off the cannon. Companies H and E, under Capts. Rodgers and Stephenson, and a part of Hudson's company, under Lieut. Todd, ·on the extreme left, behaved nobly and fought with great courage. They beat the Mexicans from their strong places and chased them like bloodhounds. Maj. Gilpin was not behind his men in bravery—he encouraged them to fight by example.

Maj. Clark, with his 6-pounders, and Capt. Weightman, with his howitzers, during the whole action rendered the most signal and essential service and contributed much toward the success of the day. The gallant charge led by Capt. Reid and sustained by Capt. Weightman, in point of daring and brilliancy of execution, has not been excelled by any similar exploit during the war.

Gen. Heredia made several unsuccessful attempts to rally his retreating forces, to infuse into their minds new courage, and to close up the breaches already made in his lines. Gen. Condé, with his troop of horse, also vainly endeavored to check the advance of the Missourians. They were dislodged from their strong places and forced from the hill in confusion.

The rout of the Mexican Army now became general, and the slaughter continued until night put an end to the chase. The battle lasted three hours and a half. The men returned to the battle field after dark completely worn out and exhausted with fatigue. The Mexicans lost 304 men killed on the field and a large number of wounded, perhaps not less than 500; and 70 prisoners, among whom was Brig. Gen. Cuilta,[1] together with a vast quantity of provisions, $6,000 in specie, 50,000 head of sheep, 1,500 head of cattle, 100 mules, 20 wagons, 25 or 30 caretas, 25,000 pounds of ammunition, 10 pieces of cannon of different calibers varying from 4 to 9 pounders, 6 culverins or wall pieces, 100 stand of small arms, 100 stand of small colors, 7 fine carriages, the general's scrutoire, and many other things of less note. Our loss was Maj. Samuel C. Owens killed and 11 wounded,[2] three of whom have subsequently died.

Thus was the army of central Mexico totally defeated and completely disorganized by a column of Missouri volunteers. The Mexicans retreated precipitately to Durango and dispersed among the ranchos and villages. Their leaders were never able to rally them.

In this engagement Col. Doniphan was personally much exposed, and by reason of his stature was a conspicuous mark for the fire of the enemy's guns. He was all the while at the proper place, whether to dispense his orders, encourage his men, or to use his saber in thinning the enemy's ranks.[3] His effective force actually engaged was about 950 men, including a considerable number of amateur fighters, among whom James L. Collins, James Kirker, Messrs. Henderson and Anderson, interpreters, Maj. Campbell, and James Stewart, deserve to be favorably mentioned. They fought bravely. It was impossible for Capts. Skillman and Glasgow to bring their companies of teamsters into the action. They deserve great honor for their gallantry in defending the trains. The soldiers encamped on the battle field, within the enemy's intrenchments, and feasted sumptuously upon his viands, wines, and poundcakes. There they rested.[4]

---

[1] Gen. Cuilta was captured in Chihuahua, Mar. 4, by Lieut. Col. Jackson and Capt. Hughes.

[2] Wounded : In Capt. Reid's mounted company—A. A. Kirkpatrick, mortally ; J. L. Mac-Gruder, mortally ; J. Barnes, arm broken ; L. A. MacLean, severely ; J. Sullivan, slightly ; J. T. Hughes, slightly. In Capt. Parsons's mounted company—W. Henkey, mortally ; W. Gordon, severely ; Sergt. A. Hughes, both legs broken ; J. B. Fleming, severely. In Hudson's mounted company—J. Wolf, slightly.

[3] His courage and gallant conduct were only equaled by his foresight and great judgment.

[4] Previous to the commencement of the battle the hostage, Ortiz, manifested considerable uneasiness and showed an evident disposition not to be carried near the scene of strife, lest he, too, should suffer in the general slaughter which he apprehended would take place among the Americans. He said to Col. Doniphan : " Your force is too weak to contend against such a force as the Mexican Army and in so strong a position. You will all be inevitably destroyed or captured and put in chains. The Mexicans will whip you beyond a doubt. I beg that you will permit me to remain out of danger." Col. Doniphan good-humoredly replied : " If I should be victorious, I will continue to treat you in a manner every way worthy your dignity. If your own people should be the conquerors, and you should fall into their hands, they will certainly do you no hurt. So, being safe in either event, you must have little cause of apprehension." When the battle was over Col. Doniphan observed to the curate : " Well, Ortiz, what think you now about the Mexicans ' whipping ' my boys?" The other replied : "Ah ! sir, they would have defeated you if you had fought like men, but you fought like devils."

While the battle was raging Capt. Glasgow, of the merchant battalion, came up to the colonel, who was standing upon the hill from which the Mexicans had been repulsed, and asked him how the day was about to issue. " Don't you see," says the colonel, " how my boys are knocking them down like ninepins ? "

Just previous to the charge the right and left wings were dismounted and every seventh man detailed to hold horses. At this moment the volley of musketry, grape, and cannister from the enemy's lines was tremendous. As Col. Doniphan passed up the lines a volunteer, who had seven horses in charge, called to him and said : " See here, Colonel ! am I compelled to stand here in this tempest of cannon and musket balls and hold horses ? " " Yes," says the colonel ; " if you are detailed for the purpose." The volunteer, quickly tying the several bridles together, dashed them down, seized his gun and saber, and started off in the charge, exclaiming as he left the colonel : " Hold hell in a fight ! I didn't come here to hold horses—I can do that at home."

As the right wing scaled the breastworks Sergt. Tom Hinckle was one of the first who crossed the intrenchments and got amongst the enemy. Having fired his yager and pistols, he was too hotly beleaguered to reload them. He laid them aside and, like Ajax Telamon, resolutely defended himself by throwing rocks.

Col. Doniphan, not like Hannibal loitering on the plains of Italy, after the battle of Cannæ, when he might have entered Rome in triumph, immediately followed up his success, and improved the advantage which his victory gave him. Early the next morning, March 1, he dispatched Lieut. Col. Mitchell, with 150 men under command of Capts. Reid and Weightman, and a section of artillery, to take formal possession of the capital and occupy it in the name of his Government. This detachment, before arriving in the city, was met by several American gentlemen escaping from confinement, who represented that the Mexican soldiery had left the place undefended, and fled with the utmost precipitation to Durango. The Spanish consul also came out with the flag of his country to salute and acknowledge the conqueror. This small body of troops entered and took military possession of Chihuahua, without the slightest resistance, and the following night occupied the cuartel near Hidalgo's monument, which stands in the Alameda.

Meanwhile Col. Doniphan and his men collected the booty, tended the captured animals, refitted the trains, remounted those who had lost their steeds in the action, arranged the preliminaries of a procession, and having marched a few miles, encamped for the night. On the morning of the 2d day of March, Col. Doniphan, with all his military trains, the merchant caravan, gay, fluttering colors, and the whole spolia opima, triumphantly entered the city to the tunes of "Yankee Doodle" and "Hail Columbia," and fired in the public square a national salute of 28 guns. This was a proud moment for the American troops. The battle of Sacramento gave them the capital, and now the Stars and Stripes and serpent-eagle of the model Republic were streaming victoriously over the stronghold of Central Mexico.

Col. Doniphan's official account of the memorable battle of the 28th of February is here subjoined:

HEADQUARTERS OF THE ARMY, CHIHUAHUA,
City of Chihuahua, March 4, 1847.

I have the honor to report to you the movement of the army under my command since my last official report.

On the evening of the 8th of February, 1847, we left the town of El Paso del Norte, escorting the merchant train or caravan of 315 wagons, for the city of Chihuahua. Our force consisted of 924 effective men—117 officers and privates of the Artillery, 93 of Lieut. Col. Michell's escort, and the remainder of the First Regiment Missouri Mounted Volunteers. We progressed in the direction of this place until the 25th, when we were informed by our spies that the enemy, to the number of 1,500 men, were at Encinillas, the country seat of Gov. Trias, about 25 miles in advance.

When we arrived on the evening of the 26th near the point we found that the force had retreated in the direction of this city. On the evening of the 27th we arrived at Sans, and learned from our spies that the enemy in great force had fortified the pass of the Sacramento River, about 15 miles in advance, and about the same distance from this city. We were also informed that there was no water between the point we were at and that occupied by the enemy; we therefore determined to halt until morning. At sunrise on the 28th, the last day of February, we took up the line of march and formed the whole train, consisting of 315 heavy traders' wagons, and our commissary and company wagons, into four columns, thus shortening our line so as to make it more easily protected. We placed the artillery and all the commands except 200 cavalry proper in the intervals between the columns of wagons. We thus fully concealed our force and its position by masking our force with the cavalry. When we arrived within 3 miles of the enemy we made a reconnoissance of his position and the arrangement of his forces. This we could easily do, the road leading through an open prairie valley between the sterile mountains. The pass of the

Sacramento is formed by a point of the mountains on our right, their left extending into the valley or plain so as to narrow the valley to about 1½ miles. On our left was a deep dry channel of a creek, and between these points the plain rises to 60 feet abruptly. This rise is in the form of a crescent, the convex part being to the north of our forces. On the right, from the point of mountains, a narrow part of the plain extends north 1½ miles farther than on the left. The main road passes down the center of the valley and across the crescent, near the left or dry branch.

The Sacramento rises in the mountain on the right, and the road falls on it about 1 mile below the battle field or intrenchment of the enemy. We ascertained that the enemy had one battery of four guns—two 9 and 6 pounders—on the point of the mountain on our right (their left) at good elevation to sweep the plain and at the point where the mountains extended farthest into the plain. On our left (their right) they had another battery on an elevation commanding the road and three intrenchments of two 6 pounders, and on the brow of the crescent near the center another of two, six, and four and six culverins, or rampart pieces, mounted on carriages, and on the crest of the hill or ascent between the batteries and on the right and left they had 27 redoubts dug and thrown up, extending at short intervals across the whole ground. In these their infantry were placed and were entirely protected. Their cavalry was drawn up in front of the redoubts in the intervals four deep, and in front of the redoubts two deep, so as to mask them as far as practicable. When we had arrived within 1½ miles of the intrenchments along the main road we advanced the cavalry still farther and suddenly diverged with the column to the right, so as to gain the narrow part of the ascent on our right, which the enemy discovering endeavored to prevent by moving forward with 1,000 cavalry and four pieces of cannon in their rear masked by them. Our movements were so rapid that we gained the elevation with our forces and the advance of our wagons in time to form before they arrived within reach of our guns. The enemy halted and we advanced the head of our column within 1,200 yards of them, so as to let our wagons attain the high lands and form as before.

We now commenced the action by a brisk fire from our battery, and the enemy unmasked and commenced also; our fire proved effective at this distance, killing 15 men, wounding many more, and disabling one of the enemy's guns. We had two men slightly wounded and several horses and mules killed. The enemy then slowly retreated behind their works in some confusion, and we resumed our march in our former order, still diverging more to the right to avoid their battery on our left (their right) and their strongest redoubts, which were on the left, near where the road passes. After marching as far as we safely could without coming within range of their heavy battery on our right Capt. Weightman, of the Artillery, was ordered to charge with the two 12-pound howitzers, to be supported by the Cavalry, under Capts. Reid, Parsons, and Hudson. The howitzers charged at speed and were gallantly sustained by Capt. Reid; but by some misunderstanding my order was not given to the other two companies. Capt. Hudson, anticipating my order, charged in time to give ample support to the howitzers. Capt. Parsons at the same moment came to me and asked permission for his company to charge the redoubts immediately to the left of Capt. Weightman, which he did very gallantly. The remainder of the two battalions of the regiment were dismounted during the Cavalry charge and followed rapidly on foot, and Maj. Clarke advanced as fast as possible with the remainder of the battery; we charged their redoubts from right to left, with a brisk and deadly fire of riflemen, while Maj. Clarke opened a rapid and well-directed fire on a column of cavalry attempting to pass to our left so as to attack the wagons and our rear. The fire was so well directed as to force them to fall back, and our riflemen, with the cavalry and howitzers, cleared the hill after an obstinate resistance. Our force advanced to the very brink of their redoubts and attacked them with their sabers. When the redoubts were cleared and the batteries in the center and our left were silenced the main battery on our right still continued to pour in a constant and heavy fire, as it had done during the heat of the engagement, but as the whole fate of the battle depended upon carrying the redoubts and center battery this one on the right remained unattacked, and the enemy had rallied there 500 strong.

Maj. Clarke was directed to commence a heavy fire upon it, while Lieut. Cols. Mitchell and Jackson, commanding the first battalion, were ordered to remount and charge the battery on the left, while Maj. Gilpin was directed to march the second battalion on foot up the rough ascent of the mountain on the opposite side. The fire of our battery was so effective as to completely silence theirs, and the rapid advance of our column put them to flight over the mountains in great confusion.

Capt. Thompson, of the First Dragoons, acted as my aid and adviser on the field during the whole engagement and was of the most essential service to me. Also Lieut. Wooster, of the United States Army, who acted very coolly and gallantly. Maj. Campbell, of Springfield, Mo., also acted as a volunteer aid during part of the time, but left me and joined Capt. Reid in his gallant charge. Thus ended the battle of Sacramento. The force of the enemy was 1,200 cavalry from Durango and Chihuahua, with the Vera Cruz Dragoons, and 1,200 infantry from Chihuahua, 300 artillerists, and 1,420 rancheros, badly armed with lassos, lances, and machetos, or corn knives, 10 pieces of artillery—two 9, four 8, and two 4 pounders and six culverins, or rampart pieces. Their forces were commanded by Maj. Gen. Hendea, general of Durango, Chihuahua, Sonora., and New Mexico; Brig. Gen. Justiniani, Brig. Gen. Garcia Condé, formerly minister of war for the Republic of Mexico, who is a scientific man and planned this whole field of defense; Gen. Uguarte and Gov. Trias, who acted as brigadier general on the field, and colonels and other officers without number.

Our force was 924 effective men, at least 100 of whom were engaged in holding horses and driving teams.

The loss of the enemy was his entire artillery, 30 wagons, masses of beans and piñola, and other Mexican provisions, about 300 killed, and the same number wounded, many of whom have since died, and 40 prisoners.

The field was literally covered with the dead and wounded from our artillery and the unerring fire of our riflemen. Night put a stop to the carnage, the battle having commenced about 3 o'clock. Our loss was one killed, one mortally wounded, and seven so wounded as to recover without the loss of limbs. I can not speak too highly of the coolness, gallantry, and bravery of the officers and men under my command.

I was ably sustained by the field officers, Lieut. Cols. Mitchell and Jackson, of the first battalion, and Maj. Gilpin, of the second battalion, and Maj. Clark and his artillery acted nobly and did the most effective service in every part of the field. It is abundantly shown, in the charge made by Capt. Weightman with the section of howitzers, that they can be used in any charge of cavalry with great effect. Much has been and justly said of the gallantry of our artillery, unlimbering within 250 yards of the enemy at Palo Alto; but how much more daring was the charge of Capt. Weightman when he unlimbered within 50 yards of the redoubts of the enemy.

On the 1st day of March we took formal possession of the capital of Chihuahua in the name of our Government. We were ordered by Gen. Kearney to report to Gen. Wool at this place; since our arrival we hear he is at Saltillo, surrounded by the enemy. Our present purpose is either to force our way to him or return by Bexar, as our term of service expires on the last day of May next.

I have the honor to be your obedient servant,

A. W. DONIPHAN,
Colonel First Regiment Missouri Volunteers.

Brig. R. JONES,
Adujant General, United States Army.

On the morning after the engagement Maj. Clarke, in reporting to Col. Doniphan the conduct of the troops under his command, holds the following language:

Capt. Weightman charged at full gallop upon the enemy's left, preceded by Capt. Reid and his company of horse, and after crossing a ravine some 150 yards from the enemy he unlimbered the guns within 50 yards of the intrenchment and opened a destructive fire of cannister into his ranks, which was warmly returned, but without effect. Capt. Weightman again advanced upon the intrenchment, passing through it in the face of the enemy, and within a few feet of the ditches and in the midst of cross-fires from three directions again opened his fire to the right and left with such effect that, with the formidable charge of the cavalry and dismounted men of your own regiment and Lieut. Col. Mitchell's escort, the enemy were driven from their breastworks on our right in great confusion. At this time, under a heavy cross-fire from the battery of four 6-pounders, under Lieuts. Dorn, Kribbin, and Labeaume, upon the enemy's right, supported by Maj. Gilpin on the left, and the wagon train escorted by two companies of infantry under Capts. E. F. Glasgow and Skillman in the rear, Maj. Gilpin charged upon the enemy's center and forced him from his intrenchments under a heavy fire of artillery and small arms. At the same time the fire of our own battery was opened upon the enemy's extreme right, from which a continued fire had been kept up upon our line and the wagon train. Two of the enemy's guns were now soon dismounted on their right, that battery silenced, and the enemy dislodged from the redoubt on the Cerro Frijolis. Perceiving a body of lancers forming for the purpose of outflanking our left and attacking the merchant train under Capts. Glasgow and Skillman, I again opened upon them a very destructive fire of grape and spherical case shot, which soon cleared the left of our line. The enemy, vacating his intrenchments and deserting his guns, was hotly pursued toward the mountains beyond Cerro Frijolis and down Arroyo Seco la Sacramento by both wings of the army under Lieut. Col. Mitchell, Lieut. Col. Jackson, and Maj. Gilpin, and by Capt. Weightman, with the section of howitzers. During this pursuit my officers repeatedly opened their fires upon the retreating enemy with great effect. To cover this flight of the enemy's forces from the intrenched camp the heaviest of his cannon had been taken from the intrenchment to Cerro Sacramento and a heavy fire opened upon our pursuing forces and the wagons following in the rear. To silence this battery I had the honor to anticipate your order to that effect by at once occupying the nearest of the enemy's intrenchments, 1,225 yards distant, and, notwithstanding the elevated position of the Mexican battery, giving him a plunging fire into my intrenchment, which was not defiladed, and the greater range of his long 9 pounders, the first fire of our guns dismounted one of his largest pieces, and the fire was kept up with such briskness and precision of aim that the battery was soon silenced and the enemy seen precipitately retreating. The fire was then continued upon the Rancho Sacramento and the enemy's ammunition and wagon train retreating upon the road to Chihuahua. By their fire the house and several wagons were rendered untenable and useless. By this time Lieut. Col. Mitchell had scaled the hill, followed by the section of howitzers under Capt. Weightman, and the last position of the Mexican forces was taken possession of by our troops, thus leaving the American forces master of the field.

CHAPTER XIX.

Col. Doniphan now having actual possession of the city of Chihuahua and virtual possession of the State; having quartered his soldiers in the public buildings near the plaza and other houses vacated by the families who fled at his approach; having stationed his artillery in a manner to command the streets and other avenues leading into the square for the perfect defense of the capital; having sent the prefecto of the city to the battle field with a number of Mexicans to bury their dead; and having set the curate, Ortiz, and the other hostages at liberty, issued the following proclamation to the inhabitants of Chihuahua:

The commander of the North American forces in Chihuahua informs the citizens of this State that he has taken military possession of this capital and has the satisfaction to assure them that complete tranquillity exists therein.

He invites all the citizens to return to their houses and continue their ordinary occupations under the security that their persons, religion, and property shall be respected.

He declares, likewise, in the name of his Government, that, having taken possession of the capital, after conquering the forces of the State, he has equally taken possession of the State.

He invites the citizens of all the towns and ranchos to continue their traffic, to come to this capital to buy and sell as formerly before the late occurrences, under the assurance they shall in no manner be molested or troubled, and, as already said, their property shall be respected; for if the troops under my command should stand in need of anything, a fair price shall be given for the value thereof with the utmost punctuality.

He likewise declares that the American troops will punish with promptitude any excess that may be committed, whether it be by the bararous Indians or by any other individual.

Lastly, we assure all good citizens that we carry on war against the armies alone and not against individual citizens who are unarmed.

We therefore only exact not that any Mexican should assist us against his country, but that in the present war he remain neutral, for it can not be expected in a contrary event that we should respect the rights of those who take up arms against our lives.

Preceding the Battle of Sacramento the American residents and merchants in Chihuahua, of whom there were about 30, received ill treatment from the Mexican populace. Indignities and insults were offered them. They were mostly kept in custody and not permitted to pass without the limits of the city. They were tauntingly told that when Col. Doniphan and his handful of men arrived there they would be handcuffed and delivered over to the populace, to be dealt with as their caprices should suggest and their humor prompt them. They even exulted in anticipation of the tortures and cruelties they meant to inflict upon the "presumptuous northern invaders." To this they often added the epithets "Texans," "Yankees," "heretics," and "pirates." When the action commenced the cannonading was distinctly heard in Chihuahua. The tide of battle was known to be raging, but the event was doubtful. When the first cannonading ceased it was announced that the Americans were defeated; that victory had perched on the Mexican flag. The resident Americans now lost all hope. The rabble triumphed and exulted over them. In a fit of immoderate excitement the greasers seized staves, knives, stones, and whatever else chance had thrown in their way, and threatened to kill them without distinction. But hark! the thunders of the battle are renewed. The merchants' hearts began to revive. The cannons' roar, the vollies of musketry, and the sharp-shooting yagers are heard until darkness envelops the earth. At length a courier, "frantic with despair," arrives in the city and exclaims, "Perdemos! Perdemos!" We are lost, defeated, ruined. Then the generals, the governor, and the retreating host came, and in hot haste passed on to Parral and thence to Durango, scarcely halting in the city to take a little refreshment. The star of the northern Republic was in the ascendant, and in the pride of their hearts the American residents shouted "victory and triumph." Only one American, James McGoffin, a Kentuckian and a naturalized Mexican, was retained a prisoner and sent to Durango. The rest were liberated.

On the 3d of March the funeral ceremonies of Maj. Owens were performed in the Catholic Church in Chihuahua with great pomp. The Mexican priests officiated on the occasion. His corpse was thence conveyed to the cemetery and interred with Masonic and martial honors. On the following day Sergt. Kirkpatrick died and was buried with similar honors. "Dulce et decorum est pro patria mori."

The same day Lieut. Col. Mitchell, accompanied by several officers and a file of men, went into the public buildings to take possession of such public property as might be found in the city, for the benefit of the United States Treasury. When he called on Mr. Potts, who claimed to be acting English consul at Chihuahua, he refused to give him the keys to the mint, alleging "that he had a private claim upon the mint and did not intend to permit the Americans to go into it." Hereupon great excitement prevailed among the soldiers, for upon the consul's refusing admittance into so spacious a building it was conjectured that the governor and a body of troops might be concealed therein. About 500 soldiers ran to their arms and made ready for the emergency. Capt. Weightman sent for his section of howitzers to be used as keys in entering the building. When their muzzles were turned upon the doors and the port fires lighted the consul, seeing no other alternative, delivered up the keys.

It has been said, with much justice, that the Mexicans both in central and northern Mexico have an unconquerable propensity for amusement and gambling. Their thieving propensities are equally irrepressible. This remark is more especially intended to apply to the lower classes, among whom there is but little of either modesty, truth, virtue, intelligence, honor, or honesty. They were frequently detected in stealing mules, horses, and other property from the American camp while in Chihuahua, and from Jackson's camp at the bull pen [1] in the suburbs of the city. No argument less potent than a teamster's wagon whip was sufficient to restrain them. They were therefore often scourged for their offenses, and that sometimes publicly. This was necessary even to the preserving of tolerable order amongst them.

The people of central Mexico, however, are, upon an average, much more enlightened and possess a higher degree of moral honesty than the inhabitants of the more northern Provinces, yet their complexion and language are very much the same. The Mexicans generally, both men and women, are exceedingly vivacious; showy and facile, and at the same time shallow in conversation; extremely fond of dress and toys; hospitable when the humor prompts them; yet indolent and addicted to every extreme of vicious indulgence; cowardly, and at the same time cruel; serving rather their appetites than following the admonitions of conscience; and possessing elastic and accommodating moral principles. Modest, chaste, virtuous, intelligent females are rarely to be met with, yet notwithstanding they are few, there are some such. Many of the females of that country are gifted with sprightly minds, possess rare personal beauty, and most gentle and winning grace of manners. Their lustrous, dark, sparkling eyes and tresses of glossy black hair constitute a fair share of their charms.

Bathing is regarded in Mexico as one of the choicest luxuries of fashionable life, to which practice both sexes are much addicted. In Chihuahua there are many bathhouses and pools of beautiful water conveniently arranged for public accommodation. These are constantly filled by the young and gay of both sexes, promiscuously splashing and swimming about with their long black hair spread out on the water without one thought of modesty.

The city of Chihuahua, and the capital of the State, was built during the Spanish viceroyalty by the Spanish capitalists and nabobs, who were allured thither from the south by the rich mines of gold and silver in the neighboring mountains. At present it contains 25,000 inhabitants. The streets about the plaza are neatly paved and curbed.

The exterior of the plaza next the streets is paved beautifully with white porphyry in such a manner as to form a promenade, furnished with numerous seats carved out of solid masses of the same material, having backs to rest against, as a sofa. This promenade was constructed for evening gossip and recreation.

In the center of the plaza mayor stands a square structure of hewn marble, about 10 feet high, having four jets supplied by a subterranean aqueduct, which discharges an abundance of cool and delightful water into an octagonal basin about 30 feet in diameter and 3 in depth, constructed also of hewn stone laid in cement and bound

---

[1] The bull pen ranks among the public buildings of Chihuahua, is situated in the suburbs of the city, is built after the manner of an amphitheater, and is spacious enough to contain 5,000 people. It is circular and is furnished with tiers of seats rising one above the other, the top of the structure being flat and sufficiently large to accommodate a vast number of spectators. Here Mexican lancers and gladiators engage in combat with the fiercest wild bulls, goaded to madness and rendered frantic by repeated thrusts of the lance, for the amusement of the people. In such sport do the Mexican people of both sexes delight. This institution is a monstrous type of the moral sentiment of the Mexican nation. If, indeed, the morals of the Mexicans generally are ascribable to the established religion of the country, it is then much to be regretted that such a system ever swayed the minds of any people.

firmly together by a joint work of lead, rendering the whole perfectly impervious to water.

The houses in Chihuahua are chiefly constructed of the adobe, cornered and fronted with hewn stone, having flat roofs, and being two stories high. Many of them are in good taste and furnished in a costly manner. The Catholic cathedral, a magnificent structure, and other public works in the city are thus alluded to by Mr. Gregg, upon whose descriptions it were needless to attempt an improvement:

The most splendid edifice in Chihuahua is the principal church, which is said to equal in architectural grandeur anything of the sort in the Republic. The steeples, of which there is one at each front corner, rise over 100 feet above the azotea. The are composed of very fancifully carved columns; and in appropriate niches of the frontispiece, which is also an elaborate piece of sculpture, are to be seen a number of statues as large as life, the whole forming a complete representation of Christ and the Twelve Apostles. This church was built about a century ago by contributions levied upon the mines of Santa Eulalia, 15 miles from the city, which paid over a percentage on all the metal extracted therefrom, a medio being levied upon each márco of 8 ounces. In this way about $1,000,000 was raised and expended in some 30 years, the time employed in the construction of the building.

A little below the Plaza Mayor stands the ruins of San Francisco—the mere skeleton of another great church of hewn stone, which was commenced by the Jesuits previous to their expulsion in 1767, but never finished. By the outlines still traceable amid the desolation which reigns around, it would appear that the plan of this edifice was conceived in a spirit of still greater magnificence than the Parroquia, which I have been describing. The abounding architectural treasures that are moldering and ready to tumble to the ground bear sufficient evidence that the mind that had directed its progress was at once bold, vigorous, and comprehensive.

This dilapidated building has since been converted into a sort of State prison, particularly for the incarceration of distinguished prisoners. It was here that the principals of the famous Texan Santa Fe expedition were confined when they passed through the place on their way to the City of Mexico. This edifice has also acquired considerable celebrity as having received within its gloomy embraces several of the most distinguished patriots who were taken prisoners during the first infant struggles for Mexican independence. Among these was the illustrious ecclesiastic, Don Miguel Hidalgo, who made the first declaration at the village of Dolores, September 16, 1810. He was taken prisoner in March, 1811, some time after his total defeat at Guadalaxara; and being brought to Chihuahua, he was shot on the 30th of July following, in a little square back of the prison, where a plain white monument of hewn stone has been erected to his memory. It consists of an octagon base of about 25 feet in diameter, upon which rises a square unornamented pyramid to the height of about 30 feet. The monument, indeed, is not an unapt emblem of the purity and simplicity of the curate's character.

Among the few remarkable objects which attract the attention of the traveler is a row of columns supporting a large number of stupendous arches, which may be seen from the heights long before approaching the city from the north. This is an aqueduct of considerable magnitude, which conveys water from the little river of Chihuahua to an eminence above the town, whence it is passed through a succession of pipes to the main public square where it empties itself into a large stone cistern, and by this method the city is supplied with water. This and other public works to be met with in Chihuahua and in the southern cities are glorious remnants of the prosperous times of the Spanish Empire.

The city is supplied with wood and charcoal brought in from the distant mountains on mules and asses. The wood is lashed on the backs of these docile animals by means of rawhide thongs, while the charcoal is put up into sacks and secured in like manner. One of these Mexican arrieros, or woodmen, will often enter the city with an atajo of several hundred of these beasts, each burdened with its cargo of fuel.

On the 7th Col. Doniphan addressed the following letter to Maj. Ryland, of Lexington, Mo.:

DEAR MAJOR: How often have I again and again determined to send you my hearty curses of every thing Mexican? But, then, I knew that you had seen the sterile and miserable country, and its description would be, of course, no novelty to you. To give you, however, a brief outline of our movements, I have to say that we have marched to Santa Fe by Bents Fort, thence through the country of the Navajo Indians to the waters of the Pacific Ocean; down the St. Juan River, the Rio Colorado, and the Gila, back again to the Rio del Norte; across the Jornada del Muerto to Brazito, where we fought the battle of which you have doubtless seen the account; thence to the town of El Paso del Norte, which was taken by us; thence across two other Jornadas and fought the battle of the Sacramento and have sent you herewith a copy of my official report of the same. We are now in the beautiful city of Chihuahua, and myself in the palace of Gov. Trias.

My orders are to report to Gen. Wool; but I now learn that instead of taking the city of Chihuahua, he is shut up at Saltillo by Santa Anna. Our position will be ticklish if Santa Anna should compel Taylor and Wool even to fall back. All Durango, Zacatecas, and Chihuahua will be down upon my little army. We are out of the reach of help, and it would be as unsafe to go backward as forward. High spirits and a bold front is perhaps the best and the safest policy. My men are rough, ragged, and ready, having one more of the R's than Gen. Taylor himself. We have been in service nine months, and my men, after marching 2,000 miles over mountains and deserts, have not received $1 of their pay, yet they stand it without murmuring. Half rations, hard marches, and no clothes; but they are still game to the last and curse and praise their country by turns, but fight for her all the time.

MEXICAN WOODMAN.

No troops could have behaved more gallantly than ours in the battle of the Sacramento. When we approached the enemy their numbers and position would have deterred any troops, less brave and determined, from the attack; but as I rode from rank to rank I could see nothing but the stern resolve to conquer or die—there was no trepidation and no pale faces. I can not discriminate between companies or individuals; all have done their duty and done it nobly.

On the 8th Dr. Connelly, an American merchant resident in Chihuahua, was sent by Col. Doniphan to Parral to hold an interview with Gov. Trias, to offer him conditions of peace and invite him back to the capital. The governor, however, refused to return, but appointed three commissioners to confer with Col. Doniphan or with such commissioners as he might designate in regard to concluding an honorable peace. Col. Doniphan's desire was to enter into treaty stipulations with the authorities of Chihuahua whereby the American merchants, after the payment of legal duties, might be suffered to remain in security, and sell their merchandise, and the State be bound to remain neutral during the continuance of the war. After much delay all negotiation was suspended between the parties without coming to any definite agreement on the subject.

On the 14th Majs. Campbell and Forsythe with 38 men left Chihuahua with the view of returning to the United States by way of the Presidio del Rio Grande, and thence across the plains to Fort Towson on Red River. Without meeting with any very serious opposition from the Indians or other cause this party reached the frontiers of Arkansas in safety, where, separating, they returned to their respective homes.

On the 18th the American troops at Chihuahua received intelligence through the Mexican papers and by Mexican rumor of the great Battle of Buena Vista or Angostura. The Mexicans represented the issue of the battle as being entirely favorable to themselves, but, taking it for granted the American arms were victorious, Col. Doniphan ordered a salute to be fired in honor of Gens. Taylor and Wool and the brave troops under their command.

Col. Doniphan had been ordered by Gen. Kearney to report to Brig. Gen. Wool at Chihuahua. Instead of finding Gen. Wool in possession of that capital as anticipated, he now had information that both he and Gen. Taylor were shut up at Saltillo and hotly beleaguered by Santa Anna with an overwhelming force. Notwithstanding this strait of affairs, Col. Doniphan felt it his duty to report to Gen. Wool wherever he might be found and afford him whatever succor might be in his power. Therefore on the 20th he dispatched an express to Saltillo bearing communications to Gen. Wool. Besides a copy of his official report of the Battle of Sacramento was the following dispatch:

> HEADQUARTERS OF THE ARMY IN CHIHUAHUA,
> *City of Chihuahua, March 20, 1847.*

SIR: The forces under my command are a portion of the Missouri Volunteers called into service for the purpose of invading New Mexico under the command of Brig. Gen. (then colonel) Kearney. After the conquest of New Mexico and before Gen. Kearney's departure for California, information was received that another regiment and an extra battalion of Missouri Volunteers would follow us to Santa Fe. The services of so large a force being wholly unnecessary in that State, I prevailed on Gen. Kearney to order my regiment to report to you at this city. The order was given on the 23d of September, 1846, but after the general had arrived at La Joya in the southern part of the State, he issued an order requiring my regiment to make a campaign into the country inhabited by the Navajo Indians, lying between the waters of the Rio del Norte and the Rio Colorado of the West. This campaign detained me until the 14th of December before our return to the Del Norte. We immediately commenced our march for El Paso del Norte with about 800 riflemen. All communication between Chihuahua and New Mexico was entirely prevented. On the 25th of December, 1846, my vanguard was attacked at Brazito by the Mexican force from this State; our force was about 450, and the force of the enemy 1,100; the engagement lasted about 40 minutes, when the enemy fled, leaving 63 killed and since dead, 150 wounded, and one howitzer, the only piece of artillery in the engagement on either side. On the 27th we entered El Paso without further opposition; from the prisoners and others I learned that you had not marched upon this State. I then determined to order a battery and 100 artillerists from New Mexico. They arrived in El Paso about the 5th of February, when we took up the line of march for this place. A copy of my official report of the Battle of Sacramento, inclosed to you, will show you all our subsequent movements up to our taking military possession of this capital. The day of my arrival I had determined to send an express to you forthwith, but the whole intermediate country was in the hands of the enemy and we were cut off and had been so for many months from all information respecting the American Army. Mexican reports are never to be fully credited; yet, from all we could learn, we did not doubt that you would be forced by overwhelming numbers to abondon Saltillo, and, of course, we would send no express under such circumstances. On yesterday we received the first even tolerably reliable information that a battle had been fought near Saltillo between the American and Mexican forces, and that Santa Anna had probably fallen back on San Louis de Potosi.

My position here is exceedingly embarrassing. In the first place, most of the men under my command have been in service since the 1st of June, have never received one cent of pay. Their marches have been hard, especially in the Navajo country, and no forage, so that they are literally without horses, clothes, or money, having nothing but arms and a disposition to use them. They are all volunteers, officers and men, and, although ready for any hardships or danger, are wholly unfit to garrison a town or city. " It is confusion worse confounded." Having performed a march of more than 2,000 miles and their term of service rapidly expiring, they are restless to join the army under your command. Still we can not leave this point safely for some days; the American merchants here oppose it violently and have several hundred thousand dollars at stake. They have sent me a memorial, and my determination has been made known to them. A copy of both they will send you. Of one thing it is necessary to inform you: The merchants admit that their goods could not be sold here in five years. If they go south they will be as near the markets of Durango and Zacatecas as they now are. I am anxious and willing to protect the merchants as far as practicable, but I protest against remaining here as a mere wagon guard to garrison a city with troops wholly unfitted for it and who will soon be wholly ruined by improper indulgences. Having been originally ordered to this point, you know the wishes of the Government in relation to it, and of course your orders will be promptly and cheerfully obeyed. I fear there is ample use for us with you, and we would greatly prefer joining you before our term of service expires.

All information relative to my previous operatins, present cnditions, etc., will be given you by Mr. J. Collins, the bearer of dispatches. He is a highly honorable gentleman and was an amateur soldier at Sacramento.

Very respectfully, your obedient servant,

A. W. DONIPHAN,
Colonel First Regiment Missouri Cavalry.

Brig. Gen. WOOL, *United States Army.*

The following letters written by the author to a friend in Missouri will show the progress and adventures of the express party from the time of their leaving Chihuahua on the 20th of March until their return on the 23d of April.

HEADQUARTERS ARMY OF OCCUPATION,
Saltillo, April 4, 1847.

MR. MILLER: It has been just one month since I wrote you from the city of Chihuahua. I am now in Saltillo, the capital of the State of Coahuilia, the camp of Gens. Taylor and Wool, 675 miles from Col. Doniphan's army. Briefly and without embellishment, I will relate the story of our adventures before arriving here. The important work of opening a communication between the Army of the West, now in Chihuahua, and the Army of Occupation in and near Saltillo was intrusted to the hands of the following 14 men, viz: J. L. Collins, interpreter and bearer of dispatches, T. Bradford, T. H. Massie, T. Harrison, J. Sanderson, I. Walker, R. D. Walker, S. Asbury, J. Andrews, G. Brown, J. Lewis, J. Moutray, R. W. Fleming, and myself, escort. There never was a more dangerous and arduous undertaking accomplished with better success by the same number of men. Every foot of the route led through the enemy's country and was attended with imminent peril. We left Chihuahua on the 20th of March and having performed almost the entire march by night, over stupendous mountains clad with horrible cactus and the maguey and through valleys of mesquite, we arrived here safely on the 2d of April. We may very properly be styled the night riders of Mexico. We traveled about 50 miles per day by the following route: From Chihuahua to the rancho Bachimbo, thence to San Pablo, thence to Soucillo on the main branch of the River Conchos; here we attempted to diverge to the left and cross the arid plains by a traversia (by-path) leading to the city of Monclova, but having traveled two days and nights in the deserts and mountains without one drop of water, and having used our utmost exertions to find the noted watering places, " Coutevo " and "Agua Chele," unsuccessfully, we were compelled to return to the river Conchos at Soucillo to avoid perishing of thirst on the arid plains. Just before returning to the Conchos we thought we would make one more effort to discover water. Messrs. Collins, Massie, Bradford, and myself ascended a high mountain and, as we thought, beheld a lake of water some 5 or 6 miles distant. We were confident we could see the banks of the lake and the green verdure circling the water's edge, as well as the waves rolling before the gentle wind. With revived hearts we set out for the refreshing element. We traveled and traveled, but the lake receded. At length we came upon a glassy sand beach (the bed of a dry lake), and the water or mirage appeared behind and around us. We were pursuing a phantom. We were perishing with internal heat and thirst. It was growing dark, and there was no prospect of obtaining water without returning to the River Conchos. Accordingly we turned about and started for the river, and having rode hard all night and until sunrise next morning, we arrived at the transparent, cool, refreshing stream. Great God, what a blessing to man hast thou made this one element, and how poorly does he appreciate it until he is cast off upon the desert!

We passed from Soucillo to La Cruz, thence to Santa Rosalia, on the Rio Florida. This town contains about 5,000 inhabitants. We passed rancho Enramida, rancho Blanco, and Guajuquilla. Three commissioners were sent out to inquire into our business, but having told them we intended to pass peaceably through the country, they permitted us to pass unmolested. This region of the country is majestically barren—there is a grandeur in the very desolation around you. The eternal mountains with the cactus bristling on their sides shut out the horizon, the rising and setting sun, and lift their bald, rocky summits high in the azure of heaven. Becoming satisfied that every effort would be made to rob us of our papers and send us as prisoners to Durango, we halted near a gorge in the mountains and examined and burnt all the letters of our friends and every other paper and letter of introduction which we had, except Col. Doniphan's official communications to Gen. Wool, and these we sewed up in the pad of one of our saddles. This we did that nothing might be found in our possession that would betray us as express men in the event we should fall into the hands of the enemy, which we had great reason to apprehend. We passed the city of Malpimi, in Durango, about midnight. On the 29th we beheld a cloud of dust before us and saw various companies of animals which looked very much like companies of cavalry. We at first supposed it was Gen. Martinez, of Durango, returning to Malpimi after the battle of Saltillo. Of course, we felt the necessity of avoiding them and accordingly directed our course toward the mountains. At length we were able to discover that, instead of being cavaly, it was several large atajos of pack mules on their way from Monterey to Chihuahua with peloncillo (cake sugar) for sale. About sundown we arrived at San Sebastian, on the Rio Nazas, where we stopped to prepare a little coffee. Don Ignacio Jirmenez, a wealthy and influential citizen of the place, collected about 100 men together and notified us that he had orders from the authorities of Durango to stop us and make us prisoners. Collins says, "Well, what are you going to do about it?" Jirmenez replies, "I shall put the order into execution." Collins: "I am going, and you can use your pleasure about stopping us." "Jirmenez: "Have you and your men passports?" Collins: "Yes, sir; we have." Jirmenez: "Let me see them." Collins, holding his rifle in one hand and revolver in the other: "These are our passports, sir, and we think they are sufficient." This ended the parley. We buckled on our pistols and bowie knives, shouldered our rifles, and left sans ceremonie. We traveled all night and all next day until sunset, and having arrived near the base of a high mountain in the State of Coahuila, we stopped again to take some refreshment and graze our animals a moment. While taking our coffee this same Ignacio Jirmenez surrounded us with a band of 75 well-armed men, and no doubt with the view of first murdering and then plundering us. We quickly formed a line of battle, heavily charged our holsters, revolvers, and rifles, and through our interpreter gave him the Spartan reply: "Here we are; if you want us come and take us." After curvetting and maneuvering around us near an hour, during which time we gained the base of the mountain, he concluded that we were a stubborn set to deal with and accordingly took the prudent plan of withdrawing his forces. There was but one sentiment in our little band, and that was to fight until the last man expired. About midnight we arrived at El Poso, where we purchased corn for our animals and took a little rest, as we had traveled night and day since we left Chihuahua.

Without further difficulty, except the failure of some of our animals, we arrived at the large and beautiful hacienda of Don Manuel Ybarro, near the city of Parras. Manuel was educated in Bardstown, Ky., is a friend to the Americans, and received us kindly. He gave us all the information we desired about the American troops and the Battle of Buena Vista. After showing us his fine houses, gardens with roses richly blooming, and premises generally, he gave us comfortable quarters during the night, a fresh supply of mules, and a guide through the mountains, in order to expedite our march to Gen. Wool's camp. Ybarro speaks good English, is a full American in feeding, and merits our highest approbation for his disinterested kind treatment. Without the occurrence of any very remarkable incident, we passed, by a very rocky, rugged, mountain traversia, the haciendas Castanuella and the Florida and arrived in Saltillo at sunset on the 2d of April. Our dispatches were forthwith delivered to Gen. Wool, but as Taylor, who has just gone to Monterey, is in command of this branch of the Army, the dispatches were sent to him early on the morning of the 3d April.

Respectfully,   JOHN T. HUGHES.

———

SALTILLO, *April 5, 1847.*

MR. MILLER: This day Mr. Collins and myself, accompanied by Gen. Wool's chief engineer, rode over the great battle field of Buena Vista, where Gen. Taylor with 5,000 men, mostly volunteers, measured his strength with Gen. Santa Anna at the head of 22,000 of the best troops Mexico ever sent into the field. Gen. Taylor, for having defeated and almost annihilated the flower of the Mexican Army with so slender a force, deserves the gratitude of the American people. Nor do the brave men who fought with him deserve less.

An awful melancholy creeps over the soul and deeply stirs the feelings and opens the fountains of sympathy as you pass over the ground covered with the mutilated deal and dyed with the blood of friend and foe. As Santa Anna says in his official report, "The ground is" truly "strewed with the dead, and the blood has flowed in torrents." We stood one moment on the spot where Col. Yell, of Arkansas, yielded up his life for his country and then admiringly turned to view the ground still crimsoned by the blood of Col. Hardin, of Illinois, and Cols. McKee and Clay, of Kentucky. The blood of the gallant dead was still red on the rocks around us. Here the last prayer and the last throbbings of many a noble heart were hushed in death forever.

The engineer pointed us to the place where the Mexican general had marshaled his hosts with a bristling forest of glittering steel. The costly trappings of the officers and the bright bayonets of the men glistened in the sheen of the sun. He then showed us where Washington's, Bragg's, Sherman's, and O'Brien's batteries with thundering roar mowed down the enemy's advancing columns, and where the chivalrous Kentuckians, the gallant Mississippians, the indomitable Illinoisans, the much-abused Indianians, and other equally courageous volunteer troops dashed into the Mexican lines, opening wide breaches and spreading fearful havoc amongst their successively advancing squadrons. The half-wasted frames of the Mexican soldiers yet lay profusely scattered over the plateau where the armies of the two republics disputed for supremacy.

Sadly we returned to Gen. Wool's tent from the field of his glorious strife. He conversed freely and pleasantly communicated to us important information respecting his great battle. He read to us his official account of the action, after which he made this flattering statement in relation to the conduct of the "Army of the West": "Missouri has acquitted herself most gloriously. Col. Doniphan has fought the most fortunate battle and gained the most brilliant victory which has been achieved during the war. I have every confidence in the bravery and gallantry of the troops under his command. Would to God I had them and their artillery here! Santa Anna might then return to Buena Vista and welcome."

Respectfully,   JOHN T. HUGHES.

———

CHIHUAHUA, *April 25, 1847.*

Mr. MILLER: On the 9th of April Gen. Taylor's dispatches to Col. Doniphan arrived at Saltillo by the hands of Maj. Howard. Col. Doniphan is ordered to march with his column forthwith to Saltillo and return to the United States by way of Matamoras and the Gulf. For the safe conveyance of the orders and the protection of the expressmen Gen. Wool sent Capt. Pike, of the Arkansas cavalry, with 26 men to act as an escort or convoy. We were also accompanied by Mr. Gregg, author of Commerce on the Prairies, having along a set of astronomical instruments for taking the latitude and longitude of places. Our party being now increased to 42 men and provided with a fresh supply of animals, we left Saltillo on the 9th and on the same day arrived at Florida, a small town about 40 miles distant. From thence we passed 35 miles to Castanuell, where we met with a very hospitable Irish lady who had married a Mexican. Here also we saw a man singularly deformed. His head and body were of the ordinary size for a man, but his arms and legs were only about 18 inches long. His appearance when he made an attempt to walk was very singular, for he could scarcely get along, except where the ground was quite level. When mounted on horseback his appearance was still more strange. This man had a wife and children. From thence, passing through the mountains, we came to the princely estate of Don Manuel Ybarro and again enjoyed his kind hospitalities and received numerous instances of his disinterested, marked friendship, for which our cordial thanks and grateful acknowledgments are due. Thence in three days we traveled about 110 miles, and came to Alimeto, having passed El Paso, San Nicolas, and San Lorenzo. Here we encamped in the plaza and took possession of two small cannon. This place contains about 1,500 inhabitants and is situated in the Valley of the Rio Nazas. The next day we traveled about 40 miles and came to the canyon in the mountains of Mapimi, where we stayed for the night. This day it rained copiously. While at this place commissioners came out from Mapimi to inquire if our intentions were pacific; that otherwse we could not be permitted to pass. Capt. Pike replied to them: "We intend to molest nothing. It is the custom of the Americans to respect life and the rights of property. At all hazards, however, we intend to pass on our way." The next morning as we approached Mapimi two of the deputies came out and entreated Capt. Pike not to pass through the town. Not knowing what forces might be concealed in the place (for troops had recently been stationed there), he took their counsel. We therefore proceeded on our way, and that night arrived at Jarilito, a deserted town, after a march of 37 miles. We were now scant of provisions. The following morning we proceeded about 9 miles to the Salt Spring, where, finding a drove of wild Mexican cattle, we pounced in amongst them with our rifles and soon had enough of beef to supply a small army. After a few hours' rest and a little refreshment we started for the Rio Cerro Gordo, a distance of 30 miles, where we arrived at sunset.

On the morning of the 18th, after a progress of 10 miles, we came to the Green Springs, near a canyon in the mountains, which the Mexicans dignify with the title of Santa Bernada. Near this stands a deserted rancho. Having nooned and regaled ourselves a little under the shade of the Alamos, we launched out upon the desert or jornada, 75 miles without water. This desert extends to Guajuquilla from Santa Bernada. Having completed about 45 miles this day, we encamped for the night on the plain, without wood or water. The next day, having traveled about 25 miles, and by this time being very thirsty, we overhauled a train of wagons belonging to one Minos, a Mexican, some of which contained oranges and peloncillo from Zacatecas, designed for the markets of Parral and Chihuahua. Eagerly we purchased a supply of oranges and sucked the luscious juice from that delicious fruit. Now revived and reinvigorated, we pressed forward to Guajuquilla, a town on the Rio Florida, containing 4,000 inhabitants, where we quartered in a spacious corral, well adapted for defense, and stationed out a night guard. These people were not friendly, but they durst not attack us through fear. Here we found several Americans who had met with a singularly hard fate. They gave me this recital of their misfortunes: "Twenty-one of us were in the employ of Speyers and Amijo, who traveled under British passports. They promised us protection, but upon our arrival at Chihuahua we were all made prisoners, and under strict guards conducted in the direction of the City of Mexico. On arriving at the little town of Zarcas we effected our escape by night and attempted to penetrate into Texas by way of Mapimi, Laguna del Tagualila, and thence to the Rio Grande. Having traveled for 14 days in the arid deserts between Mapimi and the Rio Grande, mostly without water or provision, 11 of our number perished miserably of thirst and fatigue, and the other 10, changing their course and subsisting upon the flesh of the only remaining horse we had, finally succeeded in reaching Guajuquilla." We took one of the survivors to Chihuahua; the others remained, having no means of traveling.

Thence, passing Enramada, Santa Rosalia, and San Pablo, we arrived at Bachimbo, 36 miles from Chihuahua, on the 22d, and, making an early start the next morning, we hastened forward to rejoin our companions in the capital. When we had approached within about 5 miles of the city we beheld at a distance a great cloud of dust rising in front of us. We could not at first conceive the purport of all this. In a few moments, however, a body of horsemen were seen in the distance, making toward us with great haste. We were now impressed with the belief that it was either a body of Mexican guerrilleros endeavoring to cut us off from any communication with the army or Col. Doniphan's picket guard, who, mistaking us for a party of Mexicans, had dashed out in the hopes of a skirmish. At first Capt. Pike halted the little column to make an observation. But we were soon very pleasantly undeceived, for the body of horsemen turned out to be a company of our friends, who, hearing of our approach, had come to greet us and offer us a new relay of horses. Col. Doniphan had thrice been solemnly assured that the express party were all either killed or made prisoners and sent to Durango to undergo the most cruel tortures, and had accordingly issued orders to his troops to evacuate the capital on the 25th and return to the United States by way of the Presidio del Rio Grande and San Antonio, in Texas. We now entered Chihuahua amidst the deafening peals of the great church bells, the firing of artillery, and the cordial welcomes and heartfelt congratulations of friends, who pressed around to shake us by the hands and inquire what were the orders from Gens. Taylor and Wool. Col. Doniphan, having unsealed the dispatches, announced to his soldiers that he was required to march forthwith to Saltillo, where he would receive further orders.

Respectfully,   JOHN T. HUGHES.

CHAPTER XX.

It was Col. Doniphan's intention when he dispatched the express to Saltillo to move his forces to San Pablo, in the valley of the Conchos, or to Santa Rosalia, according as he might find forage, leaving only such a garrison in Chihuahua as would be sufficient to afford protection to the American merchants.

Conformably to this design, on the 5th of April the Second Battalion, under Maj. Gilpin, and the battalion of Artillery under Maj. Clark (which now consisted of two companies commanded by Weightman and Hudson, the latter having charge of the Mexican pieces) were ordered to proceed to San Pablo. The First Battalion, under Lieut. Col. Jackson, was soon to succeed them. On the 9th, however, Col. Doniphan, while at San Pablo, received a communication from Hicks, an American at Parral, advising him that a strong Mexican force was on the march from Durango to Chihuahua to recover the capital and seize the goods of the American merchants. Col. Doniphan, not suspecting but such a project was in contemplation, from the rumors and statements which had come to him, determined to return and hold possession of the capital until he should hear from Gen. Wool. Jackson's battalion did not leave the city.

Meanwhile the American merchants had established themselves on the most active and busy streets of the city and were using every exertion to effect sales of their immense merchandise, for as yet it was uncertain what the orders of Gen. Wool to Col. Doniphan would be, and to what extent their interests might be affected. Many of them had embarked largely in the trade, and it was essential to dispose of their goods mainly before the Army (which for months had acted as a guard and convoy to their trains) should receive orders to evacuate the place. Business soon became moderately brisk, and the majority of them were successful in disposing of their heavy stocks. The aggregate amount of the importation for the year could not have been less than one million and a half of dollars at the Chihuahua prices.

"For 59 days," observes an intelligent volunteer, "we held full and undisturbed possession of the city, keeping up strict discipline with a constant guard, consisting of a camp and picket guard and a patrol during the whole night, visiting every part of the city. Various rumors were afloat of the intended march of the enemy to attack us, and sometimes report said that several thousands were on the road; but it is certain that if we had remained in the place until this day they never would have approached it with any force less than eight or ten thousand; and, having the advantage of the houses and walls, a less number never could have driven us from the city. The rights of the citizens there, as in every other place, were duly respected, and their conduct since our departure up to the latest accounts shows that this treatment was not lost upon them, for several traders who remained there have been well treated and their rights duly regarded."

Every preparation having been completed by the indefatigable exertions of the quartermaster and officers of subsistence which was necessary for the long and arduous march to Saltillo, a distance of 675 miles through an arid and desolate country, the battalion of Artillery commenced the march on the 25th of April, and was succeeded on the following day by the First Battalion. These were to await the rear and the merchant and baggage trains at Santa Rosalia, 120 miles from Chihuahua.

On the morning of the 28th a scene of the most busy and animating nature ensued. The Americans were actively engaged in hastening preparations for their departure. The Mexicans, with their serapes thrown around them, were standing at the corners of the streets in groups, speculating as to the future. The long trains of baggage and provision wagons were stretching out toward the south. Part of the merchant trains were moving off in the direction of New Mexico, taking with them little, however, except their specie or bullion. The Second Battalion, with colors thrown to the breeze, was anxiously awaiting the order to march.

Certain of the fair Mexican girls, who had conceived an unconquerable attachment for some favorite paramour of the Anglo-Saxon race with "blue eyes and fair hair," dressed in the habit of Mexican youths, were gaily dashing through the streets on their curvetting steeds. They accompanied their lovers on the march to Saltillo and bivouacked with them on the deserts.

About 10 o'clock Col. Doniphan, having delivered over to the city authorities the Mexican prisoners captured at Sacramento, to be disposed of by them as deemed advisable for the public good, quietly evacuated the capital, leaving the government in the hands of its former rulers. About 10 American merchants remained and trusted their lives to the "magnanimous Mexican people." These were chiefly such men as had great knowledge of the Mexican customs and language, and had taken the oath of allegiance to that Government. The magnificent architectural beauty of the city was left wholly unimpaired and the property of the citizens uninjured.

Two days after Col. Doniphan's departure from Chihuahua the American merchants who remained entered into a treaty stipulation with the city authorities whereby they agreed to pay the legal rates of duty upon their entire importation of goods, both sold and unsold. They were to be amply protected in their rights and liberty. The conditions of this treaty have been fully complied with by the Mexicans except in one single instance. On the 23d of June a band of ruffians violently entered the storeroom of James Aull, of Lexington Mo., and, having brutally assassinated him, plundered the house of $5,000. The assassins were subsequently apprehended and thrown into prison, but we have not learned that they received the punishment due to their crimes. The other company of merchants returned to Santa Fe by way of Coralitus and Ojo Vacca, leaving El Paso to the east. Thence they returned to Independence, where they arrived in the month of July.

Col. Doniphan, by unparalleled marches, overtook the advance at Santa Rosalia, on the 1st of May, having in four days passed Bachimbo, Santa Cruz, Soucillo, and completed 120 miles. Santa Rosalia contains about 5,000 inhabitants, and is situated at the junction of the Conchos and Florida Rivers. Here the Mexican forces under Gen. Heridia had thrown up a line of fortifications, entirely surrounding the city, except where the rivers and the bluffs were impassable, strengthened by an almost impregnable fortress. On the outside of the embankments were intrenchments, impassable by cavalry. These embankments were also strengthened by numerous bastions, in which cannon were to be employed.

Some assert that these fortifications were thrown up to defend the place against the approach of Gen. Wool, who was expected to pass that way on his march upon Chihuahua. Others aver that it was the intention of the Mexicans, if defeated at Sacramento, to remove the public archives and all their munitions of war into this stronghold and there make a desperate stand, but that losing all their cannon and means of defense in the action of the 28th they abandoned their purpose. It is true, however, that extensive preparations had been made to defend the city against an invading army.

On the 2d Lieut. Col. Mitchell, a detachment of 26 men under Capt. Pike, of the Arkansas Cavalry, and 70 men under Capt. Reid left the main body of the army and proceeded in advance to Parras, a distance of near 500 miles. The movements of the main column, however, were so rapid that the pioneer party, in case of any sudden emergency, could have fallen back upon it for support. The object of this reconnoitering party was to obtain the earliest information of either a covert or open enemy, who might meditate an attack upon the trains or seize upon some favorable moment to surprise the army, and also to procure at Parras such supplies as might be necessary for the use of the men and animals.

After a hasty march 60 miles in two days we came to Guajuquilla, on the Rio Florida, containing an industrious and agricultural population, where we obtained an abundance of forage. Here, also, the soldiers purchased chickens, pigs, cheese, eggs, bread, wine, and a variety of vegetables.

At this place there are a great number of beautiful canals, which convey the most lovely and delightful streams of water through the whole town and neighboring fields and gardens. This valley, if properly cultivated, would yield a support for a dense population. The soil is fertile and the nature of the ground is such that it is susceptible of complete irrigation.

Early the next day the commander moved his forces up the river about 6 miles to the Hacienda Dolores. Here he allowed them a short respite, ordered them to prepare provisions and fill their canteens with water before commencing the march over the desert upon which they were now to enter. This desert is 75 miles over, extending to the Santa Bernada Spring, and the road is terrible by reason of the dust. The troops having taken a few hours' rest and a little refreshment, launched out in long files upon the jornada, followed by all the baggage, provision, and merchant trains, a great cloud of dust hanging heavily and gloomily along the line of march.

After sunset a sullen, lowering cloud arose in the southwest, heavily charged with electric fluid and with frequent flashes of lighting, and hoarse, distant thunder, swept majestically over the rocky summits of the detached mountains which everywhere traverse the elevated plains of Mexico. Heavy, gloomy, pitchy darkness enveloped the earth. The road could only be seen when revealed by a sudden flash of lightning. The pennons continued to stream and flutter in the wild gales of the desert. These, together with the rising column of dust, served as guides to the soldiers in the rear. The artillery rumbled over the rocks and the fire sparkled beneath the wheels. At length heavy sleep and fatigue oppressed many, but the night march on the desert was still continued. It were folly to halt, for no water could be obtained. The soldiers were greatly wearied; some of them almost fell from their horses. Some dropped their arms and were necessitated to search after them, while the rest marched by, wagged their heads, and made sport and laughter. Some straggled off and lay down upon the desert, overpowered by sleep. Some, gifted with a richer fund of wit, a finer flow of spirits, a nobler store of mental treasure, and more physical endurance, sang "Yankee Doodle," love songs, and related stories to the groups that gathered round, as it were, to extract one spark of life to aid them on the march. About midnight a halt was ordered. The tired and sleepy soldiers tethered their animals and lay down in the dark, promiscuously, on the desert wherever they chanced to find a smooth spot of earth. They took no supper that night.

There are a great many lizards in Chihuahua and Durango, and it appeared as if this desert was their headquarters, for they crept into the men's blankets and bedding and annoyed them greatly while sleeping. Suddenly aroused from slumber by these slimy companions, the soldiers would sometimes shake their blankets, toss the scorpions and lizards and alacrans upon their sleeping neighbors, exclaiming angrily, "D——n the scorpion family." The others, half overpowered by sleep, would sullenly articulate, "Don't throw your d——d lizards here." Thus they lay, more anxious to obtain a little slumber than to escape a swarm of these repulsive reptiles.

The march was commenced early the next morning. The dust was absolutely intolerable. The soldiers could not march in lines. They were now already become thirsty, and it was yet 40 miles to water. The dust filled their mouths and nostrils and eyes, and covered them completely. They were much distressed during the whole day. Many of them became faint and their tongues swollen. The horses, and often the stubborn, refractory mules, would fail in the sand, and neither the spur nor the point of the saber was sufficient to stimulate them. Sometimes the volunteer, boiling with ire, would dismount and attempt to drag the sullen mule along by the lariat.[1] How earnestly he then desired once more to be in the land of gushing fountains, verdant groves, railroads, steamboats, and telegraph wires.

The teamsters and those with the artillery, and the animals, suffered extremely. But they endured it all with patience. After suffering every hardship, privation, and distress by marching, which

[1] See cut, p. 177.

men must necessarily experience in passing such a desert, they arrived at the spring, Santa Bernada, at sunset. Here there is a grove of willows and alamos. These afforded a pleasant shade. There is also at this place a copious, gushing spring, which furnished an abundance of water for the men and the animals. This spot, with its groves and springs, disrobed of all poetry, proved in reality to be an oasis, a smiling, inviting retreat in a desert, desolate, treeless waste of sand, rocks, and naked mountains. Here the soldiers took rest and repose.

On the 6th of May the army advanced into the State of Durango to the Cerro Gordo. This river terminates in Laguna de Xacco. The following day we arrived at the outpost, Palayo, where our advance had the previous day taken some horses and a few Mexican soldiers. This small military station is about 1 league from the town of Jarilito, which is now entirely deserted on account of the depredations and incursions of the Comanches. Since 1835 the Indians have encroached upon the frontiers of Mexico and laid

"D——mn a mule, anyhow."

waste many flourishing settlements, waging a predatory warfare, and leading women and children into captivity. In fact the whole of Mexico is a frontier. An elevated table plain extends from the Gulf of Mexico to the foot of the Cordilleras, intersected by innumerable ranges of mountains, and clustering, isolated, and conical-shaped peaks, invariably infested by bands of savages and still fiercer Mexican banditti. No effort of the Mexican Government has been able to suppress and oust these ruthless invaders of the country.

At Palayo some of the men killed a few beeves, pigs, and chickens belonging to the Mexicans, and feasted upon them at night. There was much to palliate this offense. The regiment had been marched at the rate of 35 or 40 miles per day, over a dusty, desert country, almost entirely destitute of water. Most of the men had not had a pound of meat for the last three days. Besides the exigency of the case, the State of Durango was at that very moment in arms against us. Would the most scrupulously moral man in Missouri denounce his son as a thief and robber because, after traveling more than 3,000 miles by land, and having spent the last cent of his slender resources for bread, coldly neglected by his Government, he found it necessary to kill an ox or a pig to satisfy hunger, or should think proper to mount himself on a Mexican horse, in a country which the prowess of his own arm had been instrumental in subduing? It is one thing for the philosopher to sit in his studio and spin out his finely drawn metaphysical doctrines, and another, and entirely different thing, to put them in practice under every adverse circumstance. What is most beautiful in theory is not always wisest in practice.

On the 8th the command reached the Hacienda Cadenas, 24 miles from Palayo. Here we obtained the first information of Gen. Scott's great victory of Cerro Gordo. At such welcome tidings a thrilling sensation of joy pervaded our camp. Here we took possession of another piece of cannon, which, although well mounted, Col. Doniphan restored to the inhabitants. On the 9th, a march of 22 miles brought us to the city of Mapimi, which had steadily manifested the greatest hostility to the Americans. This is a mining town. It has five furnaces for smelting silver ore and one for smelting lead ore. It is one of the richest towns in the State, excepting the capital. The Mexican forces, 3,000 strong, fled from Mapimi and Durango upon our approach, and left the State completely in our power, had Gen. Wool but permitted us to visit the capital. Gen. Heredia and Gov. Ochoa of Durango wrote to Santa Anna to send them 20 pieces of cannon and 5,000 regular troops, or the State of Durango would immediately fall into the hands of Col. Doniphan's regiment, if he saw proper to direct his march against it. Upon our arrival at Mapimi we obtained more certain intelligence of the victory of the American forces over the Mexicans at Cerro Gordo, in honor of which a national salute of 28 guns was fired by Weightman's battery. Here also a copy of Gov. Ochoa's proclamation was found, in which he earnestly exhorted the inhabitants of Durango never to cease warring until they had repelled the " North American invaders" from the soil of Mexico.

This day's march had been excessively hot and suffocating and extremely severe upon the sick. Just before reaching Mapimi, Second Lieut. Stephen Jackson, of Howard, died of an inveterate attack of typhoid fever. Lieut. Jackson was taken ill in the Navajo country, and had never entirely recovered. He was not at the battle of Brazito, being at that time sick in Soccorro; but he afterwards fought with great bravery in the more important action at Sacramento. His corpse was interred (on Sunday the 9th) with appropriate military honors. Also, the priest of Mapimi in his robes, with the Bible in his hands, and three boys dressed in white pelisses, two of them bearing torches and the third in the center with a crucifix reared upon a staff, preceded the bier, first to the Catholic Church and then to the grave, at both of which places the Catholic ceremonies were performed.

On the 10th we made a powerful march of near 40 miles to San Sebastian on the Rio Nazas. The heat and dust were almost insufferable. Don Ignacio Jermanez, who attempted to capture the expressmen, fled to the city of Durango. The army foraged upon him for the night, with the promise to pay him in powder and ball at sight. The Rio Nezas is a beautiful stream, full of fish, and empties into the three lakes, Tagualila, Las Abas, and Del Alamo. During this fatiguing march two men, King and Ferguson, died of sickness heat, and suffocation. They were buried at San Sebastian.

On the 11th the command marched to San Lorenzo, a distance of 35 miles, along a heavy, dusty road, hedged in by an immense and almost impervious chaparral. The heat was absolutely oppressive—water scarce. In this thick chaparral, Canales, with a band of about 400 robbers, had concealed himself with the view of cutting off stragglers from our army and committing depredations upon our merchant and provision trains. But our method of marching with the artillery and one battalion in front, and the other battalion in rear of the trains and droves of mules, anticipated his premeditated attack. After our arrival in San Lorenzo, a Mexican courier came to the colonel with news that Canales had made an attack upon McGoffin's train of wagons, and that McGoffin and his lady were likely to fall into his hands. A detachment of 60 men under Lieut. Gordon was quickly sent to his relief. They anticipated Canales's movement. This little village, San Lorenzo, has an overportion of inhabitants. Every house and hut was crowded with men, boys, women, and children. Almost every woman, old and young, had a child in her arms, and some of them more than one. Whether this superabundance of population is the legitimate effect of the salubrious climate or is produced by some other circumstances is left for the reader to consider. The march to-day was distressingly hot and dusty. A Mr. Mount, of the company from Jackson County, straggled off in the chaparral and has never since been heard of; he was doubtless murdered and then robbed by lurking Mexicans.

On the 12th, early in the morning, the front guard charged upon and took three Mexican prisoners; they were armed and lurking in the mezquite chaparral near the road, and were doubtless spies sent out by Canales to obtain information of our movements, but no positive proof appearing against them, they were released. As our animals were much worn down by the previous day's march, and it being impossible to procure forage for them, we only marched 15 miles to-day to the little rancho San Juan on a brazo or arm of the Rio Nazas. Here both man and horse fared badly. As our next day's march was to be over a desert region of near 40 miles without a drop of water or even a mouthful of food for our famishing animals, and also as the water had to be raised from a well into pools and vats at El Paso where the army was to encamp on the night of the 13th, Lieut. Pope Gordon and 15 or 20 men were sent at midnight in advance to draw water for the use of the Army.

The author went along as their guide, having traveled the same route on express to Saltillo. At 9 a. m. Lieut. Gordon and his advance arrived at El Paso, where we found Capt. Reid with 14 men. Capt. Reid, as elsewhere observed, had accompanied Lieut. Col. Mitchell on his way to Saltillo, with a detachment of 70 or 80 men. Upon their arrival at Parras (a city where Gen. Wool had taken up his headquarters before he formed a junction with Gen. Taylor, and which had been very friendly to the Americans in the way of furnishing supplies and taking care of Gen. Wool's sick men) they found the inhabitants in much distress. A band of Comanches had just made a descent from the mountains upon the city and killed 8 or 10 of the citizens, carried off 19 girls and boys into captivity, and driven off 300 mules and 200 horses. Besides this, they had robbed houses of money, blankets, and the sacred household gods. They besought Capt. Reid to interfere in their behalf; that although they were considered enemies to the Americans it did not become the magnanimity of the American soldiers to see them robbed and murdered by a lawless band of savages, the avowed enemies both of the Mexicans and Americans. Capt. Reid undertook to recover the innocent captives and chastise the brutal savages. This is the occasion of Capt. Reid's being at El Paso on the morning of the 13th. Just as Lieut. Gordon and Capt. Reid joined their forces the Indians, about 65 in number, made their appearance, advancing upon the hacienda from a canyon or pass in the mountains toward the south. They had all their spoils and captives with them. Their intention was to water their stock at El Paso and augment the number of their prisoners and animals. Thus boldly do the Indians invade this country. Capt. Reid concealed his men (about 35 in number) in the hacienda and sent out Don Manuel Ybarro, a Mexican, and three or four of his servants, to decoy the Indians to the hacienda. The feint succeeded. When the Indians came within half a mile the order was given to charge upon them, which was gallantly and promptly done. Capt. Reid, Lieuts. Gordon, Winston, and Sproule were the officers present in this engagement, all of whom behaved very gallantly. The Indians fought with desperation for their rich spoils. Many instances of individual prowess and daring were exhibited by Capt. Reid and his men, too numerous, indeed, to recount in detail; the captain himself, in a daring charge upon the savages, received two severe wounds, one in the face and the other in the shoulder. These wounds were both produced by steel-pointed arrows. The engagement lasted not less than two hours and was kept up hotly until the Indians made good their retreat to the mountains. In this skirmish we lost none. The Indians lost 17 killed on the field and not less than 25 badly wounded; among the former was the chief, or sachem. We recovered in this battle all the animals and spoils which the Indians had taken from the Mexicans and restored the captive boys and girls to their friends and relatives.

Let those whose moral scruples induce them to doubt the propriety of Capt. Reid's brilliant sortie upon the Indians consider that the Comanches have rarely failed to murder and torture in the most cruel manner, without discrimination, all Americans who have unfortunately fallen into their hands. The Comanches are our uncompromising enemies. Read the brutal treatment Mrs. Horn and others received from them and you can but justify Capt. Reid's conduct. In truth, he deserves the gratitude of both Mexicans and Americans for the chastisement he visited upon the heads of these barbarous wretches. The people of Parras expressed their gratitude to Capt. Reid and his men in the following handsome and complimentary terms:

Letter of thanks from the people of Parras to Capt. John W. Reid and his men after the battle of the Paso, translated by Capt. David Waldo:

POLITICAL HEAD OF THE DEPARTMENT OF PARRAS.

At the first notice that the Indians, after having murdered many of our citizens and taken others captives, were returning to their homes through this vicinity, you, most generously and gallantly, offered, with 15 of your countrymen, to combat them at the Paso, which you most bravely executed with celerity, skill, and heroism, and worthy of all encomium, meriting your brilliant success, which we shall ever commemorate. You retook many animals and other property which had been captured and liberated 18 captives, who, by your gallantry and good conduct, have been restored to their families and homes, giving you the most hearty and cordial thanks, ever feeling grateful to you as their liberator from a life of ignominy and thraldom, with the deep gratitude the whole population of this place entertain in ever-living thanks. One-half of the Indians being killed in the combat and many flying, badly wounded, does not quiet the pain that all of us feel for the wound that you received in rescuing Christian beings from the cruelty of the most inhuman of savages.

All of us ardently hope that you may soon recover of your wound, and though they know that the noblest reward of the gallant soul is to have done well for his country, yet they can not forego this expression of their gratitude.

I consider it a high honor to be the organ of their will in conveying to you the general feeling of the people of the place; and I pray you to accept the assurance of my high respect. God and liberty.

Don Ignacio Arrabe.

Parras, *May 18, 1847.*

On the evening of the 14th of May the army reached the delightful city of Parras, handsomely situated at the northern base of a lofty range of mountains running east and west, after having performed a fatiguing march of 36 miles without one drop of water, and almost without seeing one sprig of green vegetation save the pointed maguey and the bristling cactus. At Parras we found a plentiful supply of good water and forage for our perishing animals. We found Parras in reality to possess whatever of charm the imagination has thrown around one of the most beautiful of oases. We found a lovely alameda to screen us from the scorching rays of an almost vertical sun, besides a variety of fruits to satisfy the eager appetite. Parras is famous for its pretty women and for the intelligence of its population generally, many of the citizens having received an English education in the United States. The people here are much inclined to favor the institutions and Government of our country. Don Manuel Ybarro, the proprietor of a large hacienda near Parras, was educated at Bardstown, Ky., and has acted a very friendly part toward the American troops. For his numerous acts of kindness toward the author and his companions in arms he desires to return his grateful acknowledgments.

Upon Col. Doniphan's reaching Parras he received a communication from Gen. Wool, by the hands of Ybarro, in which he was authorized to purchase, on the credit of the United States, such provisions and forage as his men and animals required; he was also instructed to allow his men such respite as their condition, after so much toil and so many distressing marches, seemed to demand, and to extend to the intelligent and hospitable citizens of Parras kind treatment in reciprocation for their numerous acts of benevolence toward the sick Americans whom he had been forced to leave at that place upon his forming a junction with Gen. Taylor at Saltillo.

Though the Missourians manifested the utmost civility toward the inhabitants of Parras, one incident occurred to mar the general harmony and good feeling which had prevailed. A few disaffected Mexicans fell upon a man, Lickenlighter, in the employ of the Artillery, and with staves and stones bruised him so that he subsequently died in Monterey. This aggravated instance of cruelty, commenced by the Mexicans, excited the Artillery men and all the Missourians to such a degree that they fell upon whatever Mexicans exhibited the least insolence and beat them severely. Some say that two of them were killed, but of this nothing certain is known. Nor were the officers able to restrain the men. Capt. Pike and a portion of the advance under Lieut. Col. Mitchell, having halted at this place, now rejoined the army.

On the morning of the 17th the whole force moved off in the direction of Saltillo, and in less than five days, having completed more than 100 miles, the Missourians pitched their camps with the Arkansas Cavalry at Encantada, near the battle field of Buena Vista, where there is an abundant supply of cool and delightful water.

During this march they passed through a rugged, mountainous country, almost entirely destitute of vegetation, producing only mesquite, chaparral, clusters of dwarfish acacia, Spanish bayonet, maguey, and palmilla. This last often grows 30 feet in height and 3 feet in diameter, the body of which is sometimes used as timber for the construction of bridges. On the tops of the mountain peaks, and sometimes by the wayside, might be seen the cross, the symbol of the national faith and object of universal reverence, constructed in the rudest and most primitive manner, with a small heap of stones at its

CROSS BY THE WAYSIDE.

foot and fancifully and reverentially entwined with festoons of wild flowers. This march passed by the haciendas Ybarro, Cienega Grande, Castanuella, the princely Hacienda de Patos, and the ruins of San Juan, where there is much water. This last place had been destroyed by the Americans.

On the 22d of May the regiment was reviewed by Gen. Wool in person, accompanied by his staff, and the following complimentary order made, viz:

HEADQUARTERS, BUENA VISTA, *May 22, 1847.*

The general commanding takes great pleasure in expressing the gratification he has received this afternoon in meeting the Missouri Volunteers. They are about to close their present term of military service after having rendered, in the course of the arduous duties they have been called on to perform, a series of highly imported services, crowned by decisive and glorious victories.

No troops can point to a more brilliant career than those commanded by Col. Doniphan, and no one will ever hear of the battles of Brazito or Sacramento without a feeling of admiration for the men who gained them.

The State of Missouri has just cause to be proud of the achievements of the men who have represented her in the Army against Mexico, and she will without doubt receive them on their return with all the joy and satisfaction to which a due appreciation of their merits and services so justly entitle them.

In bidding them adeau the general wishes to Col. Doniphan, his officers, and men a happy return to their families.

By command of Brig. Gen. Wool:

IRVIN MCDOWELL, *A. A. A. Gen.*

On the 23d the Missourians marched to Gen. Wool's [1] camp, where Capt. Weightman delivered up his battery to Capt. Washington. The Mexican cannon which were captured in the action at Sacramento they were permitted to retain as the trophies of their victory. These were subsequently presented by Col. Doniphan to the State of Missouri, to be the evidences through all time to come of the valor, chivalry, and good conduct of the troops under his command. The Missouri column, now passing Saltillo, the Grand Canyon of the Rinconada, Santa Catarina, and the city of Monterey, arrived in the American camp at the Walnut Springs on the 26th, having in three days performed a march of 70 miles, during which two brave soldiers—Smith and Smart—died and were buried with becoming military honors. Maj. Gen. Taylor, having reviewed the Missouri troops on the morning of the 27th, issued the following order:

HEADQUARTERS ARMY OF OCCUPATION,
Camp near Monterey, May 27, 1847.

Col. Doniphan's command of Missouri Volunteers will proceed, via Camargo, to the mouth of the river or Brazos Island, where it will take water transportation to New Orleans.

On reaching New Orleans Col. Doniphan will report to Gen. Brooke, commanding the western division, and also to Col. Churchill, inspector general, who will muster the command for discharge and payment.

At Camargo Col. Doniphan will detach a sufficient number of men from each company to conduct the horses and other animals of the command by land to Missouri. The men so detached will leave the necessary papers to enable their pay to be drawn when their companies are discharged at New Orleans.

The Quartermaster Department will furnish the necessary transportation to carry out the above orders.

The trophies captured at the battle of Sacramento will be conveyed by Col. Doniphan to Missouri, and there turned over to the governor, subject to the final disposition of the War Department.

In thus announcing the arrangements which close the arduous and honorable service of the Missouri Volunteers the commanding general extends to them his earnest wishes for their prosperity and happiness and for a safe return to their families and homes.

By command of Maj. Gen. Taylor:

W. W. BLISS, *A. A. A. G.*

When Gen. Taylor received authentic information of the fall of Vera Cruz, the capitulation of the castle of San Juan de Ullua, and the capture of Chihuahua he published the following order to the troops under his command:

HEADQUARTERS ARMY OF OCCUPATION,
Camp near Monterey, April 14, 1847.

The commanding general has the satisfaction to announce to the troops under his command that authentic information has been received of the fall of Vera Cruz and of San Juan de Ullua, which capitulation on the 27th to the forces of Maj. Gen. Scott. This highly important victory reflects new luster on the reputation of our arms.

The commanding general would at the same time announce another signal success won by the galantry of our troops on the 28th of February near the city of Chihuahua. A column of Missouri Volunteers, less than 1,000 strong, under command of Col. Doniphan, with a light field battery, attacked a Mexican force many times superior in an intrenched position, captured its artillery and baggage, and defeated it with heavy loss.

In publishing to the troops the grateful tidings the general is sure that they will learn with joy and pride the triumphs of their comrades on distant fields.

By order of Maj. Gen. Taylor:

W. W. BLISS, *A. A. A. G.*

---

[1] To those readers who desire to peruse a full and faithful account of the operations of Gens. Wool, Taylor, Patterson, Quitman, and Scott the author would recommend the Twelve Months' Volunteer, a new and interesting history, by G. C. Furber, of the Tennessee Cavalry, recently published by J. A. & U. P. James, Cincinnati.

CHAPTER XXI.

Having left our sick men in Monterey, after a hasty march of 30 miles on the 26th, during which we passed the rivers Agua Fria and Salinas de Parras, we encamped in the small town Marin, where there was but little forage and not the semblance of either green or dry grass. The next day, passing through a country covered with an almost impervious mezquite chaparral, and over the ground where Gen. Urea's band captured Gen. Taylor's provision train and barbarously and inhumanly murdered the unarmed teamsters, whose skeletons and half-devoured frames still lay scattered promiscuously along the road, over which vultures, dogs, and wolves were yet holding carnival, and having progressed 35 miles, we encamped at a fine, bold-running spring not far from Cerralvo.

The next day, advancing about 7 miles to Cerralvo, we halted to take some refreshment. Here we witnessed the execution, by the Texan Rangers, of a Mexican guerrilla chief—one of Urea's men—who had been captured the previous night. His captors promised to spare his life upon condition that he would reveal to them where his comrades might be found. He refused to betray them, averring that he had killed many Americans, and he would kill many more if it were in his power. He added, "My life is now in the hands of my enemies; I am prepared to yield it up; only I ask that I may not be tied, and that I may be allowed to face my executioners." Having lighted his cigarrito with the utmost nonchalence, he faced his executioners (a file of six Texan Rangers), who were detailed for the purpose. They were ordered to fire. Five balls penetrated the skull of the guerrilla chief. He instantly expired.

On the 30th we encamped in Mier, situated on the small river Alcantro, and famous for having been the place where the Texans capitulated to Gen. Ampudia. The next day we reached Camargo, on the San Juan, where we obtained an abundant supply of provisions, for this place had been converted into a Government depot. This river admits of steamboat navigation. While here one of our companions, Tharp, who had performed much hard service, died of sickness. He was buried with the honors due to a brave soldier.

On the 1st of June Maj. Gilpin, with a small detachment of men, started in advance of the column, with the intention of proceeding to Reynosa, to engage transportation for the Army, by steamboats, thence to the mouth of the Rio Grande. After proceeding a few miles, one of his party, Sergt. Swain, a good soldier, having imprudently straggled on ahead by himself, was shot by Mexicans lurking in the chaparral. To avenge his death the party charged as soon as practicable upon the Mexicans, who were adroitly making their escape, and killed one of them. Four others were a short time afterwards captured by Capt. Walton, with a small detachment of men at a neighboring rancho, and carried to camp at Upper Reynosa, at which place we found Col. Webb, of the Sixteenth Regiment, United States Army. The prisoners were delivered over to him, but finding no positive evidence that they were the same who had committed the bloody deed, although one of them had blood on his clothes, they were discharged and conducted out of camp by a guard. But the company to which Swain belonged were so much enraged that, as it is said, they went out from camp and killed part of them as soon as dismissed by the guard. Of the truth of this we are not certainly informed, for those who knew would not divulge the truth, lest they should be censured by those in command, but the fire of their guns was distinctly heard.

After resting a few hours and burying the dead the march was continued down the river through the chaparral all day and all the following night. At sunrise the advance of the column arrived at Reynosa, where we were greeted by the sight of steam vessels ready to transport us to the Gulf.

Col. Doniphan, now taking the sick men on board the first transport that could be obtained, proceeded to the mouth of the river to engage shipping as early as practicable for New Orleans, leaving Lieut. Col. Jackson, Maj. Gilpin, and Maj. Clark to provide the means of transporting their respective battalions down the river. Certain of the soldiers, impatient of delay and anxious to get home, censured Col. Doniphan for leaving them at Reynosa without providing them with immediate transportation; but they did not consider how important it was that he should go in advance to Brazos Island and have ships ready engaged to convey them without delay to New Orleans. Without such precaution on the part of the commander, the whole column might have been obliged to lie many days on the beach, waiting for vessels in which to cross the Gulf. This, therefore, eventuated most opportunely, for ships were made ready in the harbor before the men arrived at the Brazos.

Meanwhile the troops at Reynosa were obliged to lie one or two days on the river bank in a comfortless and miserable plight (for it rained incessantly, and the men had no place to lie, nor tents to shelter them, but stood as cattle in the mud both day and night) before they could procure transports.

On the 4th and 5th, the men having burned their saddles and other horse rigging and sent their animals by land to Missouri, went aboard steam vessels, and on the 7th the whole force arrived safely at the mouth of the river, where they disembarked and bivouacked upon the margin of the stream until the morning of the 9th, the intermediate time being spent by the soldiers in the most refreshing and pleasant bathings in the river and the Gulf.

Lieut. James Lea, quartermaster, proceeded with his trains from Reynosa to Matamoras and turned over to the quartermaster at that place all his wagons, mules, and commissary stores·

Gen. Taylor's order requiring a " sufficient number of men " to be detailed at Camargo for the purpose of conducting " the horses and other animals of the command by land to Missouri," was not complied with; for the volunteers did not choose to obey the order, regarding the stock of but little value. However, Sergt. V'an Bibber and about 35 other men voluntarily agreed to drive the stock (of such as would allow them a compensation of $10 per head for their pains) through Texas to Missouri and deliver them in the county where the owner resided. Accordingly this party, with about 700 head of stock, leaving Reynosa on the 4th, proceeded to Camargo and thence into the United States, arriving in Missouri with the loss of near half the animals about the 15th of August.

On the 9th we walked over to the harbor at the north end of Brazos Island, whence we were to take shipping for New Orleans, and on the following day the artillery and about 250 men embarked on the schooner *Murillo*, and Col. Doniphan with 700 men embarked on the stately sail ship *Republic*, and under a favoring gale arrived safely in New Orleans on the 15th, having, in 12 months, performed a grand detour through the Mexican Republic of near 4,000 miles by land and water.

This most extraordinary march, conducted by Col. Doniphan, the Xenophon of the age, with great good fortune, meets not with a parallel in the annals of the world.

Our passage across the Gulf was speedy and prosperous. One of our number only was committed to a watery grave. This was Christopher Smith, than whom none was a better soldier. Ridge, also a brave soldier, died and was conveyed to New Orleans for interment.

We had now been in the service 12 months, had traversed the plains and solitudes of the West, had waded through the snows in the mountains of New Mexico, had traveled over the great deserts of Chihuahua, Durango, Coahuila, Nueva Leon, and Tamaulipas, half naked, and but poorly supplied with provisions, and were weary of camp service and packing up baggage. Therefore we were anxious to return to our homes and our families. When the men came within sight of the Balize—when they could but just discover through the mist low in the horizon the distant, green, looming shores of their native country, they shouted aloud in the pride of their hearts, and, Columbus-like, gave thanks to the beneficent Author of all good, not only for the prosperous voyage over the Gulf, but the unparallel success of the great expedition.

The chivalry of the South is unsurpassed; the generosity of the southern people unequaled. Their feelings are alive to every noble and magnanimous impulse. Their breasts are swayed by sentiments of true honor. Who will deny that the population of the Crescent City inspires patriotism from very proximity to the field immortalized by Jackson's victory? New Orleans, for months previous to the arrival of Col. Doniphan, had been wound up to the highest degree of military excitement and had, in truth, been the great thoroughfare for the departure and return of perhaps more than 10,000 volunteers destined for the war and returning from their various fields of glory; yet, the Missourians, rough clad, were received with unabated enthusiasm, and a cordiality for which they will ever gratefully remember their friends of the South. As they passed up the Mississippi, the streaming of flags from the tops of houses and the waving of white handkerchiefs by the ladies as a token of approval from the windows and balconies of the stately mansions which everywhere beautify the green banks of the "Inland Sea," announced to them that their return was hailed with universal joy; that their arduous services were duly appreciated; and that Louisianians are not only generous and brave but nobly patriotic. Such a reception was worth the toil of an hundred battle fields.

Isolated from every other branch of the Army, barred by intervening deserts from all communication with the Government, thrown entirely upon its own resources, compelled to draw supplies from a hostile country, and in the absence of instructions or succors, Col. Doniphan's command was left to cut its way through the country of a subtle and treacherous enemy. Destitute of clothing and the means of procuring it—not having received a dime since the day of enlistment and none then, save $42 commutation for clothing—the men almost grew as did Nebuchadnezzar, being, indeed, rough samples of Rocky Mountain life. Their long-grown beards flowed in the wind similar to those of the rude Cossacks of northern Europe, while their garments were worn to shreds, bivouacking on the rocks and sands of Mexico. Their disheveled hair, their long-grown whiskers, their buckskin apparel, their stern and uncouth appearance, their determined and resolved looks, and their careless and nonchalant air attracted the gaze and won the admiration of all people. Though they were somewhat undisciplined, yet they were hardy, unshrinking, resolute, independent, chivalrous, honorable, and intelligent men, such as, indeed, " would not flatter Neptune for his trident, nor Jove for his power to thunder."

CHAPTER XXII.

Discharge of the troops—Their return to Missouri—Reception at St. Louis—Banquets and honors—Doniphan crowned with a laurel wreath—Conclusion.

We have hitherto considered in what manner the troops under Col. Doniphan were conducted over the great solitudes to Santa Fe; how they invaded the snow-capped mountains in pursuit of the fearless Navajos; how Gen. Kearney with a small force crossed the continent and held California in quiet possession; how Col. Price succeeded to the command of the troops in New Mexico; how Col. Doniphan invaded and conquered the States of Chihuahua and Durango, thence traversing extensive deserts, treeless, barren, and waterless, oftentimes subsisting his army on half rations and less; and how, after infinite suffering and toil, he arrived at the Gulf and sailed for New Orleans.

The Missourians were now permitted to turn over to the ordnance master at New Orleans the arms they had used on the expedition and with which they had achieved signal victories. They were forthwith mustered for discharge and payment by Col. Churchill, which process was completed between the 22d and the 28th of June. Having received payment and an honorable discharge from the service they departed to their respective homes in detached parties, each one now traveling according to his own convenience and being no longer subject to command. They generally arrived in Missouri about the 1st of July, having been absent 13 months.

Anticipating the arrival of the returning volunteers, the generous citizens of St. Louis had made ample preparations to give them a hearty welcome, cordial reception, and testify to them the esteem in which their services were held by their fellow citizens. But as the volunteer soldiers, who had now become citizens, returned in detached parties and were very anxious to visit their families and friends, from whom they had so long been separated, they could not all be induced to remain and partake of the proffered hospitality. However, the company under Capt. Hudson, having in charge the captured Mexican cannon and near 300 officers and privates of different companies being in the city on the 2d of July, it was agreed that the formalities of the reception should be gone through with. Accordingly, the various military and fire companies of the city were paraded in full uniform; the people collected in great crowds; the Mexican cannon, the trophies of victory, were dragged along the streets crowned with garlands; and an immense procession was formed, conducted by T. Grimsley, chief marshall, which, after a brief, animating speech from the Hon. J. B. Bowlin and a still briefer response from Lieut. Col. Mitchell, proceeded to Camp Lucas, where the Hon. T. H. Benton delivered to the returned volunteers and a concourse of more than 7,000 people a most thrilling and eloquent address,[1] recounting with astonishing accuracy and extraordinary minuteness the events of the great campaign.

---

[1] See Benton's and Doniphan's speeches, Missouri Republican, July 3, 1847.

When the honorable Senator concluded, Col. Doniphan was loudly and enthusiastically called to the stand, whereupon he rose and responded in a very chaste and modest, yet graphic, address, in which he ascribed the great success and good fortune which continually attended him on his expedition rather to the bravery and conduct of his soldiers than to his own generalship.

For months succeeding the return to the State of the Missouri Volunteers sumptuous dinners, banquets, and balls, tables loaded with delicate viands and the richest wines, were everywhere spread to do them honor, as if thereby to compensate in some measure for past hardships and the immensity of toil and peril which they had experienced in climbing over rugged, snow-capped mountains; in contending with the overwhelming forces of the enemy; in enduring bitter cold, pinching hunger, burning thirst, incredible fatigue, and sleepless nights of watching, and in bivouacking upon the waterless, arid deserts of Mexico. But their past dangers, both from the foe and the elements, were now soon forgotten amidst the kind caresses of friends and the cordial reception with which their fellow citizens continually greeted them. The maxim which has descended from former ages, and which has met the sanction of all nations, that republics are ungrateful, has not in this instance proved true, for there was now a campaign of feasting and honors.

On the 29th of July a public dinner was given by the citizens of Independence, Mo., in honor of Col. Doniphan, his officers, and men, on which occasion the ladies, being anxious to testify their respect to the hero of Sacramento, and those who followed where he dared to lead, had prepared the laurel wreath, in all ages the "gift of beauty to valor," for the victor's brow. After the welcoming speech, by S. H. Woodson, and a thrilling and stirring response by Col. Doniphan, Mrs. Buchanan, in behalf of the ladies, delivered from the stand, in the presence of 5,000 people, the subjoined eloquent address:

Long had the world echoed to the voice of Fame when her brazen trumpet spoke of the glories of Greece and Rome. The sun looked proudly down upon Thermopylæ when Leonidas had won a name bright and glorious as his own golden beams. The soft air of the Italian clime glowed, as the splendor of a Roman triumph flashed through the eternal city. But the mantle of desolation now wraps the moldering pillars of Athens and of Rome, and Fame deserting her ancient haunts, now fills our own fair land with the matchless deeds of her heroic sons. Like the diamond in the recesses of the mine, lay for centuries the land of Columbia. Like that diamond, when art's transforming fingers have polished its peerless luster, it now shines the most resplendent gem in the coronal of nations.

The records of the Revolution, that dazzling picture in the temple of history, presents us with the astonishing sight of men whose feet had never trodden the strict paths of military discipline, defying, conquering the trained ranks of the British Army, whose trade is war. Nor did their patriotism, their energy, die with the fathers of the Revolution—their spirit lives in their sons.

The star which represents Missouri shone not on the banner that shadowed the venerated head of Washington. But the unrivaled deeds of the Missouri volunteers have added such brilliancy to its beams that even he whose hand laid the corner stone of the temple of American liberty, and placed on its finished shrines the rescued flag of his country, would feel proud to give the star of Missouri a place amidst the time-honored, the far-famed "old thirteen." The Spartan, the Athenian, the Roman, who offered on the altar of Mars the most brilliant sacrifices, were trained even from their infancy in all the arts of war. The service of the bloody god was to them the business of life, aye, even its pastime; their very dreams were full of the tumult of battle, but they who hewed asunder with their good swords the chains of a British tyrant, and they who have rendered the names of Brazito and Sacramento watchwords to rouse the valor of succeeding ages, hurried from the quiet labors of the field, the peaceful halls of justice, the cell of the student, and the familiar hearth of home to swell the ranks of the defenders of their native land.

Volunteers of Missouri, in the memory of your country, no brighter page can be found than that which records your own bright deeds. Many of you had never welcomed the morning light without the sunshine of a mother's smile to make it brighter; many of you had known the cares and hardships of life only in name; still you left the home of your childhood and encountered perils and sufferings that would make the cheek of a Roman soldier turn pale, and encountered them so gallantly that Time in his vast calendar of centuries can show none more bravely, more freely borne.

We welcome you back to your home. The triumph which hailed the return of the Cæsars, to whose war chariot was chained the known world, is not ours to give, nor do you need it. A prouder triumph than Rome could bestow is yours in the undying fame of your proud achievements. But if the welcome of hearts filled with warm love and well-merited admiration—hearts best known and longest tried—be a triumph, it is yours in the fullest extent.

The torrent of eloquence to which you have just listened, the rich feast that awaits you, are the tributes of your own sex; but we, the fairer part of creation, must offer ours also. In the name of the ladies who surround me, I bestow on you this laurel wreath—in every age and every clime the gift of beauty to valor. In placing it on the brow of him who now kneels to receive it, I place it on the brows of all who followed where so brave, so dauntless a commander led. It is true that around the laurel wreath is twined every association of genius, glory, and valor, but I feel assured that it was never placed on a brow more worthy to receive it than his on which it now rests—the hero of Sacramento.

It does not become the author to extol in unmeasured terms the gallant officers who led with such marvelous success, nor the brave men who bore with Roman fortitude and patience the fatigues of the western expedition, beyond what every candid and generous mind will readily concede. Equally the conduct of both is worthy of encomium. They performed all, and more than all, the Government expected at their hands. After the conquest of New Mexico, Gen. Kearney, with 100 men, completed an astonishing overland expedition to the shores of the Pacific, 1,090 miles distant from Santa Fe. This great march was conducted over stony mountains, barren plains, and inhospitable deserts.

Col. Doniphan and his men scaled the granite heights of the Cordilleras, amidst fathoms of accumulated, eternal snows, in the depth of winter, when the wide waste of rocks and the horrid, driving snowstorms were their most relentless enemies. Having spent three months, and performed a campaign of 750 miles in the most rugged and inhospitable regions on the continent, they return to the valley of the Del Norte. Here they refresh themselves and recruit two days, after which they commence the grand march upon Chihuahua, and gain immortal renown on the trophied fields of Brazito and Sacramento. The capital and the State, with 200,000 inhabitants, become a conquest to less than a thousand Missourians. This march was near 600 miles through barren and waterless regions.

The Nation almost trembled for the safety of Gen. Wool's column, 3,500 strong, with heavy artillery, when he set out from San Antonio on his intended expedition against Chihuahua. Many apprehended his complete overthrow and argued that it would result in a prodigal waste of means and a useless and wanton sacrifice of human life for so small a force to march against so powerful and populous a State. But the stronghold of central Mexico is in possession of the hero of Sacramento, with 924 Missourians, and the American flag floats in triumph over its walls.

Leaving Chihuahua for more extended operations and a new theater of action, they move off through the States of Durango and Coahuila, traversing parched, arid, waterless wastes for more than 600 miles, ready to succor Gen. Taylor, if beleaguered in Saltillo, or to accompany him over the Cedral Desert, in his contemplated descent upon San Louis de Potosi, having previously sent 14 express men on a most perilous enterprise to learn the general's wishes.

Their services being now no longer required, the commander in chief dispatches them to the United States, by way of Matamoras and the Mexican Gulf. They sail for New Orleans, where they are discharged. They return to Missouri from the eastward graced with the trophies of the vanquished foe, having in 12 months performed a magnificent circuit of more than 3,500 miles by land and 2,500 by water, with the loss of less than 100 of their original number.

The expedition of Cyrus against his brother Artaxerxes, and the retreat of the 10,000 Greeks, famous through all time, conducted by Xenophon and Cherisopus, forms the only parallel to Col. Doniphan's expedition recorded in history. In 15 months Cyrus and Xenophon conduct this expedition about 3,450 English miles, with the loss of several thousand brave men, and finally return to Greece, possessing nothing save their lives and their arms. In 13 months Col. Doniphan and his Missourians accomplish a similar expedition (except as to its objects) of more than 5,500 miles, returning decorated with the spoils of war and meeting with the hearty approval of their countrymen.

The distance over which Gen. Kearney marched was perhaps greater than that over which Col. Doniphan passed, but the former conducted an army only to California, returning privately, while the latter commanded and provided for his men, and that, too, without funds, until they were disbanded at New Orleans.

But where are the permanent, the beneficial, results of this wonderful, this almost fabulous, expedition of Col Doniphan? the utilitarian will inquire. The facts that the Chihuahua market, which the war had closed, was reopened for the admittance of several hundred thousand dollars' worth of American goods which otherwise would have been sacrificed, to the ruin of the merchants if not indemnified by the Government; that new and more desirable commercial relations will henceforward assuredly spring up between Chihuahua and the Western States, and on a safer and more equitable basis; that the insults and wrongs which had been repeatedly heaped on American citizens, and the decimation of the Mier prisoners, were now completely avenged by the defeat of a haughty and supercilious foe; that great light has been thrown on the political condition and geographical position of central Mexico, which had hitherto been but little explored by Americans; that the Mexican people have now been taught something of the strength of their northern neighbors; that they have acquired some knowledge of the effects of free institutions, liberty, and general education upon mankind; and that all central Mexico was thereby neutralized during the war, will sufficiently answer the important inquiry.

Thus terminated the most extraordinary and wonderful expedition of the age, attended throughout by the most singular good fortune, conducted under the auspices of Col. Doniphan, who has been very justly styled the great military pedestrian, the victor, and diplomat.

CHAPTER XXIII.

It will be remembered that on the 26th of October, 1846, Col.
Doniphan took his departure from Santa Fe on an excursion against
the Navajo Indians and was rejoined at Santo Domingo by 300 of
his own regiment, who had been previously stationed at the grazing
encampment near San Miguel, but were now ordered to proceed into
the mountains on a most serious and trying campaign. Col. Doniphan returned no more to Santa Fe.

The command of the troops in New Mexico thenceforward devolved on Col. (now Brig. Gen.) Sterling Price. For the preservation of health and activity among his troops, which consisted of the
Second Regiment, under his own immediate command; an extra
battalion, under Lieut. Col. Willock; a battalion of infantry, under
Capts. Angney and Murphy; one company of light artillery, under
Capt. Fisher; the Leclede Rangers, under Lieut. Elliott; 200 of the
First Dragoons, under Capt. Burgwin (Maj. Sumner having returned
to the United States on the 18th of October); and some additional
artillery and miscellaneous troops, under Lieuts. Dyer and Wilson,
of the United States Army, making an aggregate force of near 2,000
men, and also for the preservation of good order, quiet, and entire
submission on the part of the malcontent New Mexicans and Pueblo
Indians, Col. Price at first thus disposed of his forces:

Capt. Burgwin, with the First Dragoons, was stationed at Alburquerque to maintain tranquillity on the Rio Abajo; a squadron of 200
men, under Maj. Edmondson, was scouring about Cebolleta; a small
force under Capt. Hendley was ordered to the Valley of the Mora,
with the view of finding forage for the stock and of preserving peace
and subordination in that quarter, as well as also to check the predatory incursions of the border Indians, who were becoming quite
troublesome and deserving of chastisement; the remaining forces were
retained at the capital as a garrison.

On the 28th of October, two days after the departure of Col. Doniphan from Santa Fe, Col. Price issued an order requiring the troops
under his command to appear on parade, for drill and discipline,
twice each day. The officers were required to perform an extra drill,
that they might be better qualified to instruct the men. This discipline was rigidly adhered to. Everyone the least acquainted with
military affairs is aware how difficult a matter it is to preserve good
order and wholesome discipline in a garrison composed entirely of
volunteers. The unrestrained, independent life to which the citizen
soldier has been accustomed unfits him for garrison service. He becomes impatient of discipline and desires active, useful, honorable
employment. For this reason regular troops are much better for gar-

192

risons than volunteers, but are none their superiors in an arduous and daring campaign.

About the 1st of December the most distinguished of the malcontents began to hold secret cabals and consultations and to plot the overthrow of the actual existing Government. Oftentimes the conspirators, like Cataline and his accomplices in guilt, would withdraw into some retired room in the capital, or on the flat top of some unfrequented building, and there at the silent hour of midnight machinate a scheme for the massacre of all the Americans, the establishment of a new government, and installation of new governors. The leaders of this dark and desperate conspiracy were Don Tomas Ortiz, who aspired to be governor of the Province; Don Diego Archulette, who had been nominated as commanding general; and Seniores Nicholas Pino, Miguel Pino, Santiago Armijo, Manuel Chavez, Domingo Baca, Pablo Dominguez, Juan Lopez, and may others, all men of great and restless ambition and expectants of office if the conspiracy should have a favorable issue.

The 19th of December, at midnight, was the time at first appointed for the revolt to commence, which was to be simultaneous all over the department. In the meantime each one of the conspirators had a particular part of the State assigned him, to the end that they might gain over the whole people of the Province. The profoundest secrecy was to be preserved, and the most influential men, whose ambition induced them to seek preferment, were alone to be made acquainted with the plot. No woman was to be privy to these things, lest they should be divulged.

Each having pledged himself to the others on the cross that he would be faithful and vigilant in consummating their designs as speedily and successfully as possible, departed, some into one place and some into another. For his part Tomas Ortiz, who had been second in command to Armijo, the late governor, went to El Bado, that he might stir up the people there; Diego Archulette hastened to the Valley of Taos, to make known his plans and solicit aid in that quarter; Domingo Baca departed to the Rio Abajo to excite the inhabitants and procure assistance there; Pablo Domingueb and Miguel Pino proceeded to the settlements on the River Tesuca, to enlist them in the enterprise; and the priest Leyba would propose the same to the people at San Miguel and Las Bagas.

For the more certain success of the revolution, the conspirators assembled in secret conclave in the capital on the night of the 15th of December to consult, mature their plans, and arrange the method of attack. Don Sanchez, when apprehended and brought before the tribunal, testified that Don Diego Archulette commenced the discourse: " I make the motion that there be an act to nominate a governor and a commander general, and I would nominate Tomas Ortiz for the first office, and Diego Archulette for the second." This was unanimously carried, and the act signed by every individual present. After this was concluded they commenced a discourse relative to the method of surprising the Government at Santa Fe, and taking possession of the place. They decided upon the following plan: " On Saturday evening, the 19th of December, all were to assemble with their men at the parish church. Having divided themselves into several parties, they were to sally forth, some to seize the pieces of artillery, others to go to the quarters of the colonel, and others to the palace of the governor (if he should be there), and if not, to send an order to Taos to seize him, because he would give the most trouble. This act was also agreed on by all. The sound of the church bell was to be the signal for the assault by the forces concealed in the church, and those which Don Diego Archulette should have brought near the city—midnight was the time agreed on, when all were to enter the plaza at the same moment, seize the pieces of artillery, and point them into the streets. The meeting now dissolved."

Owing to a want of complete organization and concert, and that the conspiracy was not yet fully matured, it was concluded to suspend the attack for a time, and fix on Christmas eve night for the assault, when the soldiers and garrison would be indulging in wine and feasting, and scattered about through the city at the fandangos, not having their arms in their hands. All the Americans without distinction throughout the State, and such New Mexicans as had favored the American Government and accepted office by appointment of Gen. Kearney, were to be massacred or driven from the country, and the conspirators were to seize upon and occupy the Government. This enterprise, however, failed of success, being detected, exposed, and crushed by the vigilance of Col. Price, his officers and men.

The conspiracy was detected in the following manner: A mulatto girl, residing in Santa Fe, had married one of the conspirators, and had by degrees obtained a knowledge of their movements and secret meetings. To prevent the effusion of blood which would inevitably be the result of a revolution, she communicated to Col. Price all the facts of which she was in possession, and warned him to use the utmost vigilance. The rebellion was immediately suppressed.

But the restless and unsatisfied ambition of the leaders of the conspiracy did not long permit them to remain inactive. The rebellion had been detected and smothered, but not completely crushed. A second and still more dangerous conspiracy was plotted. The most powerful and influential men in the State favored the design. An organized plan of operations was adopted. The profounded secrecy was preserved. While all appeared to be quiet and secure, the machinations of the conspirators were maturing and gaining strength. Even the officers of State and the priests gave their aid and counsel. The people everywhere, in the towns, villages, and settlements, were exhorted to arm and equip themselves, to strike for their faith, their religion, and their altars, and drive the "heretics," the "unjust invaders of the country," from their soil, and with fire and sword pursue them to annihilation. On the 19th of January this rebellion broke out in every part of the State simultaneously.

On the 14th of January Gov. Charles Bent, attended by an escort of five persons, among whom were the sheriff, circuit attorney, and the prefecto, left Santa Fe and proceeded to Taos. Upon his arrival there he was applied to by the Pueblo Indians to release from prison two of their number who, for some misdemeanor, had been incarcerated by the authorities. The governor told them they must await the ordinary process of the laws.

On the 19th of the same month the governor and his retinue were murdered in the most cruel and inhuman manner by the Pueblos and Mexicans at the village San Fernando. On the same day seven other

Americans, after standing a siege of two days, were overpowered, taken, and butchered in cold blood at the Arroyo Hondo; also four at the town Mora and two on the Colorado.[1]

The insurgents had assembled in strong force at La Canada, under command of Gens. Ortiz, Lafoya, Chavez, and Montoya, with the view of making a descent upon Santa Fe. Col. Price having ordered Maj. Edmondson and Capt. Burgwin, with their respective commands from the Rio Abajo, on the morning of the 23d, at the head of 353 men,[2] and four mountain howitzers, marched against the insurgents, leaving Lieut. Col. Willock, with a strong garrison, in command of the capital. The weather was extremely inclement, and the earth covered with snow.

On the evening of the 24th Col. Price encountered the enemy at Canada, numbering about 2,000 men, under the command of Gens. Tofaya, Chavez, and Montoya. The enemy were posted on the hills commanding each side of the road. About 2 o'clock p. m. a brisk fire from the artillery under the command of Lieuts. Dyer, of the Regular Army, and Harsentiver was opened upon them, but from their being so much scattered it had but little effect.

The artillery were within such short distance as to be exposed to a hot fire, which either wounded or penetrated the clothes of 19 or 20 men who served the guns. Col. Price, seeing the slight effect which the artillery had upon them, ordered Capt. Angney with his battalion to charge the hill, which was gallantly done, being supported by Capt. St. Vrain, of the citizens, and Lieut. White, of the Carroll companies. The charge lasted until sundown. Our loss was 2 killed and 7 wounded. The Mexicans acknowledge a loss of 36 killed and 45 taken prisoners. The enemy retreated toward Taos, their stronghold. Col. Price on the 27th took up his line of march for Taos, and again encountered them at El Embudo on the 29th. They were discovered in the thick brush on each side of the road, at the entrance of a defile, by a party of spies, who immediately fired upon them. Capt. Burgwin, who had that morning joined Col. Price with his company of dragoons, hearing the firing, came up, together with Capt. St. Vrain's and Lieut. White's companies. A charge was made by the three companies, resulting in the total rout of the Mexicans and Indians. The battle lasted about half an hour; but the pursuit was kept up for two hours.

The march was resumed on the next day, and met with no opposition until the evening of the 3d of February, at which time they arrived at the Pueblo de Taos, where they found the Mexicans and Indians strongly fortified. A few rounds were fired by the artillery that evening, but it was deemed advisable not to make a general attack then, but wait until morning. The attack was commenced in the morning by two batteries under the command of Lieuts. Dyer and Wilson, of the Regular Army, and Lieut. Harsentiver, of the Light Artillery, by throwing shells into the town. About meridian, a charge was ordered and gallantly executed by Capt. Burgwin's com-

---

[1] The following persons fell victims to the conspiracy : At Taos—C. Bent, governor ; S. Lee, sheriff ; J. W. Leal, circuit attorney ; C. Virgil (Mexican), prefecto ; N. Baubien, son of Judge Baubien ; and Jirmia, a Mexican. At the Arroyo Hondo, 12 miles from Taos—S. Turley, A. Cooper, W. Harfield, L. Folque, P. Roberts, J. Marshall, and W. Austin. At the Rio Colorado—M. Head and W. Harwood. At the Mora—L. Waldo, R. Culver, Noyes, two others.
[2] See Col. Price's official dispatch, Feb. 15. 1847.

pany, supported by Capt. McMillan's company and Capt. Angney's battalion of infantry, supported by Capt. Burbee's company. The church, which had been used as a part of the fortifications, was taken by this charge. The fight was hotly contested until night, when two white flags were hoisted, but were immediately shot down. In the morning the fort was surrounded. The old men, the priest, and the matrons, bringing their children and their sacred household gods in their hands, besought the clemency and mercy of their conquerors. Pardon was granted. In this battle fell Capt. Burgwin, than whom a braver soldier or better man never poured out his blood in his country's cause.

The total loss of the Mexicans in the three engagements is estimated at 282 killed; the number of their wounded is unknown. Our total loss was 15 killed [1] and 47 wounded.

Learning of the insurrectionary movements on the 20th of January, Capt. Hendley, who was in command of the grazing detachment on the Pecos, immediately took possession of Las Bagas, where the insurgents were beginning to concentrate their forces. He now ordered the different grazing parties to unite with him and prepare for offensive and defensive warfare. In a short time he was joined by various detachments, increasing his numbers to 225 men.

Lieut. Hawkins, with 35 men, was dispatched on the 22d to escort a train of wagons into Las Bagas, the Mexicans having sent out a party to plunder them. He soon met Capt. Murphy, with a train of wagons, convoyed by a detachment of Capt. Jackson's company, having in his possession about $300,000 in specie. The convoy returned about one day's march to guard the provision train, while the specie train moved on, escorted by Lieut. Hawkins.

Capt. Hendley, leaving the greater part of his force at Las Bagas, on the 22d, with 80 men started for the Mora, where he had learned the Mexicans were embodied, 200 strong. He arrived before the place on the 24th, found a body of Mexicans under arms prepared to defend the town, and while forming his men in a line for attack, a small party of insurgents were seen running from the hills. A detachment was ordered to cut them off, which was attacked by the main body of the enemy. A general engagement immediately ensued, the Mexicans retreating and firing from the windows and loopholes in their houses. Capt. Hendley and his men closely pursued them, rushing into their houses with them, shooting some and running, others through with bayonets. A large body of the insurgents had taken possession of an old fort and commenced a fire from the loopholes upon the Americans. Capt. Hendley with a small party had taken possession of an apartment in the fort, and while preparing to fire it, he was shot by a ball from an adjoining room. He fell, and died in a few minutes. Our men having no artillery, and the fort being impregnable without it, retired to La Vagas. The enemy had 25 killed and 17 taken prisoners. Our loss was 1 killed and 3 wounded.

Thus fell the brave Capt. Hendley, almost in the very moment of victory; and while we lament his loss, it is some consolation to know

---

[1] Killed: Capt. Burgwin, Lieut. Van Valkenburg, Sergts. Caldwell, Ross, and Hart, and Privates Graham, Smith, Papin, Bower, Brooks, Levicy, Hansuker, Truax, Austin, and Bebee.

that he died like a soldier. His body was taken to Santa Fe, where he was buried with all the honors of war.[1]

On the 1st of February, the death of Capt. Hendley, as well as that of Messrs. Waldo, Noyes, Culver, and others, was avenged by Capt. Morin and his men, in the complete demolition of the village Mora. The insurgents fled to the mountains. The dead bodies of the Americans who had been assassinated were conveyed to Las Bagas for interment.

The battles of La Canada, Embudo, Pueblo de Taos, and the Mora, in all of which the insurgents were vanquished with heavy loss, suppressed the insurrection, and once more restored quiet, law, and order throughout the territory. On the 6th of February, Montoya, one of the leaders of the conspiracy, who had styled himself the Santa Anna of the North, was court-martialed and sentenced to be hung. He was executed on the 7th,[2] in the presence of the Army. Fourteen others who were concerned in the murder of Gov. Bent were tried, convicted, and executed in a similar manner, in the neighborhood of Taos.

Leaving a detachment of Infantry in the valley of Taos, under the command of Capt. Angney, Col. Price returned to Santa Fe, where he continued to discharge the highest civil and military functions of the Territory. At a subsequent period, however, Capt. Angney was relieved by Lieut. Col. Willock's battalion of Cavalry.

The leading instigators of the revolution having fallen in battle, been executed upon a charge of treason, or escaped the punishment merited by their offences by flight to the mountains, the country once more enjoyed a short repose. The insurgent armies were dispersed. The people returned from the hills and mountains, whither many of them had fled for refuge during the excitement, to their respective homes, and resumed their daily avocations. Peace and harmony once more reigned throughout the Province.

---

[1] The remains of Capts. Hendley and Burgwin, several, lieutenants, and Sutler Albert Wilson were exhumed at Santa Fe and brought to Fort Leavenworth, where they were interred on the 22d of September, 1847, except those of Capt. Hendley, which were conveyed to Richmond and buried on the 23d.

[2] The court-martial consisted of six officers, Capts. Angney, Barbee, and Slack; Lieuts. Ingalls, White, and Eastin, the latter being judge advocate of the court.

CHAPTER XXIV.

Increased vigilance of the troops—Suspicion—Battle of the Red River Canyon—Murder of Lieut. Brown—Battle of Las Bagas—Six prisoners executed—Attack on the Cienega—Indian outrages—Robberies—Lieut. Love—Capt. Mann—The new levies.

After the suppression of the rebellion in New Mexico the troops were posted in almost every part of the country. A greater degree of vigilance was observed and stricter discipline enforced. The conduct of the Mexicans was watched with the utmost scrutiny. No house was permitted to retain arms or other munitions of war; nor was any Mexican cavalier suffered, as had hitherto been the case, to ride with impunity about the country and through the American camps, displaying his weapons and warlike trappings, making estimates of the American forces, and keeping a strict espionage upon their movements. The American soldiers, roused to indignation by the brutal massacres and frequent assassinations which had already blackened the annals of the campaign and thrown a dark shade over the conquest of the country, scarcely spared the innocent and unoffending. However, no acts of violence were perpetrated.

The soldiers slept upon their arms. They never left their quarters, or rode out of the city, or visited the villages, or passed through the country without their arms in their hand. They were always prepared, both night and day, for any sudden emergency that might arise, with such suspicion and animosity did the Americans and New Meixicans now regard each other. A suspicious quietude reigned throughout the Territory, but it was only that the rebellion might break out afresh on the first favorable opportunity.

On the 26th of May, 1847, Maj. Edmondson, with a detachment of 200 men under Capts. Hollaway and Robinson and Lieuts. Elliott and Hughes, were vigorously attacked by a large body of Mexicans, Apache, Comanche, and Kiawa Indians combined, at the " Red River Canyon," about 120 miles from Santa Fe. The enemy were supposed to number about 500. The action commenced about sunset, and continued until dark. The defile was narrow, and on either hand the spurs of the mountains were rugged and inaccessible to cavalry. The pass led through a morass or quagmire, so difficult of passage that many of the horses stuck fast in the mud. The cavalry could not act to any advantage. Maj. Edmondson therefore dismounted the men and cautiously advanced against the enemy under the heavy fire. The enemy was repulsed; but gaining fresh courage, he renewed the attack with more vigor than ever. The Americans now slowly retired in good order a few hundred paces, and occupied a more favorable position for defense. The retreat was covered by Lieut. Elliott, with the Laclede Rangers. It was now dark. The next moring Maj. Edmondson led his force through the canyon to renew the attack, but the enemy had retreated. In this engagement the Americans lost 1 man killed, and had several slightly injured. The Mexicans and Indians suffered a loss of 17 killed and no doubt many more wounded.

On the 26th of June, the horses belonging to Capt. Horine's company of mounted men, stationed under Maj. Edmondson, at Las Bagas, were stolen by the Mexicans and driven into the neighboring mountains. On the 28th Lieut. Brown and Pvts. McClanahan and Quisenbury, together with one Mexican as a guide, were dispatched in pursuit of them. Not returning on the following day as they intended, their companions rightly conjectured that they had been murdered. On the 5th of July a Mexican lady came into Las Bagas and stated that three Americans and one Mexican had recently been slain and their dead bodies consumed to ashes.

Maj. Edmondson, immediately after receiving this information, posted out a strong picket guard, with instructions to permit no one to enter the camp without first being brought before him. On the same day, Private William Cox, of Capt. Hollaway's company, while hunting in the mountains, discovered three suspicious-looking Mexicans endeavoring to shun him, whereupon he captured and brought them into camp. They were separately examined by Maj. Edmondson, but not being able to extort from them a satisfactory answer, one of them was hanged by the neck several times and until he had almost expired. When let down the third time he stated that three Americans and one Mexican had recently been murdered and their dead bodies burnt, near Las Bagas. When this confession was extorted, Maj. Edmondson quickly ordered the detachment, which consisted of 29 cavalry, 33 infantry, and one 12-pound mountain howitzer to prepare for the march, expecting to reach town before daylight the next morning.

Maj. Edmondson ascertaining that he would not be able to reach Las Bagas as soon as he desired, hurried on with the cavalry, leaving orders for the infantry and artillery to follow in his rear with all possible haste. On reaching the place he divided his men into two parties, under the command of Capts. Hollaway and Horine. They were now ordered to charge at full speed on the right and left at the same moment and gain possession of the town. The charge was gallantly made. The Mexicans commenced a precipitate retreat toward the mountains. A part of the Americans fired upon them, while the others entered the town. In less than 15 minutes 10 Mexicans were slain, the fugitives were captured, and the town, with 50 prisoners, taken. The Americans sustained no loss. The dead body of Lieut. Brown, having the cross suspended from the neck, was not burned, but secreted among the rocks. Such reverence is paid to the cross by the most cruel men. The clothes, guns, sabers, holsters, pistols, bowie knives, and trinkets of these unfortunate men were discovered secreted in various houses. Their ashes were also found. The greater part of the town was reduced to ashes, only a sufficient number of houses being left to shelter the women and children. Also the mills, a few miles from Las Bagas, which belonged to the alcalde, who was known to have participated in the murder of Lieut. Brown's party, was consumed.

The prisoners, by order of Col. Price, were conveyed to Santa Fe, where they were tried before a drumhead court-martial, and six of them sentenced to death. This sentence was accordingly put into execution in Santa Fe on the 3d of August in the presence of the army.

On the 9th of July a detachment of 31 men belonging to Capt. Morin's company, stationed on the Cienega, 18 miles from Taos, was furiously attacked two hours before daylight by 200 Mexicans and Pueblo Indians combined. Five of our men were killed [1] and nine wounded. The remainder of the party retired under the banks of the Cienega, which position they gallantly held until Capt. Shepherd arrived with his company and assisted them in vanquishing the enemy.

In the spring of 1847 the Indians, principally the Pawnees and Comanches, infested the Santa Fe road, committed repeated depredations on the Government trains, fearlessly attacked the escorts, killed and drove off great numbers of horses, mules, and oxen belonging to the Government, and in several instances overpowered and slew or captured many of our people. They openly declared that they would cut off all communication between the Western States and New Mexico and capture and enslave every American who might venture to pass the plains.

In pursuance of these views a large body of Indians, on the 22d of June, attacked a returning Government train near the Grand Arkansas, drove off 80 yoke of oxen, and in sight of the teamsters, whose force was too weak to offer effectual resistance, wantonly and cruelly slaughtered them for amusement and for the gratification of their savage propensities.

On the 26th Lieut. Love's convoy, with $300,000 in specie, encamped near the Arkansas. He was furiously assailed by a body of 500 savages, who had taken their position in the road and lain in wait to surprise at dawn. They succeeded in frightening the stock. One hundred and fifty yoke of oxen, in an estampeda, wildly scampered off and crossed the river, followed by the Indians, yelling and firing amongst the herd. Twenty of Lieut. Love's men pursued to recover the cattle, while the rest remained to protect the train. They charged the Indians about 1 mile, who retired; but this was a ruse to lead them into an ambuscade. At this moment more than 100 Indians sallied forth from an ambush, intercepted their retreat, and fiercely attacked them. They were now completely surrounded by the savages. The engagement became close and severe. At length the Americans charged through the enemy's ranks and made good their retreat. The loss of the Indians in this action was 25 killed and perhaps double that number wounded. The Americans, in killed and wounded, lost 11. The savages were mounted on horses and armed with guns, pistols, lances, shields, and bows and arrows.

On the 27th of October, 1846, Capt. Mann's train of 24 Government wagons was encamped 30 miles below the crossing of the Arkansas. The next morning two of the best mules were missing. The captain and Yates started in search of them. They had not proceeded far when they saw signs of Indians. They returned to camp, geared up, and started off, leaving Woodson and Stricklin a short distance in the rear with one wagon.

---

[1] The killed were Lieut. Larkin, W. Owens, J. A. Wright, W. S. Mason, and —— Wilkinson. The loss of the enemy was not ascertained.

At this crisis several hundred Indians came charging and yelling furiously from the hills and some attacked the train, while others surrounded the two men with the wagon. The trains were halted and the wagons corraled. Woodson and Stricklin were rescued, but the wagon, which contained the captain's scrutoire and three years' outfit of clothing, was taken, rifled, and burned. The American loss was 1 killed and 4 wounded; loss of the Indians not ascertained. The Indians now surrounded the corral. Night approaching, Capt. Mann and his men determined to gear up, take the wounded, and decamp. Accordingly a white flag was hoisted, and the train moved off. In a short time they were overtaken by the savages, who told them they desired to be friendly. A halt was ordered and the wagons again corraled. About 10 o'clock at night the Indians came rushing and yelling like a legion of devils and drove off 280 mules, leaving only 12 behind. The party now decamped, left the trains, and traveled on foot 30 miles, carrying the wounded, where they overtook Capt. McIlvaine, who sent back for the wagons. Here they fortified, 4 miles below the crossing, and sent the wounded to Fort Bent.

About the 1st of July, 1847, a regiment of volunteer infantry, raised in Illinois, and commanded by Cols. Newby and Boyakin, were outfitted at Fort Leavenworth and dispatched across the Plains to relieve the troops under Col. Price at Santa Fe whose term of service would soon expire. This is the Sixth Illinois Regiment.

Also between the 5th and 20th of August a battalion of infantry, under command of Lieut. Col. Easton, and a full regiment of cavalry, commanded by Cols. Ralls and Jones and Maj. Reynolds, all Missouri volunteers, departed from Fort Leavenworth, destined for Santa Fe. This is the fourth regiment and the fourth separate battalion of volunteers Missouri has furnished for the War with Mexico.

About the 27th of September the Fifth Separate Battalion of Missouri Volunteers, under Lieut. Col. Powell, left Fort Leavenworth for its destination on the Oregon route. This is denominated the Oregon battalion, and it will be employed in constructing a cordon of military posts from western Missouri to the Oregon territory. It is a cavalry corps.

Between the 1st and 15th of August, Gen. Price, and the troops under his command, returned to Missouri, where they arrived about the 25th of September, having lost more than 400 men in battle and by disease. A garrison of five companies, three of volunteers and two of regulars, was left in Santa Fe under Lieut. Col. Walker. Gen. Price has returned to Santa Fe. His force is now about 3,000 men.

In consequence of the recent repeated aggressions of the Indians on the Santa Fe road, the Executive determined to send against them a body of troops. Accordingly, on the 24th of July, a requisition was made on the State of Missouri for five companies of volunteers, two of cavalry, two of infantry, and one of artillery. This corps, the Sixth Separate Battalion of Missouri Volunteers, commanded by Lieut. Col. Gilpin, was outfitted at Fort Leavenworth and took its departure thence for the Plains on the 6th of October, where it will be employed in quelling and overawing the savages who beset the Santa Fe road for booty. This is called the Indian battalion.

These new levies are now in their various fields of operation. Little else remains for them to accomplish but to secure the conquests which have already been made. If, however, their subsequent achievements should be deemed worthy of historic record they may be embraced in a future edition of this work.

The author has now finished his labors, and if he has afforded entertainment for the curious, truth for the inquisitive, novelty for the lover of romance, instruction for the student of history, or information for the general reader, he feels himself amply rewarded for his pains. Should anyone, however, think that the narrative herein given of the expedition is unfaithful or incomplete, let him consider how difficult it is to write history, how impossible it is to feast every appetite, and how diverse are the sentiments of mankind.

O